Acting White?

Acting White?

Rethinking Race in "Post-Racial" America

DEVON W. CARBADO

and

MITU GULATI

OXFORD

UNIVERSITY PRESS

OXFORD
UNIVERSITY PRESS

Oxford University Press is a department of the University of Oxford.
It furthers the University's objective of excellence in research, scholarship,
and education by publishing worldwide.

Oxford   New York
Auckland   Cape Town   Dar es Salaam   Hong Kong   Karachi
Kuala Lumpur   Madrid   Melbourne   Mexico City   Nairobi
New Delhi   Shanghai   Taipei   Toronto

With offices in
Argentina   Austria   Brazil   Chile   Czech Republic   France   Greece
Guatemala   Hungary   Italy   Japan   Poland   Portugal   Singapore
South Korea   Switzerland   Thailand   Turkey   Ukraine   Vietnam

Oxford is a registered trademark of Oxford University Press
in the UK and certain other countries.

Published in the United States of America by
Oxford University Press
198 Madison Avenue, New York, NY 10016

Library of Congress Cataloging-in-Publication Data
Carbado, Devon W.
Acting white?: rethinking race in "post-racial" America / Devon W. Carbado and Mitu Gulati.
p. cm.
Includes bibliographical references and index.
ISBN 978-0-19-538258-7
1. Discrimination in justice administration—United States.   2. Justice,
Administration of—Social aspects—United States.   3. Discrimination in
employment—United States.   4. Racism—United States.   5. Stereotypes
(Social psychology)—United States.   I. Gulati, Mitu.   II. Title.
KF384.C37 2013
340.089'96073—dc23
2012019811

ISBN 978-0-19-538258-7

1 3 5 7 9 8 6 4 2
Printed in the United States of America
on acid-free paper

For Giovanna Tringali
—DWC

For Prea, Amma, and Kimba
—MG

CONTENTS

Acknowledgments   ix

Prologue: Acting Out the Racial Double Bind   1

1. Why *Act* White?   21

2. Talking White   46

3. Acting Like a Black Woman   68

4. Acting Like a (White) Woman   80

5. (Not) Acting Criminal   96

6. Acting Diverse   116

7. Acting Within the Law   134

8. Acting White to Help Other Blacks   149

Epilogue: Acting Beyond Black and White   167

Notes   171

Index   193

ACKNOWLEDGMENTS

The list of those who supported this book is too long for us to be able to do justice to. We began talking about and arguing over these ideas more than a decade ago, when we were first-year law students. We remember the time and place, roughly. It was either Property or Contracts, where the two of us got into a heated argument over the Rodney King case verdict and the resulting riots in Los Angeles that year. We were fortunate to have David Charny as a teacher. He managed to turn our squabble into something productive. He showed us that we were struggling with the same issues, and pushed us to think harder about answers we thought were either obvious or nonexistent. We miss him dearly.

Randall Kennedy and David Wilkins were also supportive of our engaging questions of race and law in our scholarship, as were Elizabeth Schneider and Joan Williams, two feminist scholars who were visiting professors at Harvard Law School while we were students. Outside of Harvard, Martha Fineman was an early and a significant mentor. She not only insisted that we write up our ideas; she provided a venue in which we could present and publish them—a feminist conference at Cornell Law School and the *Cornell Law Review*, respectively. "Working Identity," our first foray into the racial performance phenomenon emerged from that context. Still, it bears mentioning that, notwithstanding Martha's invitation and generous support, "Working Identity" would not have been written without the encouragement and critical feedback from several of our UCLA colleagues, and in particular, Kimberlé Crenshaw, Laura Gomez, Jerry Kang, Cheryl Harris, and David Sklansky.

There was karma in the fact that our initial ideas were formed out of arguments over events in Los Angeles. One law school, UCLA School of Law, took the risk of hiring us together, thereby enabling us to continue our arguments. To the members of that year's hiring committee, Rick Abel, Evan Caminker, Jody Freeman, Jerry Kang, Phil Trimble, and Eric Zolt, we owe an everlasting debt.

Pieces of what you will read in *Acting White?* have their seeds in a series of prior articles. These articles include: *Intra-Racial Diversity*, 60 UCLA L. Rev. (2013, forthcoming); *After Inclusion*, 4 Ann. Rev. of L. and Soc. Sci. 83 (2008) (with Catherine Fisk); *The Story of Jespersen v. Harrah's: Makeup and Women at Work*, in Employment Discrimination Stories 105, 120–24 (Joel Wm. Friedman ed., 2006) (with Gowri Ramachandran); *Race to the Top of the Corporate Ladder: What Minorities Do When They Get There*, 61 Wash. & Lee L. Rev. 1645 (2004); *The Law and Economics of Critical Race Theory*, 112 Yale L.J. 1757 (2003); *(E)Racing the Fourth Amendment*, 100 Mich. L. Rev. 446 (2002); *The Fifth Black Woman*, 11 J. Contemp. Legal Issues 701(2001); *Conversations at Work*, 79 Or. L. Rev. 103, 132-35 (2000); and *Working Identity*, 85 Cornell L. Rev. 1259 (2000), the article with which we began this intellectual journey. While we have broadened, elaborated upon, and in some instances expressly repudiated the ideas expressed in these prior works, it was those articles that suggested to us that a book of this sort was in order.

We would be remiss not to mention the many intellectual sparring partners, including co-authors, with whom we have thrown around ideas about this book over the years. Among those are Kathy Abrams, Rick Banks, Kate Bartlett, Paul Butler, Paulette Caldwell, Ann Carlson, Mary Anne Case, Mario Barnes, Guy-Uriel Charles, Frank Rudy Cooper, Sumi Cho, Stephen Choi, Anne Coughlin, Kimberlé Crenshaw, Scott Cummings, Martha Fineman, Catherine Fisk, Rich Ford, Katherine Franke, Tracey George, Laura Gómez, Lani Guinier, Janet Halley, Angela Harris, Cheryl Harris, Luke Harris, Jerry Kang, Kim Krawiec, Gillian Lester, Don Langevoort, Jerry Lopez, Deborah Malamud, Ann McGinley, Carrie Menkel-Meadow, Jennifer Mnookin, Rachel Moran, Stephen Munzer, Martha Nussbaum, Charles Ogletree, Angela Onwuachi-Willig, Eric Posner, Gowri Ramachandran, Russell Robinson, Stephanie Robinson, Elizabeth Scott, Patrick Shin, David Sklansky, Clyde Spillenger, Ronald Sullivan, Sarah Sze, Kendall Thomas, Frank Valdes, Leti Volpp, Adrien Wing, Kenji Yoshino, and Noah Zatz.

We have benefitted from the help of numerous research assistants, including Peter Carr, Michael Dulong, Antonio Kizzie, Jelani Lindsey, Kelly Song, Zain Sharazi, Katherine Stewart, Kelvin Sun, and Hentyle Yapp. Briana Brake and Susanna Pfeffer provided invaluable administrative assistance. Thanks is due to our law schools, the Duke Center for Race, Law & Politics, UCLA's Critical Race Studies Program, UCLA's Williams Institute, the Fletcher Foundation and the African American Policy Forum's Writers Workshop, for providing research support and/or travel grants that supported the production of this book. Finally, thanks to our editor, David McBride, for his engagement with our work and for his patience and understanding.

Writing, thinking, and arguing about the issues in this book was not only a labor of love, it was fun. We have tried to infuse *Acting White?* with that spirit. Our hope is that you experience it as you read the book.

Acting White?

Acting Out the Racial Double Bind (or Being Black Like Obama)

Being an African American in a predominantly white institution is like being an actor on stage. There are roles one has to perform, storylines one is expected to follow, and dramas and subplots one should avoid at all cost. Being an African American in a predominantly white institution is like playing a small but visible part in a racially specific script. The main characters are white. There are one or two blacks in supporting roles. Survival is always in question. The central conflict is to demonstrate that one is black enough from the perspective of the supporting cast and white enough from the perspective of the main characters. The "double bind" racial performance is hard and risky. Failure is always just around the corner. And there is no acting school in which to enroll to rehearse the part.

Yet, blacks working in white institutions act out versions of this "double bind" racial performance every day. It is part of a broader phenomenon that we call "Working Identity." Working Identity is constituted by a range of racially associated ways of being, including how one dresses, speaks, styles one's hair; one's professional and social affiliations; who one marries or dates; one's politics and views about race; where one lives; and so on and so forth. The foregoing function as a set of racial criteria people can employ to ascertain not simply whether a person is black in terms of how she looks but whether that person is black in terms of how she is perceived to act. In this sense, Working Identity refers both to the perceived choices people make about their self-presentation (the racially associated ways of being listed above) and to the perceived identity that emerges from those choices (how black we determine a person to be).

Paying attention to Working Identity is important. Few institutions today refuse to hire any African Americans. Law expressly prohibits that form of discrimination and society frowns upon it. Indeed, most institutions profess a commitment to diversity, so much so that "diversity is good for business" is now a standard corporate slogan. Companies that invoke that mantra will have at least one black face on the company brochure or website.[1] Moreover, employers want to think of themselves as "colorblind." That perception is hard to sell if all the employees are white. Finally, to the extent that there are some blacks in the workplace, the employer can use them as a shield against charges of racism or racial insensitivity: "How can you say we are racist. Obviously, we wouldn't adopt a policy that would hurt our African American colleagues."

The reality today, therefore, is that most firms want to hire *some* African Americans. The question is, which ones? Working Identity provides a basis upon which they can do so. Employers can screen their application pool for African Americans with palatable Working Identities. These African Americans are not "too black"—which is to say, they are not racially salient as African Americans. Some of them might even be "but for" African Americans—"but for" the fact that they look black, they are otherwise indistinguishable from whites. From an employer's perspective, this sub-group of African Americans is racially comfortable in part because they negate rather than activate racial stereotypes. More generally, the employer's surmise is that these "good blacks" will think of themselves as people first and black people second (or third or fourth); they will neither "play the race card" nor generate racial antagonism or tensions in the workplace; they will not let white people feel guilty about being white; and they will work hard to assimilate themselves into the firm's culture. The screening of African Americans along these lines enables the employer to extract a diversity profit from its African American employees without incurring the cost of racial salience. The employer's investment strategy is to hire enough African Americans to obtain a diversity benefit without incurring the institutional costs of managing racial salience.

At least ten implications flow from what we have just said. Together, they constitute the core issues our book engages:

1.   Discrimination is not only an inter-group phenomenon, it is also an intra-group phenomenon. We should care both about employers preferring whites over blacks (an inter-group discrimination problem) and about employers preferring racially palatable blacks over racially salient ones (an intra-group discrimination problem).

2.   The existence of intra-group discrimination creates an incentive for African Americans to work their identities to signal to employers that they are racially palatable. They will want to cover up their racial salience to avoid being screened out of the application pool.

3.   Signaling continues well after the employee is hired. The employee understands that she is still black on stage; that her employer is watching her racial performance with respect to promotion and pay increases. Accordingly, she

becomes attuned to the roles her Working Identity performs. She will want the employer to experience her Working Identity as a diversity profit, not a racial deficit.

4. Working Identity requires time, effort, and energy—it is work, "shadow work." The phenomenon is part of an underground racial economy in which everyone participates and to which almost everyone simultaneously turns a blind eye.

5. Working Identity is not limited to the workplace. Admissions officers can screen applicants based on their Working Identity. Police officers can stop, search, and arrest people based on Working Identity. The American public can vote for politicians based on their Working Identity. Here, too, there are incentives for the actor—to work her identity to gain admissions to universities, to avoid unfriendly interactions with the police, and to gain political office.

6. Working Identity is costly. It can cause people to compromise their sense of self; to lose themselves in their racial performance; to deny who they are; and to distance themselves from other members of their racial group. Plus, the strategy is risky. Staying at work late to negate the stereotype that one is lazy, for example, can confirm the stereotype that one is incompetent, unable to get work done within normal work hours.

7. Working Identity raises difficult questions for law. One can argue that discrimination based on Working Identity is not racial discrimination at all. Arguably, it is discrimination based on behavior or culture rather than race. Therefore, perhaps the law should not intervene. And even assuming that this form of discrimination is racial discrimination, it still might be a bad idea for the law to get involved. Do we really want judges deciding whether a person is or isn't "acting white" or "acting black"—and the degree to which they might be doing so? It is difficult to figure out what role, if any, law should play.

8. Working Identity transcends the African American experience. Everyone works their identity. Everyone feels the pressure to fit in, including white, heterosexual men. But the existence of negative racial stereotypes increases those pressures and makes the work of fitting in harder and more time consuming. African Americans are not the only racial minority that experiences this difficulty, though our focus in the book is primarily on this group.

9. Nor is race the only social category with a Working Identity dimension. Women work their identities as feminine or not. Men are expected to act like men. Gays and lesbians are viewed along a continuum of acting straight or not. Racial performance is but part of a broader Working Identity phenomenon.

10. We all have a Working Identity whether we want to or not. Working Identity does not turn on the intentional, strategic behavior of the actor.

An employer might perceive an African American as racially palatable even if that person does not intend for the employer to racially interpret her in that way. Irrespective of strategic behavior on the part of the employee, the employer will racially judge her based not only on how she racially looks but also on how the employer perceives her to racially act.

Acting Like Obama

Americans understand the dynamic of being black on stage more than they might even realize. Barack Obama's ascendancy to the forefront of American politics has put the phenomenon into the public domain. Obama racially acted his way into the most significant role in the world, president of the United States. To do so, he successfully performed the racial "double bind," persuading white voters that he was not "too black" and black voters that he was "black enough."

Obama's persuasion techniques are almost always subtle. His performances are rarely racially didactic. Perhaps this is because we, his ever-watching political audience, are often (but as we shall see, not always) subtle about the racial roles we expect him to play. It is difficult for us to talk openly about a person's degree of blackness, as though racial identity were a thermometer. Few want to be accused of suggesting that a "real" black person should act one way or another. Leave it to late-night television to dispense with that worry.[2] A *Saturday Night Live* sketch featured cast members playing Jesse Jackson and Al Sharpton discussing whether America is ready for a black president. Their answer: it depends on the person's degree of blackness, or "scales of soul." They then proceed to ask whether Obama's degree of blackness will change as America gets to know him. Different social factors move Obama up and down the scales. The fact that his name is Barack moves him up to a higher degree of blackness. But that he was called Barry in high school moves him down. That he was raised by a single mother moves him up, but the fact that he was raised in Hawaii moves him down. His marriage to a black woman moves him up—and so does the fact that in the past he dated white women.

One can challenge the accuracy of both the biographical elements of Obama's family history and personal associations and whether they move people up and down some scale of blackness along the lines the skit suggests. Nonetheless, the skit reflected a phenomenon about which people were (sometimes only quietly) talking. In none of these discussions did anyone assert that Obama was white, though some emphasized that his mother was white and argued that the public discourse about his race obscured that fact. The issue was almost entirely about Obama's degrees of blackness. Both black and white voters were taking his racial temperature.

For Hollywood stars, such as Sarah Jessica Parker and George Clooney, Obama's racial temperature was just right: not too hot (which is to say, "not too black") and not too cold (which is to say, "not too white"). Other white voters read Obama's racial temperature that way as well. Two decades ago, when we were in law school and Obama had just finished his stint as the president of the *Harvard Law Review*, it was inconceivable to us that it would some day become fashionable for Hollywood stars to get behind a black man for president, let alone Barack Obama. Who would have thought that whites would be lining up to offer their support, leading the "yes we can" charge and proudly bearing Obama bumper stickers on their cars—even before many in the black community joined the effort? Who would have thought that a significant part of the Democratic political machinery would pick Obama over Hillary Clinton? This was all unimaginable. And yet all of this actually happened. The explanation—or at least part of it—was that Obama was not "too black," but still "black enough."

On Being Not "Too Black"

Obama is biracial—the son of a black man from a small village in Kenya and a white woman born in Kansas. He grew up largely with the white part of his family in Hawaii. His professional and academic credentials are impeccable—Harvard Law School graduate, president of the *Harvard Law Review*, law professor at the University of Chicago, among other accomplishments. From Obama's very early public appearance at the Democratic National Convention in 2004, he seems to have understood that his political future would turn on his ability to work his identity for a white audience. He seems to have understood that he could not enact a racial performance that his white audience would perceive as being "too black." He pitched his speech at the Democratic Convention to avoid being racially pigeonholed in that role.

> Now even as we speak, there are those who are preparing to divide us, the spin masters, the negative ad peddlers who embrace the politics of anything goes. Well, I say to them tonight, there is not a liberal America and a conservative America—there is the United States of America. There is not a Black America and a White America and Latino America and Asian America—there's the United States of America. The pundits,

the pundits like to slice-and-dice our country into Red States and Blue
States; Red States for Republicans, Blue States for Democrats. But
I've got news for them, too: We worship an awesome God in the Blue
States, and we don't like federal agents poking around in our libraries in
the Red States. We coach Little League in the Blue States and yes, we've
got some gay friends in the Red States.... We Are One People.[3]

The speech created a buzz. His audience loved it. Applause could be heard
for days.

Yet, nothing Obama said was particularly remarkable. Granted, the speech was
delivered with rhetorical flare, elegance, and grace. And, yes, Obama was, dare
we say, articulate. But the substance of the speech was at best perfectly fine—
nothing more—and not nearly as interesting or sophisticated as his subsequent
speech on race, about which we will say more later. What *was* striking about
Obama's performance, particularly from the perspective of a white audience,
was that a black political figure was talking passionately about American politics
without making them feel racially uncomfortable or racially guilty. At least some
white Americans could have interpreted Obama's performance as offering them
a kind of racial cover ("we are not racist because we support Obama"). This is
not hyperbole. There are discrimination cases in which the defendant's response
to the allegation of discrimination is basically to say: "I supported Obama for
president, therefore I cannot be a racist."[4]

But even if white Americans were not experiencing Obama in terms of
racial cover, they were certainly experiencing him in terms of racial palatability. Nothing in Obama's comments hinted at racial division, racial antagonism,
or racial conflict. Indeed, nothing in his speech hinted at civil rights. This
was not the Reverend Jesse Jackson. This was not Congressman John Lewis.
This was not Al Sharpton. Then presidential hopeful, Joseph Biden, pretty
much said as much. He described Obama as "the first mainstream African-
American who is articulate and bright and clean and a nice-looking guy."[5]
For *Washington Post* columnist Eugene Robinson, much of Biden's description was code for Obama's racial palatability to white voters. According to
Robinson:

There was a sharp reaction, mostly focused on Biden's incomprehensible
reference to personal hygiene. For my part, I never made it past "articulate," a word that's like fingernails on a blackboard to my ear.... Will won-
ders never cease? Here we have a man who graduated from Columbia
University, who was president of the *Harvard Law Review*, who serves
in the U.S. Senate and is the author of two best-selling books, who's

a leading contender for the Democratic presidential nomination, and what do you know, he turns out to be articulate. Stop the presses....

Yes, I'm ranting a bit. But before you accuse me of being hypersensitive, try to think of the last time you heard a white public figure described as articulate. Acclaimed white orators such as Bill Clinton and John Edwards are more often described as eloquent....What's intriguing is that Jackson and Sharpton are praised as eloquent, too—both men are captivating speakers who calibrate their words with great precision. But neither is often described as, quote, articulate. Apparently, something disqualifies them....

I realize the word is intended as a compliment, but it's being used to connote a lot more than the ability to express one's thoughts clearly. It's being used to say more, even, than "here's a black person who speaks standard English without a trace of Ebonics."

The word articulate is being used to encompass not just speech but a whole range of cultural cues—dress, bearing, education, golf handicap. It's being used to describe a black person around whom white people can be comfortable, a black person who not only speaks white America's language but is fluent in its body language as well.[6]

Biden recognized that he had committed a *faux pas* and apologized for any offense his comments might have caused. He had "no doubt that Jesse Jackson and every other black leader—Al Sharpton and the rest—will know exactly what I meant."[7] Jackson was forgiving, Sharpton less so. When Biden called Sharpton to apologize, Sharpton began the conversation with a note about his personal hygiene: "I told him I take a bath every day." For Sharpton, Biden's comments were less a verbal gaffe and more an effort on Biden's part to "discredit Mr. Obama with his base" by distinguishing him from political figures like Sharpton and Jackson.[8] It was an effort to demonstrate that Obama was not "black enough."

Obama, for his part, considered Biden's comments "unfortunate" and "historically inaccurate." According to Obama, "African-American presidential candidates like Jesse Jackson, Shirley Chisholm, Carol Moseley Braun and Al Sharpton gave a voice to many important issues through their campaigns, and no one would call them inarticulate."[9] This might well be so. But little if anything about Obama's campaign linked him to these political figures. More to the point, white voters continued to draw an intra-racial line between Obama, on the one hand, and other black political actors, on the other. Obama was a different kind of black politician, a new category of black.[10] He was racially palatable. He was racially comfortable. He was not "too black."

On Being "Black Enough"

But was he black enough? The fact that he lived on the south side of Chicago, attended a black church, and married a black woman all helped to shore up his racial authenticity. His relationship to basketball helped too. Obama seems to love the sport. And at least he thinks he is pretty good at it. Moreover, he prefers the Carolina Tar Heels to the Duke Blue Devils. "So what?" at least some of you must be asking. What's the relevance of that? Others of you, particularly the sports fans, might even be offended; we shouldn't make assumptions about a person's race or degree of blackness based on the sports team that person chooses to support. That goes too far.

And, indeed, race may have absolutely nothing to do with Obama's preference for Carolina. Perhaps when he lived in Chicago, he became a Michael Jordan fan. Any Chicago Bulls fan worth his salt knows of MJ's Carolina pedigree. Or, maybe this was simply an election strategy and had nothing to do with race. Obama needed to win North Carolina. His team would have known that there are more Tar Heel fans among the voters in that state than Blue Devil fans.[11]

But, just maybe, Working Identity is implicated here as well. Recall the *Saturday Night Live* skit. It would not have escaped Obama and his advisers that the basketball program at Duke has long been accused of pursuing only those black players who some argue "act white," whereas Carolina has long been perceived as the more authentically black team. Retired basketball player Jalen Rose made this point about Duke in an ESPN documentary:

> For me, Duke was personal. I hated Duke. And I hated everything I felt Duke stood for. Schools like Duke didn't recruit players like me. I felt like they only recruited black players that were Uncle Toms.

In a subsequent interview, Rose elaborated:

> Well, certain schools recruit a typical kind of player whether the world admits it or not. And Duke is one of those schools. They recruit black players from polished families, accomplished families. And that's fine. That's okay. But when you're an inner-city kid playing in a public school league, you know that certain schools aren't going to recruit you. That's one. And I'm okay with it. That's how I felt as an 18-year-old kid.[12]

Whether there is any merit to Rose's story is an open question (one of us teaches at Duke and would prefer to think that there isn't). The point is that, in the context of deciding which of the two teams should advance to the very end of the NCAA tournament, Obama and his advisers presumably understood the implications of picking Carolina over Duke. Assuming that Rose's characterization was at least partially shared by many in the black community, and particularly in North Carolina, where Obama desperately needed the black vote, this was a no-brainer. Preferring the Tar Heels would help with the black vote without alienating whites because UNC-Chapel Hill is more popular in the state anyway (it is the flagship state university). Picking Duke, on the other hand, could have compounded the extent to which some African Americans already perceived Obama to be insufficiently black—indeed, the kind of black that, according to Rose, Duke sought to recruit, the kind of black person who is not "black enough."

For comedian and television personality Bill Maher, Obama is at times exactly that kind of black person. Expressing disappointment with Obama's handling of the British Petroleum (BP) oil spill, Maher commented that Obama "is a little professorial. He saw someone [on the Gulf Coast] and said 'I have been briefed on your pain.'" Pulling no punches, Maher went on to add: "I thought when we elected a black president we were going to get a *black* president. This [BP oil spill] is where I want a *real* black president. I want him in a meeting with BP CEOs, you know, where he lifts up his shirt so they can see the gun in his pants. That's [in a "black" man's voice] 'we've gottamotherfu**ing problem here?' Then shoots someone in the foot."[13]

Maher was not the first to ask whether Obama is authentically black or black enough. Author Debra Dickerson commented that Obama is not "black" from an American political and cultural viewpoint because that term refers to those descended from West African slaves.[14] Obama—who she says is "as black as circumstances allow"[15]—has not experienced the burdens of the legacy of slavery. Princeton professor Cornel West also raised questions about Obama's racial identity and commitments. He did so in the context of criticizing Obama's decision to announce his presidential candidacy from the location where Abraham Lincoln's political career began, the Old State Capitol in Illinois, rather than from the State of the Black Union, Tavis Smiley's annual gathering.[16] According to West, Obama "speaks to white folks and holds us [African Americans] at arm's length."[17] The Reverend Al Sharpton, who is now a staunch Obama supporter, was, at the time of Obama's presidential run, even more pointed. "We cannot put our people's aspirations on hold for anybody's career, black or white," Sharpton observed.[18] "Just because you are our color doesn't make you our kind."[19] For Sharpton, the fact that Obama looked black (in the sense of having "our color") didn't mean that he acted black (in the sense of being one of "our kind").

To be fair to both West and Sharpton, one could say that they were simply noting that it was less than clear whether, if elected president, Barack Obama would be focused on the various dimensions of black inequality. Neither was concerned about whether Obama acts black or white per se. But a black person's political commitments and connections to the black community are factors some African Americans employ to ascertain whether a person is sufficiently black, as the Working Identity criteria we listed earlier attests. Just ask Supreme Court Justice Clarence Thomas. It is largely because of his political commitments and relationship to the black community that some African Americans continue to use the unfortunate term "Uncle Tom" to describe him.[20] West and Sharpton were not suggesting quite this much in their 2008 criticism of Obama, but they were commenting on the extent to which they perceived Obama to be *authentically* black. While neither West nor Sharpton even implicitly raises questions about Obama's blackness today (though West has been consistently critical of Obama's presidency), both deemed it appropriate and important at the time to comment on what Russell Robinson might call Obama's perceived "authenticity deficit."[21]

The issue has not gone away. There is now a literature exploring aspects of Obama's racial authenticity.[22] For example, Angela Onwuachi-Willig and Mario Barnes have argued that "[p]art of Obama's campaign strategy seemed to include an active disregard of race or 'racial' figures, even when they seemed difficult to ignore."[23] As evidence, they point to the fact that "when Obama accepted the Democratic nomination for the presidency on the forty-fifth anniversary of Dr. Martin Luther King, Jr.'s 'I have a Dream' speech, he never spoke the Reverend's name or even asserted the words 'black' or 'African American' during his speech."[24] Similarly, Eduardo Bonilla-Silva and Victor Ray maintain that Obama "distanced himself from most leaders of the civil rights movement, from his own reverend, from his own church, and from anything or anyone who makes him 'too black.'"[25] Finally, Frederick Harris has weighed in, provocatively raising the question of whether Obama's racial distancing suggests that we might "still [be] waiting for our first black president."[26] His point, at least implicitly, is that in terms of political commitments, Obama is not black enough.

Getting the Double Bind Racial Performance Right

Part of what intrigues us about Obama's Working Identity is that, quite apart from Obama's "true" behavioral inclinations, whatever those might be, he likely makes conscious choices about how to work his identity. When, for example, he learns about the BP oil spill or the plans to build a Muslim community center near Manhattan's Ground Zero, he can react with emotion, anger, erudition, and so on. These are choices. But Obama exercises these choices under enormous constraints. As we have said, he has to negotiate a racial "double bind." He has to be black enough to get buy-in from African Americans, but not so black that he loses the white vote. The difficulty for Obama is in knowing beforehand what racial performances will satisfy these two racial demands. When he gets this right, the results are striking.

Recall candidate Obama's now-famous speech on race. Many describe it as one of the greatest American speeches. It signaled the audacity of hope and stressed that we can become a more perfect union through racial healing, responsibility, and cooperation.[27] The enthusiastic response to his speech, while understandable, obscured that Obama's racial "double bind," the fact that he could afford to be neither "too black" nor "not black enough" is precisely what produced the historic address. More specifically, the speech was a reaction to what came to be known as Reverend Wright's "God Damn America" speech:

> The government gives them the drugs, builds bigger prisons, passes a three-strike law and then wants us to sing "God Bless America." No, no, no, God damn America, that's in the Bible for killing innocent people. God damn America for treating our citizens as less than human. God damn America for as long as she acts like she is God and she is supreme.[28]

The endless circulation of Wright's words, spoken four years earlier, created a firestorm of controversy. Obama was potentially in trouble. For more than twenty years and up until that moment, Wright had been Obama's pastor. In addition to marrying the Obamas, he had baptized their two daughters. Obama's initial reaction was to explain that Wright "is like an old uncle who says things I don't always agree with." This did little to squash the controversy. More was required. Few would have predicted that the "something more" would be a major speech on race. Such a speech could render him not simply "the candidate of race," to borrow the words of Rush Limbaugh, but the black candidate of race. The circulation of Wright's statements changed the calculus. The statements essentially blackened Obama. At least initially, when Obama was still suffering from an authenticity deficit, he could not simply have repudiated Reverend Wright. That would have made him not "black enough" in the eyes of some black voters.

Obama negotiated these competing racial demands—that he be "black enough" but not "too black"—by giving a speech in which he engaged race both in historical and contemporary terms. In the context of doing so he condemned and contextualized the minister's fiery comments. While Obama made clear that some of Wright's sermons reflect "a profoundly distorted view of this country—a view that sees white racism as endemic, and that elevates what is wrong with

America above all that we know is right with America," he also pointed out that Reverend Wright's church, "like other predominantly black churches across the country,...embodies the black community in its entirety....The church, contains in full the kindness and cruelty, the fierce intelligence and the shocking ignorance, the struggles and successes, the love and yes, the bitterness and bias that make up the black experience in America."[29]

Moreover, Obama specifically discussed ongoing racial inequality, noting that American schools are still segregated "fifty years after *Brown v. Board of Education,* and the inferior education they provided, then and now, helps explain the pervasive achievement gap between today's black and white students."[30] Racism, he maintained, is not something that resides "in the minds of black people"; it is a real problem that must be addressed "not just with words, but with deeds."[31]

That Obama criticized, but did not repudiate, Wright, and at the same time spoke unequivocally about the persistent problem of race, reduced the likelihood that people (especially blacks) would consider him not "black enough." Indeed, among the blacks who welcomed the speech, some worried that it might have made him "too black" in the eyes of whites.

This did not happen. Obama's poll numbers had dipped after Wright's comments became public, but the candidate recovered his ground after the speech. This political recovery was not just a function of the fact that Obama's speech reflected his now-familiar rhetorical signature—elegance, sophistication, and balance—but was also because, in addition to calling attention to racism, he spoke of our collective capacity to beat it. Moreover, he urged African Americans to link their "particular grievances—for better health care, and better schools, and better jobs—to the larger aspirations of all Americans—the white woman struggling to break the glass ceiling, the white man who's been laid off, the immigrant trying to feed his family."[32] He called for racial solidarity, not racial balkanization, and racial unity, not racial division. Further, he admonished blacks to take "full responsibility for our own lives—by demanding more from our fathers, and spending more time with our children, and reading to them."[33] The themes of racial cooperation, racial unity, and black social responsibility throughout his speech reduced the likelihood that people (especially whites) would consider him "too black."

That Obama was negotiating the line between being "black enough" and not "too black" in his speech is reflected in his own words: "At every stage of the campaign, commentators have deemed me either 'too black' or 'not black enough.'"[34] There is reason to believe that this awareness shaped the very way in which Obama structured his presidential bid. According to the *New York Times,* Obama directed members of his staff to devise a strategy, based on existing research, not only for how he should manage the question of race throughout the campaign, but also for how he should make Americans "comfortable with the idea of putting a black family in the White House."[35] In this sense, Obama's staff was advising him not only on matters of policy but also on how he should work his identity. Whether Obama continues to receive or request such advice is hard to know. What is clear is that his Working Identity is always on the political table.

Consider the case of Trayvon Martin, a seventeen-year-old black male who was shot and killed by George Zimmerman, allegedly in self-defense. The story quickly became headline news and required Obama to work his identity in response. Trayvon was wearing a hooded sweatshirt at the time, and some attributed his death to that fact. According to Geraldo Rivera, for example, the hoodie was "as much responsible for Trayvon Martin's death as George Zimmerman was."[36] From Rivera's perspective, in effect, the hoodie took away Trayvon's innocence and turned him into a "bad" black. "Trayvon Martin's you know, god bless him, he's an innocent kid, a wonderful kid, a box of Skittles in his hand. He didn't deserve to die," Rivera commented.[37] "[I]f he didn't have that hoodie on, that— that nutty neighborhood watch guy wouldn't have responded in that violent and aggressive way."[38] For Geraldo, the lesson from all of this is clear: "[P]arents of black and Latino youngsters particularly [should] not…let their children go out wearing hoodies." He added, "People look at you [in a hoodie], and what's the instant identification? What's the instant association?…[S]omeone stickin' up a 7-Eleven…[A] mugging on a surveillance."[39] Concern about these associations has caused Rivera to instruct his own "particularly dark-skinned…son Cruz (24)" not to wear hoodies.[40]

The shooting, statements about hoodies, and the police (mis)handling of the investigation, created a furor. Initially, Obama said nothing. Then, in response to pressure from leaders in the black community (who pointed out that he had not hesitated to reach out to the Georgetown law student whom Rush Limbaugh had called a "slut"), he intervened,[41] observing that: "If I had a son, he'd look like Trayvon."[42] This carefully crafted statement reminded all Americans that Obama is black and reminded African Americans that Obama conceives of himself as black. Moreover, the statement signaled that, because Obama exists within a black family context, he and his family are vulnerable to racism. Essentially, Obama was saying: If I had a son, he'd be black; as such, he would be subject to the kind of risk that resulted in Trayvon Martin's death. All of this subtle signaling solidified Obama's connection to African Americans. In that moment, he was "black enough."

At the same time, Obama's comments did not alienate white Americans. This is because they were not explicitly racialized. Few quarreled with Obama's statement "If I had a son, he'd look like Trayvon." How could they? It is descriptively accurate at least in the sense that if Obama had a son he would indeed look black. This is hardly a controversial claim, and at any rate, is not the kind of statement that would make Obama "too black." Like his speech on race, then, this was another successful "double bind" racial performance.

Much is at stake with respect to whether Obama successfully performs the racial "double bind." Small missteps in acting "too black" or not "black enough" can negatively impact the public's reactions to his domestic and foreign policy initiatives. How Obama works his identity shapes and is shaped by the positions he takes on Iran, the Middle East peace process, the financial crisis, immigration reform, and marriage equality. As we write this, in mid-2012, a presidential campaign is under way. And this time, entitlement programs are likely to be at the heart of the debate. Obama's opponents are going to push him to defend these programs, knowing that the widespread perception is that the primary beneficiaries are black.[43] This could render Obama the "welfare president," an idea that could still take root in and grow from the same fertile racial ground as the "welfare queen." This is not far-fetched. Prior to dropping out of the Republican primary, Newt Gingrich repeatedly referred to President Obama as the "food stamp president."[44] And, more recently, Mitt Romney, the Republican nominee for president, has released a series of negative advertisements falsely stating that Obama seeks to eliminate welfare-to-work requirements that make the receipt of welfare contingent upon fulfilling certain work obligations. These advertisements, like Gingrich's comments, forward the idea of Obama as the "welfare president." Were white Americans to perceive Obama in that way, it could move him up the scales of blackness, rendering him "too black."

From the other side of the "double bind," Obama will likely continue to contend with questions about whether he is "black enough." In this respect, one can query whether his recent position supporting marriage equality for gay and lesbian couples will move him down the scale. This seems unlikely, both because the African American community's views on gay marriage, like those of other racial groups, are in flux and because Obama's intervention has generated a robust debate among black churches and among African Americans more generally on this very issue. None of this debate has been about whether this church or that one, or this African American or that one, is "black enough." Instead, the debate has been about whether the Bible supports same-sex marriage and whether, as an historically subordinated group, African Americans in particular should be supportive of LGBT rights. Quite apart from how this debate comes out, there is every reason to believe that, going forward, Obama will continue to have to shore up his relationship to African Americans—but without racially threatening or alienating white Americans. This "double bind" racial performance is part of a broader script that Obama's position on the most visible stage in the world requires him to enact.

Beyond Obama

Obama is not alone in his dilemma. African Americans in predominantly white institutions experience similar performance pressures all the time. They, too, have to negotiate a racial "double bind." They, too, are black on stage. Although "double bind" racial pressures in the workplace can take a variety of institutional forms, perhaps the best example is the employer who wants his African American employee to be black enough to function as racial window dressing for the firm (for example, by serving as *the* African American representative on important committees) but not so black as to create racial conflict or discomfort in the workplace (for example, by agitating for robust diversity initiatives within the institution).

That many African Americans find themselves negotiating the line between being "black enough" but not "too black" suggests that they are not passive objects of discrimination, waiting for the experience to happen to them and complaining about it after the fact. They proactively work their identities to avoid discrimination in the first place. This is what Johnny Williams did in the context of his job search subsequent to completing his MBA degree from Booth School at the University of Chicago. After a miserable time in the 2010 job market, Williams embarked on a set of strategies to increase his market appeal. One involved removing all references to race from his resume. "His membership, for instance, in the African American business students association? Deleted."[45] According to an article by Michael Luo of the *New York Times*, Williams's logic was this: "If they're going to X me, I'd like to at least get in the door first."[46]

Williams's account was part of a more general story the *New York Times* ran about the racial gap in employment opportunities for white and black college graduates. Roughly a week later the *Times* ran another article by Luo, "'Whitening' the Resume."[47] It focused on the resume-whitening strategies African Americans employ to minimize the salience of their blackness. These strategies are not about "passing" in the sense of presenting oneself as white to escape the burdens and disadvantages of being black. Indeed, because some institutions are expressly interested in diversifying their ranks, it is sometimes helpful to be identifiable as black. The question is, how black? In whitening his resume, Williams was not denying his race. He was trying to appear less black "to at least get in the door."[48]

Williams's story converges with a central theme of *Acting White*, namely, that the resume-whitening phenomenon is a mechanism some African Americans use to appear racially palatable or not "too black." Invoking the experience of another African American, the *New York Times* article hit the nail on the head: "Activism in black organizations, even majoring in African-American studies can be signals to employers"—signals that suggest that one is too black.[49] Eliminating those explicit racial markers is one way of "calming down on the blackness," to quote Yvonne Orr, who has worked for fifteen years in fund-raising for nonprofits.[50] Looking for work in Chicago, Orr "removed her bachelor's degree from Hampton University, a historically black college, leaving just her master's degree from Spertus Institute, a Jewish school. She also deleted a position she once held at an African-American nonprofit organization and rearranged her references so that the first references listed were not black."[50] In adjusting her resume, Orr was following her mother's advice. Notwithstanding the fact that Orr's parents had been members of the Black Panther Party in the 1960s, Orr's mother instructed her daughter that she didn't need to "shout out, 'I'm black'" on her resume.[51] In effect, Orr's mother was advising her on how to work her identity to be more racially palatable to prospective employers.

Decision-makers—whether voters, employers, law enforcement officials, or school admissions officers—implicitly or explicitly demand that African Americans work their identities to satisfy decision-makers' racial expectations. Failure to work one's identity can result in losing elections, unpleasant and even deadly interactions with law enforcement, losing out on jobs, being passed over for promotions, and denial of admission to educational institutions. The disadvantages are not a product of simply being black. They are a product of how black a decision-maker perceives a particular person to be. In this respect, what we describe is not so much an interracial discrimination problem (decision-makers preferring whites over blacks) but rather an intra-racial discrimination problem (decision-makers preferring some blacks over others). The eight chapters that follow explore the different contexts in which this form of discrimination can occur and explain why the phenomenon should concern us.

Chapter 1, "Why Act White?" asks a central question about Working Identity: why would a person of color do it? Why might an African American, for example, "act white" or not act "too black"? The answer is, to be racially palatable to the majority race. Being racially palatable is hard against the background of negative stereotypes associated with one's race. Chapter 1 describes the incentives for African Americans to work their identities to disconfirm these racial stereotypes. There are a myriad of strategies a person might use. These include strategic passing (I might look black, but I am not *really* black), racial comforting (I won't make you feel guilty about being white), and racial distancing (I don't hang out with other black people). All these strategies have costs. To the extent that an employee is overly concerned with negating racial stereotypes, he may take on too much work (to prove that he is not lazy), attend too many social events (to prove that he is "one of the guys"), refuse to ask for help when he needs it (to avoid the impression that he is unqualified), or avoid other racial minorities who might mentor him (to signal that he is racially colorblind). In short, an employee who is worried about negating racial stereotypes may end up with more work and fewer resources than his white counterparts. Chapter 1 sets out these and other costs of Working Identity.

Chapter 2, "Talking White," explores the ways in which conversations at work are implicated in the Working Identity phenomenon. For the most part, people invoke "talking race" to discuss either accent discrimination (for example, an employer who refuses to hire a person because she sounds "too Asian") or racial discrimination (for example, a landlord who invites a prospective tenant to see an apartment because the person "talked white" but then refuses to rent the apartment to that person upon discovering that the person is black). Chapter 2 highlights a more subtle speech dynamic that disadvantages African Americans in the workplace: what an African American says at work can confirm or negate stereotypes of black people and make her more or less racially salient as an African American. Talking white, then, is not just about accent, it is also about substance. Substantively, anything an African American says that diminishes the extent to which her employer or her co-workers perceive her to be black is "talking white." On the flipside, anything an African American says that increases the extent to which she is perceived to be black is "talking black." Within majority-white workplaces, talking white is more advantageous to the employee than talking black. Chapter 2 explains why.

Chapter 3, "Acting Like a Black Woman" focuses on Working Identity dynamics as they affect black women. Black feminists have long argued that black women are doubly burdened, inside and outside the corporate context, because of the intersection of their race and gender. Scholars often cite *Rogers v. American Airlines*, an important anti-discrimination case, to make this point.[53] Renee Rogers was terminated from her job as a flight attendant because she wore her hair in braids. In part, the plaintiff's argument was that American Airlines's policy prohibiting its employees from wearing braids disparately impacted black women—that is, it impacted black women more than any other social group. Chapter 3 demonstrates how the *Rogers* case also implicates Working Identity. Hair is a part of a person's Working Identity. In the corporate

context, black women who wear their hair in braids or dreadlocks are less palatable and more racially salient than black women who do not. An employer
can interpret the decision to braid or dread one's hair as a decision not to "act
white," or as a decision to act "too black."

Our hope is that chapters 1 through 3 will persuade readers that we should
take the Working Identity phenomenon seriously. Some readers might be persuaded and still wonder whether Working Identity is something the law can
and should manage. As it turns out, the law is already managing a version of this
problem. Chapter 4, "Acting Like a White Woman," demonstrates one context
in which this is so. Central to chapter 4 is the widespread recognition that a
woman's vulnerability to discrimination is a function of her Working Identity, or
the way she expresses her gender. Institutions treat women differently depending on whether they are perceived to be masculine or feminine. A case involving
a Nevada casino that terminated a white female bartender because she refused
to wear makeup demonstrates this point. We discuss this case to illustrate the
relationship between Working Identity and sex discrimination cases involving
white women. To the extent that courts take performance dynamics seriously in
the context of gender cases involving white women, it is worth thinking about
whether they should do so with respect to race as well, a question we pick up in
chapter 7. Before doing so, we take the discussion beyond the corporate context in chapters 5 and 6.

Chapter 5, "(Not) Acting Criminal," focuses on racial profiling. Identity performances play a crucial role in the context of both police interactions and public
policy discussions about racial profiling. To avoid being stopped by the police,
black people might drive less frequently than they otherwise would, drive less
flashy cars when they do, and avoid wearing hoodies while driving. To terminate
a police encounter, a black person might refrain from asserting his right (to signal that he is a "good black"), be overly cooperative (to signal that he is not an
angry black man), consent to searches he has a right to refuse (to signal that he
is not carrying drugs). In each example, the Working Identity strategy is to perform law-abidingness against a background stereotype of criminality. The strategy is also at play in public policy discussions about racial profiling. For example,
at the height of the public campaigns against racial profiling, the campaign of
the American Civil Liberties Union (ACLU) against racial profiling included
the circulation of images of well-dressed and seemingly respectable black men.
Its implicit message is that because racial profiling is affecting the lives of "good"
black men, the practice should be abolished.

Chapter 6, "Acting Diverse," focuses on affirmative action. The Supreme
Court has been clear that diversity is a compelling justification for affirmative

action. In accepting this rationale, the Court rejected a number of others, including the existence of societal discrimination, role modeling, and the underrepresentation of minorities in certain professional and occupational settings. Focusing on higher education, chapter 6 raises the question of whether the diversity rationale for affirmative action encourages admissions officers to screen applicants to ascertain whether they are "too diverse" or not "diverse enough," a corollary of the "too black" or not "black enough" problem we discuss. We provide concrete examples to illustrate the different ways in which university officials may intra-racially select among African American applicants, preferring some over others, depending on how these applicants have worked their identities in their applications.

Our final two chapters focus on solutions. Chapter 7, "Acting Within the Law," outlines two broad anti-discrimination approaches judges might take to tackle the Working Identity problem. Neither is completely satisfying. Thus, chapter 8, "Acting White to Help Other Blacks" explores whether solutions may lie at the level of individual action. There is a growing sense that the representation of people of color at the top of institutions will produce trickle-down benefits to those on the bottom. Chapter 7 questions this assumption. The presence of people of color at the top of the corporate hierarchy may do little to help those at the bottom. Indeed, notwithstanding the strong notion in the black community that African Americans should "lift as we climb," incentives exist for African Americans at the top of the ladder to pull it up behind them once they land on higher corporate ground. Doing so helps them to blend in, to solidify the firm's impression of them as racial exceptions, and to maintain their status as "good blacks." Working to increase the number of blacks in a firm is a surefire way to racially stand out.

The epilogue notes some of the objections we heard once we began circulating our book manuscript. We respond to those concerns and in doing so share our optimism—that the Working Identity phenomenon and intra-racial discrimination will soon move from the margins of legal discourse into more mainstream conversations about race, law, and equality. Shifting racial discourse in this way is important. Anti-discrimination law and the reputational harms of maintaining all-white work environments substantially diminish the likelihood that employers will discriminate against *all* blacks. Employers who want to discriminate are likely to do so by discriminating against a subset of blacks based on their Working Identity. This creates an incentive for black prospective employees to signal that they are "good" by adopting precisely some of the strategies Michael Luo's *New York Times* articles mentioned. We need to have a much better sense of the extent to which people are engaged in these strategies.

We need to think much harder about what, if anything, the law can do. And we need to identify much better mechanisms for holding a range of institutional decision-makers—employers, police officers, admissions officials—more accountable to the extent that they engage in intra-racial distinctions of the sort this book describes. Our optimism is that *Acting White?* will put us closer to accomplishing these goals.

Why *Act* White?

In Comedy Central's hit, *The Chappelle Show*, host Dave Chappelle presents a number of skits under the rubric of "when keeping it real goes wrong." Each skit illustrates the cost of being true to one's convictions, or "keeping it real" (See figure 1.1). One of these skits helps frame this chapter. It features a black male executive, Vernon Franklin. As it opens, we see Vernon walking confidently though the corridors of the corporation for which he works. He is on his way to what appears to be the prized corner office. In the next shots, he is shown sitting at his desk, both poring over his work and leisurely reading the newspaper. He seems comfortable and happy.

Subsequently, we see him in a conference room with several other executives, all of whom are white. As he moves through the halls, to his office, to the

Figure 1.1 Dave Chappelle.
Source: © Laura Farr/ZUMA/Corbis.

conference room, a narrator offers an account of Vernon's life and relationship to the corporation that introduces and contextualizes the "when keeping it real goes wrong" moment that lies just ahead:

NARRATOR: Vernon Franklin was an exceptional young man. He was the valedictorian of his high school class, won several scholarships, and became the first person in his family to attend college. He got a good job and worked 14-hour days six days a week, quickly becoming the youngest vice president in the history of the Viacorp Corporation, ending the cycle of violence and drug addiction that had plagued his family for generations. The offices of his company were wrapping up the usual Thursday meeting in the south conference room, when Frank Murphy, the man who had mentored Vernon, made an awkward comment.

FRANK: Vernon, great job, buddy. You da man!! Give me some skin, huh? (stretches out hand for hi five)

NARRATOR: Vernon got along with all of the people he worked with, which in his heart of hearts, made him feel like an Uncle Tom. Though he could have ignored the simple comment his mentor made, Vernon decided to "keep it real."

VERNON: Get your mother fucking hand out of my face. You heard me motherfucker, get your hand out of my face! What you think this is man? Just shake my hand like a man! Got to give me some five, on the back-hand side, and all this crazy jive. That's bullshit. (Begins to do stereotypical racially comedic shuck and jive dance routine.) Want a little soft shoe? Should I juggle some Oreos over here for you boss? Fuck all that shit, nigga.

FRANK: Vernon, buddy… (reaches out to grab Vernon's arm).

VERNON: Get your mother fucking hands off me, Frank! This ain't a game!

FRANK: This ain't the Vernon I know.

VERNON: Allow me to re-introduce myself, my name is Hov! (famous rap lyric). You never heard that before have you? Rap music is dangerous! I used to beat motherfuckers up just like you. Just for walking around my way!

FRANK: (Stands up) Vernon, Vernon, buddy.

VERNON: You better sit the fuck down, Frank. I said sit down, bitch! Thug Life! Think it's a game, nigga? (barks twice imitating rapper, DMX) Wu-Tang!!

The scene cuts to the consequences of Vernon's blowup, as we see Vernon pumping gas and washing car windows at a local gas station after being fired for his tirade. The narrator ends this way: "Vernon Franklin, once a heartwarming story of perseverance. Today, a startling example of when keeping it real goes wrong."

Chappelle's "when keeping it real goes wrong" highlights the theme of this chapter: working within an organization entails negotiating and working one's identity. This includes managing the impressions of one's supervisors, co-workers, and subordinates. How employees do so may surprise you. Think of an organization that values effort (and not just outcomes). Assume that effort is difficult to demonstrate, and that the organization awards promotions to those who show that they are expending lots of effort. Under this scenario, the employee is in something of a pickle. How does she show that in completing a particular task she gave it her all? Consider the following few ways in which the employee might do so.

In the context of having a casual conversation at the workplace, the employee might mention how tired she is as a result of having had to work all through the previous two nights. More obliquely, she might comment that she has a wonderful view of the sunrise from her office, or she might cultivate a harried and tired look to suggest that she is very busy. She might leave her jacket in the office and the lights on when she leaves early so as to suggest that she was at work later than she was. Or she might e-mail documents late at night. The list of effort-suggestive actions or "signaling strategies" goes on. The point is that if effort is a criterion for promotion, and if it is difficult to observe, employees have an incentive to work their identities in ways that suggest to the employer what otherwise might not be readily apparent.

What does this have to do with "acting white"? After all, employees of all identities feel pressured to signal to their employers that they belong and possess the right institutional stuff to succeed. White people, people of color, men, women, heterosexuals, and gays and lesbians all have to work their identities to fit into and thrive in their workplaces. Our claim is that the problem is worse for people of color than it is for whites, worse for women than it is for men, and worse for gays and lesbians than it is for heterosexuals. Focusing on race, we will explain why this is so.

As an initial matter, it is helpful to explain what we mean by *identity*. Nothing deep or philosophical. Think of identity as falling into one of two categories: *sense of self identity* (how we define and perceive ourselves) and *ascriptive identity* (how others define and perceive us). Admittedly, this distinction is artificial because how we see ourselves is shaped by how others see us. For example, a person's view of herself as outgoing, creative, and witty is based in part on other people experiencing her in those ways. Nevertheless, the distinction helps, if only because, at the end of the day, most of us do develop particular views of ourselves. We sometimes call this our *self-image*. While one's self-image can certainly change over time, at any given moment, we are likely to have one.

This chapter places these definitions of identity in the context of a broader discussion about race and professional identity in the workplace.[1] We argue that because people of color often perceive themselves to be the subjects of negative stereotyping, they are likely to feel the need to do significant amounts of identity work to counter those stereotypes. What is worse, these stereotypes are often in tension with the institutional norms around which the workplace is organized. As a result of this tension, persons of color must master the ability to negotiate between their sense of self and their sense of who the institution wants them to be.

As an example of how this negotiation might work, assume an employer that values hard work or effort from its employees. The firm also rewards even more amorphous qualities, such as collegiality, teamwork, and trust. Because each of these characteristics is hard to observe, employees seeking success in a corporate environment have an incentive to signal that they are hardworking, collegial, team oriented, and trustworthy. To signal collegiality, an employee might go out drinking with her colleagues, attend the firm's social events, or participate on company sports teams. True, the foregoing actions may not be enough, or even necessary, to demonstrate collegiality.[2] But when employers value attributes that are hard to observe, individual employees have an incentive to take actions that suggest that they have those attributes.[3]

How will the employee decide what actions he should take to signal to the employer that he exhibits one of those prized attributes? The answer turns on a negotiation, on how he chooses to negotiate his identity at work. Consider a shy and reserved employee who enjoys his job. He is happiest when he goes to work and performs his duties with little or no non-job-related interactions with his co-workers. He does not enjoy, and thus would rather not attend, official or unofficial after-work social events. However, he is aware that his organization values and encourages collegiality. Indeed, while he believes that because many of the people considered for promotion have the same credentials and overall work quality and productivity, he knows that collegiality is also an important criterion for promotion.

If this employee is interested in advancing, he will make a decision about how to best balance his preferred routine of nonsocialization while maximizing his opportunities for advancement. Thus, he will engage in a negotiation.[4] The negotiation is between his sense of self and his sense of the institutional values involved (in this case, collegiality).[5] He may decide that he cannot compromise his sense of identity, that he is happy with his routine, and that engaging in office small talk or attending after-work events would interfere with that happiness. He may also choose not to explore other ways of maximizing his opportunities for advancement.

Alternatively, the employee may decide that while he would rather not socialize with his colleagues, he should nonetheless do so to improve his chances of promotion. Whatever he decides, he will take a series of actions that reflect his decision. This is an example of an employee being engaged in a continual process of negotiating and working his identity.[6] The choice of how to work identity is a negotiation to the extent that it reflects a conflict resolution.[7] The employee seeking advancement has an incentive to resolve the conflict between his sense of identity and his sense of the institutional or workplace identity he needs to project to signal to his employer that he has the qualities the employer values.

The preceding hypothetical may sound somewhat abstract. To make this negotiation dynamic more concrete, we will break the process down into four stages and apply each stage to Chappelle's "when keeping it real goes wrong" clip.

The Four Stages of Racial Negotiation

Stage 1. Here, the employee has a sense of himself. This sense of self allows him to distinguish between two kinds of personal conduct: identity-affirming conduct that comports with his sense of identity and identity-negating conduct that runs afoul of the employee's sense of his identity. This identity-affirming/identity-negating dichotomy is reflected in common expressions, such as "I sold out," "I compromised my beliefs," and "It was so unlike me to do X."[8] Assume that Vernon, the character in Chappelle's clip, considers himself to be a person with integrity who does not acquiesce to stereotypes about African Americans.

Stage 2. Assume now that the employee forms an impression about the criteria that the institution values. Let us stipulate that in Vernon's workplace, the criteria include both collegiality and being thick-skinned and not overly sensitive about race.

Stage 3. At this point, the employee realizes that a conflict exists between his sense of self as a person with racial integrity and his sense of the people the institutional values—namely, those who are collegial and not overly racially sensitive. This is the moment in the clip when Vernon realizes that, while showing his mentor and senior colleague "some skin" in the form of a high five would advance the perception that he is collegial and demonstrate that he is not overly racially sensitive, doing so would compromise his sense of self as a person with racial integrity.

Stage 4. Here, Vernon has to decide whether to resolve the conflict, and how precisely he wants to do so. This is the negotiation. He could decide, like Sammy Davis, Jr., that "I've got to be me."[9] Or, like Polonius in Hamlet, his mantra might be "to thine own self be true."[10] His performance will reflect this negotiation—he will either not show his senior colleague "some skin" or he may compromise and high five his mentor. In the clip, as noted earlier, Vernon chooses the former and finds himself fired from his job and cleaning car windows as a result.

All employees, regardless of their identities, feel pressure to fit into the workplace. Every employee is subject to the negotiation dynamic we describe. Everyone works identity. However, race can increase the likelihood that one's sense of self will be in conflict with criteria that an institution values, and, correspondingly, race can increase the pressure one feels to compromise one's sense of identity. This is because racial stereotypes often conflict with institutional criteria. When this is the case, the employee's assumption is that the employer's stereotypes about her are at odds with the criteria that the employer values. The stronger the employee's perception of this conflict, the stronger the incentives are for her to signal—by working her identity—that she possesses the criteria that the institution values, and the stronger the incentive for the employee to compromise her identity.

Think about this in terms of bargaining power. All other things equal, an employee would rather not compromise her sense of identity; she would rather not have to work her identity to demonstrate that who she is at work corresponds with who the employer wants her to be. Her bargaining power to avoid this compromise and the extra identity work it entails is a function of existing negative stereotypes about her identity. The stronger the stereotypes, and the greater their conflict with institutional norms, the weaker her bargaining power. The weaker her bargaining power, the more she has to compromise her identity and engage in the extra identity work to signal that she fits in.

If we are right that the existence of negative racial stereotypes (particularly as they conflict with institutional norms) creates an incentive for employees to work their identity to negate those stereotypes, the next question is, what forms will these identity performances take? We offer six possibilities: racial comfort, strategic passing, using prejudice, racial discomfort, selling out, and buying back. Before we more fully describe these Working Identity strategies, three caveats are in order. First, in suggesting that there are categories of Working Identity, we are not arguing that one can predict whether, when, and how an employee will adopt them. Second, we are not making an empirical claim that every Outsider at some point or another will adopt one or more of the strategies we describe. Our argument is that the existence of negative stereotypes creates incentives for Outsiders to utilize them, not that Outsiders necessarily will. Third, the six Working Identity categories we delineate are clearly related. We describe each one separately for conceptual clarity. We begin with racial comforting.

Racial Comforting

This occurs when Outsiders work their identities to make Insiders feel comfortable with their outsider status.[11] For example, a perception may exist that a Muslim or Chinese American has conflicted feelings of loyalty to the United States.[12] Assume that promotion in a scientific laboratory involved in weapons research is a function of success on the most important projects. Junior scientists are picked for these projects not only on the basis of their scientific abilities but also for their loyalty and the ability to work in teams. Assume that, based on stereotypes, the senior scientists at the laboratory recognize that the junior Muslim and Chinese American scientists are exceptional in terms of scientific ability, but deem them untrustworthy and individually rather than team-oriented. What kinds of strategies might these Outsiders take in order to comfort (i.e., appear less foreign and more "American" to) their senior colleagues?

They could emphasize the fact that they attended American colleges, were members of fraternities, or played quintessential American team sports like football and baseball. They could avoid associating with other Muslims or Asians and instead associate only with white Americans. They could change their names to more American-sounding ones. They could also announce that they have never visited Asia or the Middle East and do not speak any of the languages from that region. They could make jokes about the "stupid terrorists" having "weird accents." They could display American flags on their cars and lockers—and outside their homes. Such actions may serve to comfort Insiders and assure them that the Outsider is more of an Insider, effectively "one of the guys," despite his Outsider status. Depending on how successful the Outsider is at providing racial comfort, he may even become an honorary Insider, or, to employ the more specific racial term, an "honorary white."

As another example of providing racial comfort, consider the case of a white male employee who tells jokes about a Chinese character. The employee puts on the stereotypical Chinese accent commonly heard in the movies and on television. An Outsider hearing this joke could laugh, stay silent, or point out that his co-worker is being racist. Laughing would supply racial comfort. If the Outsider laughs, it increases the likelihood that his white co-worker will probably view him as a person of color who can take a joke, is not obsessed with race, and with whom he is likely to feel (racially) comfortable.[13] Alternatively, if the Outsider suggests that the caricature is racist and offensive, it increases the likelihood that the white male employee will perceive the Outsider negatively—that is, as a person who is humorless, too racially sensitive, and therefore uncomfortable to be around. Should the outsider decide to challenge the joke, he will paradoxically be viewed as someone who is not racially neutral and who thrives on playing the race card.

The preceding discussion might lead one to conclude that "acting white" always produces racial comfort and that "acting black" always produces racial discomfort. This is not, in fact, the case. Sometimes the reverse is true.[14] Consider this point with respect to the movie *Crash*.[15] In it, Terrance Howard plays the role of an African American director, Ken. After he finishes shooting a scene and yells, "cut and print," his white producer and senior colleague, Fred, played by Tony Danza, approaches him with some concerns over how one of the black actors, Jamal, is speaking in the scenes.

FRED: Ken, Ken, you got a second?

KEN: Yea, Fred, I just want to grab some coffee.

FRED: Yea, listen, I think we need another take, buddy.

KEN: A huh? That looked pretty terrific man.

FRED: This is gonna sound strange, but is Jamal seeing a speech coach or something?

KEN: What do you mean?

FRED: Haven't you noticed uh, I think this is weird for a white guy to say, but have you noticed, he's talking a lot less black lately?

KEN: (laughs) No, I haven't noticed that.

FRED: Really? Like in this scene he was supposed to say "don't be talkin bout that" and he changed it to "don't talk to me about that."

KEN: (laughs again) Wait a minute, wait a minute you think because of that the audience won't recognize him as being a black man? Come on.

FRED: Is there a problem, Ken?

KEN: Excuse me?

FRED: (stares at Ken) Is there a problem, Ken?

KEN: (obviously uncomfortable) No . . . we don't have a problem.

FRED: I mean, that's all I'm saying is it's not his character. Eddie's supposed to be the smart one, not Jamal right? I mean, you're the expert here, but to me it rings false.

KEN: We're going to do it one more time.

FRED: Thanks, buddy.

This scene reflects a more generalizable problem in Hollywood. As Hilton Als put it in a March 10, 2010, *New Yorker* article on the topic, "The sad fact is that, in order to cross over, most black actors of Mackie's generation must "*act* black" before they're allowed to act human." Just as "acting black" is a way for black actors to fit into Hollywood, it can also be a way for black people to fit into other aspects of American life. We do not mean to suggest, then, that "acting white" always provides racial comfort. Sometimes, "acting black" is what is called for.

Strategic Passing

One way to describe passing is to say that it is a phenomenon in which an Outsider fools Insiders into believing that the Outsider is one of the Insiders. In this sense, passing is a 100% comfort strategy because the Outsider pretends to be one of them.[16] We refer to passing of this sort as *complete passing*. For example, a light-skinned African American may pass for white, a gay or lesbian may pass as a heterosexual, a Hindu may pass as a Muslim, a Jew may pass as a gentile, or a man may pass as a woman. In each of the examples, the passing is complete in the sense that, as far as the average observer is concerned, the Outsider is an Insider. On the other hand, the fact that Outsiders can pass has historically made Insiders uncomfortable. White anxieties about blacks passing for white run deep, and the discourse about the "down low" reflects a similar anxiety about gay black men passing for straight.[17]

With respect to race, this 100%, or complete, passing strategy applies only to a small subset of Outsiders, because most nonwhites cannot fully pass. Therefore, we focus on partial passing strategies, wherein the Outsider's status is known, but she works her identity to modify the stereotypical assumptions about or otherwise suppress the salience of that status. A person might partially pass in two ways: distancing herself from the Outsider group or embracing the Insider group.

With respect to racial distancing, a Latina who is bilingual might refuse to speak Spanish. A black person might avoid associating with other black people. A Korean American might change her name from Mi-Young to Julie or even have eyelid surgery.[18] In none of these instances is the person attempting to fully claim a white identity. However, each strategy may reflect an attempt to downplay or minimize racial difference. By characterizing partial passing in this way we are not suggesting that Outsiders should highlight their differences, racial or otherwise. Nor are we arguing for multiculturalism, whatever that might mean. We simply note that passing entails people both fully "escaping" their Outsider identity (complete passing) and selectively "escaping" the attributes of their Outsider identity (partial passing) and that racial distancing is one way they can do the latter.

The other way Outsiders can partially pass is by affirmatively identifying or associating with institutions, cultural practices, and social activities that are stereotypically perceived to be white.[19] They might, in other words, express an affinity for "stuff white people like." There are websites devoted to listing such "stuff." Here is the top-fifty list from stuffwhitepeoplelike.com:

- #50 Irony
- #49 Vintage
- #48 Whole Foods and Grocery Co-ops

- #47 Arts Degrees
- #46 The Sunday *New York Times*
- #45 Asian Fusion Food
- #44 Public Radio
- #43 Plays
- #42 Sushi
- #41 Indie Music
- #40 Apple Products
- #39 Netflix
- #38 *Arrested Development*
- #37 Renovations
- #36 Breakfast Places
- #35 *The Daily Show/Colbert Report*
- #34 Architecture
- #33 Marijuana
- #32 Vegan/Vegetarianism
- #31 Snowboarding
- #30 Wrigley Field
- #29 80s Night
- #28 Not having a TV
- #27 Marathons
- #26 Manhattan (now Brooklyn too!)
- #25 David Sedaris
- #24 Wine
- #23 Microbreweries
- #22 Having Two Last Names
- #21 Writers Workshops
- #20 Being an expert on YOUR culture
- #19 Traveling
- #18 Awareness
- #17 Hating their Parents
- #16 Gifted Children
- #15 Yoga
- #14 Having Black Friends
- #13 Tea
- #12 Non-Profit Organizations
- #11 Asian Girls
- #10 Wes Anderson Movies
- #9 Making you feel bad about not going outside
- #8 Barack Obama
- #7 Diversity

- #6 Organic Food
- #5 Farmer's Markets
- #4 Assists
- #3 Film Festivals
- #2 Religions their parents don't belong to
- #1 Coffee

Obviously, one should read this list with both tongue in cheek and an awareness of the problematic stereotyping these items reflect. The point is that more than a few of us believe that there *really* are some things that white people like that, by implication, African Americans do not; and some things that black people like that, by implication, white people do not. Assuming this perception exists, one way an African American can partially pass is to like the "stuff" that white people like. Drawing on the above list, he might do so by professing to enjoy indie music, organic food, the theatre, and Wes Anderson movies. As with racial distancing, this person is not attempting to pass for white. He is attempting to downplay or minimize the extent of his racial difference.

As noted, a 100% comfort or passing strategy does not force an Insider to challenge stereotypes that he holds about Outsiders because the Insider does not know he is interacting with an Outsider. But when a black employee engages in partial passing, does it change how the employer thinks about black people? The possibility exists that employers will treat Outsiders who perform partial passing as exceptions. Statements such as "we like you despite your being (gay, lesbian, Asian American, Latina/o, etc.)" or "we don't really think of you as (gay, lesbian, Asian American, Latina/o)" exemplify this dynamic.[20] With respect to race, we call this *racial exceptionalism* and its beneficiaries *racial exceptions*.

One reason to be worried about racial exceptionalism is that it enables Insiders to use their association and friendship with the "racial exceptions" as a shield against charges of discrimination. Most of us have heard, and maybe made, the argument: "How can you say that I'm being racist when I am friends with X?" To go back to the Trayvon Martin shooting incident discussed in the prologue, George Zimmerman's father said something like this to explain why Zimmerman's shooting of Martin would not have been racially motivated.[21] And, as we also explained in the prologue, there are racial discrimination cases in which defendants frame their defense to charges of discrimination in this way. More generally, racial exceptions encourage employers to avoid confronting their use of stereotypes. The fact that the employer believes that some black people are racial exceptions—a minority who don't fit the stereotype—means that, from the employer's perspective, the majority of black people do fit the stereotype. The partially passing Outsider employee thus becomes the exception to otherwise valid stereotyping rules.[22]

Our use of the terms *complete passing* and *partial passing* might suggest that there is a "true" identity out of which the employee is passing. We do not mean to convey this idea. At bottom, passing is about racial recognition and the rules we employ to racially categorize individuals. Consider, for example, Mary, a light-skinned woman who, based on ancestry, would be defined as black. If she successfully adopts a complete passing strategy, she may no longer be recognizable as being black. But, if people discovered her ancestry, they would likely assert that she isn't really white. One need not argue that Mary's "true" identity is black to make this point.

Change the hypothetical so that Mary is now dark skinned. Should Mary engage in partial passing, she is less recognizable as black—that is, while she is phenotypically black, the employer does not perceive her to be black with respect to her Working Identity. The employer might even conclude that Mary is a "but for" black person—"but for" her phenotype, the employer would not know that Mary is black.[23] Again, understanding this dynamic does not require one to believe that Mary's "true" racial identity is black.

We should be clear to point out that the phenomenon of partial passing is not limited to people who intentionally adopt this strategy. Roughly, there are three categories of employees about whom one might be concerned: (1) employees who intend to partially pass, (2) employees who engage in conduct knowing that such conduct can be interpreted as partial passing, but who are not doing it solely for that reason,[24] and (3) employees who are oblivious to how their conduct might be interpreted. Those in the first category are responding to the incentives we earlier described. However, even if the employee is not consciously responding to the incentive to racially fit into the workplace, and even if the employee does not intend to partially pass, the fact that Insiders may interpret her conduct as partially passing raises concerns about race and professional identity, which we explore more fully in later chapters. For now it is enough to recognize that, whether or not an employee intends to pass, her professional standing within an institution can be enhanced or diminished depending on whether and to what extent her Working Identity can be interpreted as partial passing.[25]

A final point about partial passing is that there is no reason to assume that a person who partially passes is uncommitted to advancing the interests of members of her Outsider group. Partial passing is not necessarily the same thing as "selling out," a phenomenon we discuss more fully later. Indeed, the employee might adopt partial passing strategies precisely to get inside of and then change an institution. More colloquially, a black male employee might employ partial passing to operate institutionally as an "undercover brother."[26] Whether such strategies work is a different matter, as is the question of whether people ultimately internalize the identities they seek to perform. We are simply suggesting that people might be motivated to partially pass because they are committed to making things better for their racial group, not just themselves.

Exploiting Stereotypes

Thus far, we have discussed the burdens that stereotypes tend to impose. Under some circumstances, however, employees might be able to use stereotypes to their advantage. Within competitive environments, where advancement depends on the kinds of projects to which an employee is assigned, Insiders inevitably benefit from prejudices against Outsiders. Other things equal, an Insider with the presumption that he is likely to be collegial, team-oriented, and trustworthy is more likely to be selected for a desirable project than an equivalent Outsider. Unfair enough, but Outsiders might engage stereotypes to counteract this.

For example, the Korean American who is stereotyped as being hardworking, technically inclined, uncreative, and lacking in leadership skills might be able to take limited advantage of this otherwise negative image.[27] Take an organization in which work is done in teams and a select few of these employees are later promoted to leadership positions. Teams need leaders as well as followers. Teams need creativity, but they also need people to do the unpleasant, boring, and technical tasks. To gain an advantage for the non-leader slot, the Korean American may decide that it is best for him to portray himself as technically-oriented and lacking in creativity

A cost of this type of behavior is confirming prejudice. The Outsider may succeed in obtaining a job or a promotion, but end up confirming a stereotype that may have overall negative effects. For example, by confirming the "drone" stereotype, he will hurt other Korean American employees' chances of competing for a leadership position. In other words, to the extent that the Korean American strategically presents himself as technically-oriented, not only does he entrench the drone stereotype, he establishes racial precedent within his workplace culture for the performance. This precedent potentially burdens other Korean American employees.

Providing Discomfort

Some Outsiders may work their identities to create discomfort. The Outsider may choose to emphasize his or her Outsider status in a way that makes Insiders uncomfortable. The Outsider may, for example, consistently point out instances of unfairness against Outsiders. Most people tend to think of such behavior as authentic or politically principled. But sometimes such behavior is strategic in that the goal may be to satisfy an institutional need. To the extent the institution can handle some dissent, the discomfort strategy may work to provide the institution with legitimacy by creating the image of a democratic institution.

Outsiders also might adopt the discomfort strategy as a way to set the ground-work for a discrimination claim by identifying and calling attention to examples of discrimination within the institution.

Selling Out

An Outsider can make arguments that work to the advantage of Insiders so that Insiders can then claim that their arguments are not self-interested or even racial. For example, a claim made by an Insider at a predominantly white institution concluding that a particular episode was not racial does not carry as much weight as a similar claim made by an Outsider. The argument might be employed, explicitly or implicitly, to legitimize the Insider's perspective.[28] The employee may then be rewarded for adopting this strategy. Thus, the notion of *selling out*.

The term *selling out* is fraught with controversy. At the end of the day, it might not even be descriptively useful, since people often differ significantly on the question of whether a person has or has not sold out. Some believe that for-mer President Bush rewarded Clarence Thomas, a black man, for selling out, by nominating him to the Supreme Court.[29] As we indicated in the prologue, we are not interested in figuring out who is or is not selling out. Our point is to say that Outsiders can consciously act or be perceived by the employer as acting against the interests of other Outsiders in favor of Insiders. The term *selling out* is one but certainly not the only way to capture either of those circumstances.

Buying Back

Outsiders who think that their performance of comfort may have been costly to their community may adopt a buy-back strategy to make amends. These indi-viduals may engage in both comfort and discomfort strategies. For example, the Asian American who emphasizes his technical skills to take advantage of the ste-reotype that Asian Americans are good at technical subjects may recognize the costs of his actions and support other Outsider claims of institutional discrimi-nation to buy back, or make amends, for the cost. A more cynical view is that an Outsider who engages in comfort strategies may engage in some visible discom-fort strategies to retain status in the Outsider community, while simultaneously maintaining a certain amount of legitimacy within the Insider institution.

The foregoing Working Identity strategies are situational. Meaning that whether and how an Outsider performs them depends on the specific institu-tional context in which the Outsider is situated. These strategies also have costs, some of which we now describe. In outlining these costs, we do not mean to suggest that all identity-related decisions are a product of conscious strategizing. Just as stereotyping operates on an unconscious level, outsider responses to stereotyping can operate on an unconscious level as well.[30] However, the assumption that people consciously think about how to work their identities is a useful heuristic device for understanding a more complex phenomenon.[31]

The Costs and Burdens of Identity Performances

Working Identity Is Work

Few would dispute the claim that employees subject to negative stereotypes have an incentive to try to negate those stereotypes; that eliminating negative stereotypes generally requires additional work; and that those not subject to the same stereotypes do not have to perform that work.[32] Given that racial minorities, and blacks in particular, are generally subject to negative stereotypes, it follows that they likely end up doing more work to negate those stereotypes than their white counterparts. One indication of the extent to which this might be so are the responses we got on presenting draft chapters of this book at several conferences at which minority professionals or academics were the majority. In these settings, the dominant reaction was something like: "It's about time we focus on this issue. It's a problem. A burden. And no one is talking about it." The people with whom we engaged about the matter didn't use the term "Working Identity." But, the comments we got, almost to a person, was that part of fitting into predominantly white workplaces entails toning down the extent to which one is nonwhite—and that doing so is a burden.

To appreciate how this burden might operate, consider a hypothetical black male law professor. The possibility exists that stereotypes about his identity will be at odds with stated or unstated criteria that (he thinks) the institution values.[33] Table 1.1 captures some examples; the institutional values/employer criteria are to the left; the stereotypes are to the right.

With the six pairings from the table in mind,[34] assume that the black male is a law professor in his first year of teaching, and that the law school dean has assigned him to teach criminal procedure. The course explores constitutional constraints on police investigation practices. When do police officers need warrants? Under what circumstances can they seize us? When do the *Miranda* warnings apply? One of the first cases the professor is likely to teach is *Terry v. Ohio*.[35] This case establishes the stop-and-frisk doctrine. If a police officer has reasonable suspicion that a person has engaged or is about to engage in criminal conduct, she may stop and detain the suspect for limited questioning.[36] If at any time

Table 1.1

Institutional Norm	Racial Stereotype
Race neutral/colorblind	Race man/color-conscious stereotype
Apolitical	Ideological
Strong work ethic	Lazy
Qualified workers	Unqualified
Status quo workers	Anti-institutional
Good institutional citizenship	Uncooperative and uncollegial

during the encounter the officer develops reasonable suspicion that the suspect is armed and dangerous, she may subject the suspect to a "frisk"—that is, a limited search of the suspect's outer clothing, a "pat-down."[37] In teaching this case, any first-year law professor must at least think about two concerns: whether to employ the Socratic method and how to substantively engage *Terry v. Ohio*. We are interested in how these choices are differentially freighted for the black male law professor.

The Socratic method may not be the new professor's preferred pedagogical approach. Yet it remains the dominant approach in law schools. If he were not worried about issues of authority in the classroom—and the extent to which being black already positioned him as not being the prototypical law professor—he might adopt a less traditional approach. For example, he might break the students up into small groups, ask them to discuss the material, and then have them report back to the class.[38] Given the background assumptions about his identity,[39] however, such an approach would not necessarily signal creativity. Instead, it could signal unpreparedness, intellectual softness, and disorganization.[40] A white male professor, on the other hand, is more likely to be rewarded for bucking the traditional approach to legal education (he might be seen as innovative, creative, and maybe even brave).

Moreover, employing the Socratic method effectively is difficult. But for racial assumptions about his identity, the professor might also adopt a teaching approach that requires a different kind of intellectual work: lecturing. It takes work to convey complicated doctrinal ideas through Socratic engagement. The teacher must think carefully about the questions, anticipate the responses, and move the conversation in a coherent and accessible way.[41] It might be easier and safer for this professor to teach the material to the students via a lecture. This way, he remains in control of the conversation.[42]

Further, the professor might also think that problems with the Socratic method exist, and that it operates to disproportionately benefit Insider students.[43] This suspicion might especially be true of classes with few students of color.[44] However, employing a teaching method other than the Socratic method could result in an image of the professor as non-traditional, illegitimate, intellectually rigid, closed-minded, uninterested in student ideas, and unable to think on his feet.[45] In other words, the employment of the lecture format could be interpreted as the employment of a script.[46]

There is also the substantive question of how the professor will frame *Terry v. Ohio.*[47] The case was decided in 1968 and includes an interaction between a white officer and three men, two of whom are black.[48] In teaching the case, one could ignore the political context in which the case was litigated,[49] the racial dynamics of the encounter between the defendants and the police,[50] and the race-based way in which Justice Warren structured the opinion.[51] Alternatively, one could focus on all those factors. During such a discussion, the professor might choose to reveal his own encounters with the stop-and-frisk doctrine on the street.

Assume that student evaluations play an important role in the tenure and promotion process at this institution.[52] Assume also that the student body is overwhelmingly white. If so, the professor might choose not to focus on—or might even ignore—the racial aspects of the case. That approach, from our perspective, would be problematic. Given the professor's fears about what sort of assumptions the students might make if he talks about race,[53] the professor might make the pragmatic choice to avoid race, for fear that talking about it would result in his receiving negative evaluations.[54]

Suppose, however, that the professor chooses to address the racial aspects of the case. He thinks that this is the right thing to do normatively, intellectually, and pedagogically. The fact that he makes this choice, however, does not mean that his pragmatic concerns about tenure and promotion have disappeared. Instead, the professor is likely to attempt to negotiate his pragmatic concerns about teaching evaluations and tenure with his political, intellectual, and pedagogical concerns about race. He will have to find ways to meaningfully integrate politics, history, and race into a discussion of the narrow doctrinal questions presented by the *Terry* opinion,[55] while avoiding alienating students or creating the impression that he is partial and obsessed with race. This approach involves extra work, which is directly related to the background racial assumptions that people make about the professor's identity.[56] None of these concerns would apply, at least not in the same way, if this professor were a white male.[57]

The above hypothetical and a bunch of anecdotes, of course, do not constitute real evidence. Ultimately, the question of how much work goes into Working Identity is an empirical one. After all, one could argue that, in the age of diversity initiatives and a variety of anti-discrimination laws, blacks don't have to work their identities very much at all. Strengthening this argument would be the idea that, if employers harbor negative stereotypes about blacks, it could actually be

advantageous to black employees in the sense of lowering the employer's expectations with respect to job performance. For example, against the backdrop
of stereotypes that blacks are lazy, the employer could be pleasantly surprised
by a black employee whose work ethic is ordinary. If that is the case, the black
employee would not have difficulty fitting in, or so one might argue. Indeed, that
employee would find it fairly easy to exceed the employer's stereotypical expectations that set the performance bar low. Put another way, the fact that there
are very negative stereotypes of blacks might mean that those who achieve even
minimal success will be hailed as conquering heroes, even when they are only
performing on par with or even below their white male co-workers. While we
remain comfortable in our assertion that if the employee perceives that she is
subject to negative stereotypes, she is likely to exert effort to try and negate those
stereotypes, there are arguments that cut in the other direction.

The Associational Pressure of Colorblindness

A second burden of identity performances derives from the pervasive notion
that our society, our workplace culture, and our social interactions ought to be
colorblind.[58] Under a colorblind norm, whites cannot intentionally discriminate
against people of color based on race. They cannot use racial slurs or otherwise
engage in overt racial conduct that creates a hostile work environment for people of color. But colorblindness regulates more than that. It implicitly polices the
workplace associations of people of color.

To appreciate how, consider a large law firm at which associates are expected
to bill more than fifty hours a week. Because of this expectation, firm associates
have limited time to interact with other lawyers in their firm outside of work
assignments. In this context, eating lunch together becomes an important way
for associates to develop and sustain relationships within the firm. If the firm has
a colorblind workplace norm, it would not be problematic for the same group
of white male associates in the law firm to go to lunch together everyday. Such
racial associations would not run afoul of a workplace norm of colorblindness.
Few white people in the law firm would interpret these all white, all male daily
gatherings as a form of white, male racial bonding or as revealing a tendency
on the part of the white male associates to form racial cliques. On the contrary,
these associations might be understood to reflect the collegiality of the individual members of the lunch group.

Now suppose that within this same firm Latinas/os develop a practice of
going to lunch with each other once a week. This is unlikely to be viewed as
evidence of collegiality. The risk instead is that Insiders in the firm will interpret this as an identity-based association. Even a monthly lunch gathering of

Latinas/os could be sufficiently racially salient to create the impression of racial cliquishness,[59] of people "sticking to their own kind." To the extent that racial cliquishness is at odds with collegiality,[60] there is a disincentive for Outsiders to associate at work.

But why do racial associations on the part of whites carry a different social meaning than racial associations on the part of people of color? With reference to the above example, one answer might be that the white associates did not racially define their association as a white-only association; it just happened that their lunch gatherings were white and male. However, with respect to the Latinas/os, their monthly meetings were organized around the very fact of their racial or ethnic identity. This reasoning does not persuade us. Even a situation involving Latina/o daily lunches that are not organized intentionally along identity lines will still be perceived as racially cliquish. This is because the social meaning of employee associations—for example, Latinas/os going to lunch together—does not depend solely or most significantly on the racial intent behind the association, but on the racial composition of that association.

The reason the racial composition of the association matters relates to the one-directional way in which the colorblind norm works. The colorblind norm does not require whites to avoid other whites or to associate with people of color. This norm does, however, implicitly require people of color to avoid other people of color (the negative racial duty) and to associate with whites (the affirmative racial duty). Understood in this way, the colorblind norm operates as a color conscious burden.[61] Colorblindness, therefore, does not actually mean race neutrality.[62] In the context of professional institutions, the norm racially allocates identity work, requiring people of color, but not white people, to think and be careful about their racial associations.[63] The question of whether the workplace norm of colorblindness is violated turns on whether people of color associate with each other or with whites. Consequently, white-with-white and white-with-people-of-color associations are perceived as colorblind. However, people of color with people-of-color associations will likely be perceived as color conscious.

We are not saying that colorblindness has no effects on white employees or predominantly white professional environments. As indicated above, the norm of colorblindness creates a disincentive for whites to engage in intentional discrimination or exhibit behavior that is overtly racially offensive. Colorblindness might even cause some white employees to be overly cautious about what they say about race for fear of being labeled racist or racially insensitive. In short, our focus on how colorblindness affects the racial association of non-white employees is not intended to suggest that colorblindness has no regulatory effects on whites.

The Costs of Compromising

Identity performances can result in people of color compromising their sense of identity. This is not to say that people have true identities or essences. We have already argued that there is no such thing. The point, as we explained at the beginning of this chapter, is that there are moments in which a person's performance of identity contradicts some normative or social image that person has of herself. Dismissing this "sense of self" as false consciousness, obscures the extent to which each of us makes daily decisions based on who we think we are at any given moment. Compromising that sense of self—over and over again—can be painful.[64]

The Costs of Poor Performances

Outsider Working Identity also involves two types of extra risks. First, the risk exists that others will identify the performative element of an Outsider's behavior as strategic and manipulative. Suppose a black employee's white colleague is attempting a humorous caricature of a fellow employee. Stipulate that the black employee instead thinks the caricature is racist. The black employee does not react negatively. He thinks that by doing so would feed his white colleague's stereotype of Outsiders as people who are obsessed with race. Instead, our black employee joins the laughter. If, however, the white colleagues perceive that the laughter is halfhearted and fake, it may be worse for the black employee's prospects than if he had objected to the caricature or refused to laugh. In other words, to the extent that the Outsider is perceived as acting strategically, his actions will be discounted and resented. Therefore, the Outsider not only has to perform, but he has to perform well. To do so likely requires the acquisition of cultural capital, or familiarity with and an understanding of mainstream cultural norms.[65]

The Backfire Costs

Second, because Outsiders are subject to multiple stereotypes, the risk exists that taking steps to negate one kind of negative stereotype will activate another one. Take the case of an organization that values assertiveness and in which Susan is one of a few female employees. She recognizes that other women before her have failed in the organization in part because of a stereotype that women are unassertive. Therefore, Susan decides to be assertive in meetings and in her dealings with colleagues and subordinates. Susan's doing so can backfire. Her male colleagues will not see the assertiveness as positive, but rather as a sign that she is angry and pushy, and to use the gendered term, "bitchy."

Or to recall the example we used in the prologue, imagine that, in an organization that values both effort and intellectual ability, a black male employee perceives that negative stereotypes about him exist on both counts. He works longer hours than normal to negate the stereotype of a lazy black man. However, that strategy creates the risk that working late will be interpreted as an inability to get work done as quickly as the others.

Consider now a male Indian employee who is worried about the perception of Indian men as sexist. To negate that stereotype, he takes up cooking. But instead of negating the stereotype of the sexist Indian man, his decision to take up cooking triggers the colonial image of the servile South Asian, the colonial subject. The point is that Outsiders are typically subject to not one, but a number of interconnected stereotypes. And it is possible that a strategy to repudiate one stereotype, like laziness, will confirm another, like intellectual incompetence.

Finally, think of an Asian American male assistant professor who wants to project a collegial image. Assume that his institution is one in which faculty meetings tend to be sites of tension and unpleasant political discussions, such as discussions about affirmative action faculty hiring and student admissions. Assume also that the institution values collegiality and views the tensions that arise over racial issues as disturbing collegiality. If the Asian American faculty member disagrees with his colleagues about a particular controversial issue, he risks being viewed as uncollegial. Given these conditions, the Asian American male faculty member might attempt to demonstrate his collegiality by refraining from disagreeing with his colleagues. If no other stereotypes about Asian American men existed, the non-intervention/non-participation strategy might improve the Asian American male's faculty standing. However, given the multiplicity of stereotypes about Asian American men, this stereotype-repudiating strategy could end up confirming stereotypes about Asian American men being docile, timid, and lacking in political and intellectual courage.[66]

While the foregoing does not exhaust the costs, risk, and burdens of Working Identity, the discussion suggests some of the disadvantages Outsiders face as a result of existing stereotypes about their race. These costs are linked to employee, not employer, behavior. Nothing we have said thus far involves the employer actively discriminating against Outsiders. The disadvantage we describe exists because of the tension between stereotypes about Outsider identities and the norms that professional institutions value.

None of this is to argue that Insiders are unaffected by the Working Identity phenomenon. As we have stated several times, and want to stress again here, Insiders work (and are perceived to work) their identities as well. A male heterosexual partner at a law firm, for example, might worry about being stereotyped

as being insensitive to racial, gender, and sexual orientation inequality. He might
work his identity to signal that he is more progressive than others might assume.
He could do this in casual conversation ("though I really like *Mad Men*, the show
needs to better deal with race, particularly given the historical context in which
the show takes place"), relationship building (by reaching out to junior associates of color, inviting them to lunch, dinner, etc., and generally providing mentoring), and institutional policy making (urging the firm to implement sexual
harassment training).[67] Indeed, one of our current projects is on why and how
Insiders work their identities. While this book gives short shrift to that issue, we
want to make clear that the Working Identity phenomenon transcends particular social categories.

***

At least seven implications flow from the arguments about Working Identity we
have advanced in this chapter. First, people who work their identities are performing work. We might frame this work as a type of shadow work—unacknowledged
as a formal matter, largely unregulated as legal matter, but implicitly expected as
an institutional matter. While it is problematic that employees might have to work
their identities at work in order to succeed, the jury is out on the question of how
the law should intervene. The evidentiary questions would be messy. How would
an employee prove that, because of racial stereotypes, she felt pressured, and
worked her identity to fit into the workplace? How would the employer disprove
this claim? In part for this reason, we reserve our doctrinal argument for instances
in which the employer, for example, refuses to hire or promote someone because
that person acted "too black" or failed to "act white." That would be analogous to
a scenario in which an employer refused to hire or promote a woman who acted
too much like a woman (feminine) or failed to act like a man (masculine). The
purpose of this chapter is to introduce the Working Identity phenomenon and
explain how the existence of racial stereotypes creates an institutional imbalance
in terms of how much identity work racial Outsiders have to perform.

   Second, employees need not believe that their employers are consciously and
invidiously racially motivated to have an incentive to work their identity. All of
us have implicit biases that shape how we see and think about race.[68] To borrow from Jerry Kang, our perception is far from "immaculate," even when we
try to see people as blank racial slates.[69] This was the basic thrust of Malcolm
Gladwell's *Blink*. Drawing from the academic research, Gladwell concludes that
implicit bias "is at the root of a good deal of prejudice and discrimination."[70]
African American corporate employees will likely understand this and thus be
incentivized to work their identity even if they do not believe that their employer
will intentionally discriminate against them.

Third, the Working Identity phenomenon makes clear that phenotype is not the only basis upon which people make racial judgments. Of course, phenotype remains important. The point is that phenotype does not fully determine a person's vulnerability to discrimination. This is true even with respect to passing. The phenomenon of blacks passing as white, or as Cheryl Harris puts it, *tres*passing—entering the social world of white identity without permission— required black people to both look and act the part of whiteness.[71] People who insufficiently worked their identity as white would not succeed in passing for white, their physical appearance notwithstanding. Our aim has been to explore the Working Identity phenomenon in the context of what we have called partial passing. Here, people are not working their identity out of their race (phenotype prevents most black people from doing that); they are working their identity out of being racially salient ("acting white" enables many people to succeed in that effort).

Fourth, colorblindness is implicated in the Working Identity story we have told. Almost every workplace is structured around the norm of colorblindness. To the extent that racial salience threatens colorblindness, Outsiders have an incentive to work their identity to diminish their racial difference.

Fifth, we are using the "acting white" term loosely; sometimes to describe instances in which people of color obscure, downplay, or expressly repudiate the racial group to which they presumptively belong; and sometimes to describe instances in which people of color engage in conduct or activities that are not typically associated with people of their race. None of this means that there is some true or real way to "act white." There is not. It simply means that we racially judge people based on perceived racial conduct or behavior, and not just on perceived racial physicality or phenotype. With respect to the former, there has been a fair amount of discussion about whether part of the reason for the performance gap between black and white students is the belief on the part of black students that doing well academically is "acting white." Without weighing into that debate, our view is that the "acting white" phenomenon transcends it.

Sixth, the Working Identity phenomenon challenges the idealized model of race discrimination. This model features a racist employer who excludes a highly qualified black applicant in favor of a less qualified white applicant. It is a model in which the employer holds all the cards. The black job applicant has no hand to play. The outcome of the game turns on whether the employer plays the hiring card or the exclusion card.

The scenario gets complicated if we assume that the black applicant has agency with respect to deciding how to work her identity. Here, the applicant doesn't sit passively waiting to see whether the employer plays the exclusion or the hiring card. Instead, she exercises agency by working her identity to influence which of those cards the employer ultimately plays. This notion of agency is foundational to the Working Identity thesis.

As we discussed earlier, the dynamic of the employee who works identity to negate negative stereotypes can exist even if the employee doesn't believe or is unsure about whether the employer actually harbors those stereotypes. The existence of negative stereotypes as a general matter is enough to induce black employees to exercise the agency necessary to perform stereotype-negation strategies. It is the safe thing to do, a "just in case" form of racial protection. An analogy here might be to the pedestrian who looks both ways before crossing at a stop sign "just in case" a driver—intentionally or not—drives through the sign without stopping.[72]

This traffic analogy is apt in another sense. We want pedestrians to look both ways before and as they cross the road, notwithstanding the existence of traffic laws requiring drivers to stop. To the extent that people don't look before they cross, we hold them at least partially responsible for any accident that ensues. Does it make sense to extend this comparative fault analysis to the Working Identity phenomenon? More specifically, do we want blacks and other Outsiders to do their part negating stereotypes, notwithstanding the existence of work-place anti-discrimination laws? If they don't negate those stereotypes, should we hold them partially responsible for any discrimination that results?

One could argue that if the discrimination is a function of perceived ste-reotypes, it may well be that the employee, not the employer, is the cheapest cost avoider. Under this view, the socially optimal outcome might simply be for employees to perform stereotype-negating behavior. That would eliminate the problem altogether, or so the argument might go. The persuasiveness of this claim turns both on how one assesses the costs of Working Identity (we think they are significant, though we concede that the question is an empirical one) and on whether one thinks that a particular employee can render herself invulnerable to the attribution of negative stereotypes (which we do not think is possible). To the extent that stereotypes are simply a part of the air we breathe, every interaction a black employee has with her employer or co-workers can potentially produce a racial circumstance in which the employee confirms some preexisting stereotype about blacks and therefore becomes vulnerable to an adverse employment decision. Unless one passes in the sense of completely masking one's Outsider identity, one is always vulnerable to the stereotypes that apply to one's group. This racial vulnerability argues against a liability regime that imposes the costs of avoiding discrimination on the black employee.[73]

A final implication of our argument derives from our claim that an employ-ee's Working Identity is constituted not only by what she does but also by what she says. How an employee talks at work—and what she says—increases or decreases the extent to which her co-workers will perceive her as an Outsider who doesn't racially fit in. This creates an incentive for nonwhite employees to put their conversations at work to work. Recall our discussion of the bilingual Latina, who adopted an English-only workplace identity in order to diminish her racial salience. This is part of a broader speech/race dynamic that we discuss in chapter 2. As we will show, when we speak, what we say, and how we say it, can each shape the Working Identity others perceive us to have.

2

Talking White

In 2009, the powerful Democratic senator from Nevada, Harry Reid, found himself in a pickle. The source of his problem was a private comment he had made to a reporter during the 2008 presidential campaign to the effect that Barack Obama had a reasonable chance of success thanks in part to his "light skin," overall appearance, and the fact that he spoke "with no Negro dialect unless he wanted to have one."[1] (See figure 2.1.)

Figure 2.1 President Obama and Senator Harry Reid.
Source: © JASON REED/Reuters/Corbis.

While the term "Negro dialect" is jarring, particularly when uttered by a high-profile figure like Reid, it wasn't Reid's poor choice of words alone that generated criticism. In other words, the controversy was not simply about Reid's use of the term "Negro." Troubling as that term might be, few would equate it with what we now sanitize and regularly express as the "N-word." What generated the controversy was the assumption underlying Reid's statements: that one can "sound black," "act black," and "look black." From Reid's perspective, because Obama did not "sound black," "act black," and "look (that?) black," it was plausible that he could become the next president of the United States.

In making this observation, Reid was in effect articulating a more colorful version of the Working Identity thesis *Acting White?* advances. The thrust of his comments transcends Obama's identity and political trajectory and is applicable to many African Americans who find themselves in white-dominated workplaces. The proposition is that the less black African Americans appear to be in these environments, the more likely they are to succeed in them. Reid, a wily politician and a realist, was stating this truth. His point, at bottom, was that the degree to which one is perceived as black determines how successful one is in life.

With respect to skin color, this is hardly a debatable proposition. As Boyce Watkins noted during the flare-up over Reid's comments, "[T]he truth is that for the past 400 years, light-skinned Blacks have been preferable to darker-skinned African Americans in almost every walk of life from beauty, to employment, to politics."[2] In this respect, Reid was simply pointing out the obvious, and reminding us that we are a long way away from any kind of "post-racial America."

Fair enough. But what about Reid's reference to "Negro dialect"? Does "sounding too black," like "looking too black," close career doors or make it harder to walk through them? Does "talking white" have the opposite effect? Boyce Watkins doesn't say. Perhaps this is because the very notion that people "talk black" or "talk white" disturbs us. What exactly does "talking black" or "talking white" mean? Presumably, to say that a person "talks white" or "talks black" is to assume that people of a particular race have a particular language, dialect, or rhetorical style in which they speak. That sounds downright offensive—tantamount to old-school racism.

Yet, the argument we make in this chapter is that the phenomenon of people "talking white" or "talking black" is real in the sense that our racial perceptions are based on sound, not just on sight. Race is something we "hear" as well as "see." Ask Joseph Phillips, a black actor who entered prime time through his role as Lt. Martin Kendall, the husband of Denise Huxtable, on *The Cosby Show*. In his book *He Talk Like a White Boy*, Phillips explains that the title captures a set of experiences he had as both an adolescent and an adult. According to Phillips:

> The day after my high school graduation, I was at my friend Jerald's house. His older sister was commenting on the previous day's ceremony and complimented me on my commencement address. "You gave a good speech," she said. "You sounded really smart," to which she added, "You sounded white." I looked at her cross-eyed and asked, "Did you hear what you just said?"
>
> Of course this was not the first time I had heard this, nor would it be my last. The charge of sounding white had haunted me all through school and would haunt me well into my professional acting career. "Joseph, do it again and this time try to sound more black." I have been black all my life. How can I be *more* black?[3]

Phillips's narrative is in line with research suggesting that "talking white" (or "talking black") is a measureable social phenomenon. As mentioned in chapter 1, much of this research invokes the "talking race" phenomenon as an example of either accent discrimination[4] (for example, an employer discriminating against a person who speaks "black-accented" English in favor of one who speaks "Standard" English)[5] or racial discrimination (e.g., a landlord inviting a prospective tenant who "talked white" on the phone to see an apartment and upon discovering that the person is black indicates that the apartment is no longer available).[6]

While both examples help to reveal how patterns of speech can make us more or less vulnerable to discrimination, there is a more subtle speech dynamic that disadvantages Outsiders in the workplace: what an Outsider says in the workplace can confirm or negate stereotypes of that Outsider and make that Outsider more or less racially salient. The "talking white" dynamic is not just about speaking with a certain accent; it is also about the content of what we say. Under this formulation of "talking white," anything an African American says that has the potential to minimize the extent to which others perceive her to be black is "talking white." On the flipside, anything she says that increases the extent to which others perceive her to be black is "talking black." Within majority-white workplaces, "talking white" is more advantageous to an employee than "talking black." This creates an incentive for black employees to work their speech so as to reduce the likelihood that their co-workers and managers will perceive what they say as "talking black."

In more general terms, the problem is not just about "talking black", it is also about "talking female" or "talking gay" or "talking Latino" or "talking like an Asian woman." In each case, the problem is the same: Outsiders manage what they say to minimize the extent to which they are perceived as Outsiders. This constraint can disadvantage the employee in four significant ways.

First, if an Outsider feels that anything she says can and will be used to make her racially salient, she is constrained in terms of her ability to use conversations at work to enhance her workplace reputation. Who we are, and who our colleagues perceive us to be, is shaped by how we speak and what we say. Workplace conversations both form and reflect workplace identities. This is especially true in environments like academia where employees largely work on their own and have limited interactions with their colleagues. A professor's reputation as smart, collegial, rigorous, witty, charming, and so forth, will be based, to a meaningful extent, on statements made during seminars and faculty meetings, that is, in workplace conversations. The nexus between workplace identity, professional reputation, and workplace communications creates an incentive for employees at work to put their conversations *to work*. To the extent an employee's conversations are constrained because of her perception that she is "talking black," her ability to use her conversations positively to construct her workplace identity is limited.

Second, an employee who harbors a concern about "talking black" is not likely to criticize the governance structure of the workplace. Other things being equal, a black employee in a white-dominated workplace who perceives that his co-workers hold a stereotype of blacks as hostile and unable to fit in is likely to be more cautious in criticizing his employer's policies and practices than a white male counterpart would be. The latter would be less concerned (if at all) about his speech confirming stereotypes. By and large, white employers do not hold stereotypes of other whites as likely to be hostile and disloyal with respect to corporate culture. And white men presumptively fit into corporate culture and define its norms and practices.

Third, an employee's ability to have certain conversations can influence the kind of work she ends up doing. For example, an employee's perception that she is subject to stereotyping may impact whether she accepts or declines a particular assignment. If she thinks that her employer stereotypes black women as lazy, she is likely to say yes when asked to take on additional projects, even when she is already busy, to avoid triggering the lazy stereotype. Stereotypes diminish her workplace bargaining power and, thus, her ability to negotiate her workload. As we will show, the cost of taking on too many tasks (particularly what we call "lumpy citizenship tasks," discussed later) undermines an Outsider's ability to succeed in the workplace and can end up confirming stereotypes of Outsider incompetence.

Fourth, an employer may be aware that the existence of stereotypes effectively silences some employees both by deterring them from saying no to certain assignments and by making them less likely to be critical of the workplace. To the extent that employers are so aware, it is rational for them to exploit the employee's vulnerability.[7] Exploitation is especially likely in work-place cultures in which employees have some power to say no to their employer's requests to perform assignments. Other things being equal, the easier it is for the employer to "get to yes" with a particular employee, the more likely it is that the employer will ask that employee to take on certain undesirable tasks. Even if the employer does not *intend* to exploit the vulnerability of its Outsider employees along these lines,[8] the employer may still end up over-allocating work to them.[9] So long as the Outsider perceives that she has been stereo-typed, she is likely to accept—without complaint—more of the less-desirable assignments than she otherwise would.

Any one of the foregoing constraints can have deleterious effects on the Outsider employee. In the next sections, we use the example of a black employee to illustrate how. We begin our discussion by describing how an employee's concerns about both "talking black" and negating stereotypes constrain her ability to strategically employ her workplace conversations. We then show how this dynamic can result in the employer over-allocating work to African American employees. We conclude with possible solutions.

Putting Conversations to Work in High-Visibility Settings

Employees have an incentive to put their conversations at work *to work*. There are two ways an employee might do this. First, she can engage in clear and effective conversations with her colleagues. Doing so would presumably enhance her reputation in the workplace. This seems obvious enough. Second, the employee can use her conversations to signal to the employer that she has the personal characteristics her employer values. The more difficult these characteristics are to observe, and the more valuable she perceives them to be to the employer, the stronger the incentive to signal them.

Consider the following hypothetical scenario. The scene is a law school faculty seminar. The speaker presents a paper on Justice Scalia's opinion in *Whren v. United States*, a case involving two young African American men who were stopped for a traffic violation and then arrested when the police found drugs in their vehicle.[10] According to Justice Scalia, the officers who made the arrest did not violate the Fourth Amendment because their investigation was objectively reasonable, regardless of their *actual* motivation for the investigation.[11] The speaker argues that Justice Scalia had failed to consider the incentives the "objectively reasonable" standard creates for police officers. If there is no inquiry into motivation, he maintains, police essentially have carte blanche to practice racial profiling.[12]

A senior faculty member opens up the floor for questions. Attending the seminar is a junior faculty member who specializes in international business law. In a few months she will be up for tenure. She has not had much of a presence at faculty seminars, and this is the last one of the year. She raises her hand and says to the speaker:

JUNIOR FACULTY MEMBER: I know you didn't get to present your entire paper, but as I understand it, the basic thrust of your argument is X.

The speaker nods his head to agree.

JUNIOR FACULTY MEMBER THINKS: *I hope my senior colleagues realize that I've read the paper.*

SENIOR FACULTY MEMBER THINKS: *A nice, crisp question. I always thought she was quick on her feet.*

JUNIOR FACULTY MEMBER CONTINUES: It seems to me that your project is less about the Fourth Amendment, and more about how legal formalism functions to deny the realities of race. We see this all the time, for example, in Fourteenth Amendment jurisprudence where the Court's ideological commitment to race neutrality or colorblindness obscures the realities of race.[13]

The speaker nods his head again.

JUNIOR FACULTY MEMBER THINKS: *They probably didn't know that I could think outside my intellectual box.*

SENIOR FACULTY MEMBER THINKS: *Where does she get the time to stay on top of literature outside her field? Obviously she's read some of that incomprehensible crit stuff—and articulates it better than they do! None of that pointless jargon in what she said.*

JUNIOR FACULTY MEMBER CONTINUES: Now, even as I agree with your account of what *Whren* does and doesn't do, you have provided us with no indication as to how courts can actually manage this problem. You don't use this term in your paper, but lots of people refer to the phenomenon you describe as DWB—Driving While Black.[14] Again, I think this is a real problem. Parenthetically, I think that white people are stopped pretextually as well, and you might want to think about how that social reality affects your analysis. But that might just be a quibble. My larger point is that it is unclear how, in practical terms, courts should deal with this problem. Isn't that, after all, the real question?"[15]

The speaker, taken aback by this barrage, looks crestfallen. He reaches for his bottle of water.

> JUNIOR FACULTY MEMBER THINKS: *How about that, colleagues? I'm real-world oriented, solution-driven, nuanced, racially sensitive—but not too sensitive (pretextual stops are a problem for white people as well). What's more, I crushed the speaker with that last question—but in a very collegial way.*
>
> SENIOR FACULTY MEMBER THINKS: *She is truly engaged. This reflects well on our institution. If only we could find more female candidates like her to hire. If only my other female colleagues were as engaged as she is.*

This scenario is exaggerated. As we indicated in chapter 1, an employee might signal in more subtle ways. The point is that in "low-visibility" settings (such as a large law school faculty), what one says during the few moments of "high visibility" (such as at seminars or faculty meetings) takes on importance. This creates an incentive for the employee to use her speaking opportunities to signal that she has the characteristics her employer values. The employer, in turn, "screens" her statements to evaluate whether she in fact has those characteristics.

The foregoing dynamics are further complicated by the existence of racial stereotypes. Stereotypes create the risk not only that Outsiders will be misinterpreted but also that their conversations will send negative signals about their identity. One way that Outsiders can mitigate these risks is by "talking white." But as we will explain, "talking white" can mean not talking at all (in the sense of refraining from criticizing one's employer's policies, procedures, or governance structures), saying yes to time-consuming work assignments that take a lot of time but do little to advance one's career, and not asking the institution for resources that could advance one's career.

Chilling Institutional Speech and Silencing Institutional Criticism

To appreciate how an Outsider's concerns about being misinterpreted can chill her speech about institutional governance matters, consider a workplace where professional disagreement with company policy is not only encouraged but also expected. Unprofessional disagreements, however (disagreements the employer views as motivated by self-interested politics), are considered improper and diminish an employee's advancement opportunities. In this workplace culture, an employee seeking advancement has an incentive to shape her criticisms of company policy so that the employer will not misinterpret them as unprofessional disagreements.

An employee's ability to have her criticisms correctly interpreted as professional disagreements depends, in part, on her reputation at work, or her *workplace standing*. Workplace standing comprises both the employer's judgment of the employee's worth and the employee's sense of this judgment. We discuss them in turn.

First, the employer's opinion of the employee influences the way the employer interprets an employee's criticism. The identity of the speaker helps to define the content of the speech. If the employer is unsure about whether the criticism is professional—that is, if the employee is ineffective in clearly and unambiguously communicating the meaning of her criticism to her employer—the employer will resolve this uncertainty based on the image the employer has of the employee. The stronger the employee's workplace standing, the more likely it is that the employer will read her criticisms to be professional. Conversely, if the employee has a weak workplace standing, the employer is more likely to conclude that the criticisms are unprofessional. Where an employee's conversations at work can be interpreted positively or negatively, the employer will resolve the ambiguity by using the image, or stereotype, the employer has of the employee.[16]

Consider the following hypothetical: A black female employee in a white, male-dominated workplace is on the firm's hiring committee and has been asked to offer her views on its current hiring practices. She suggests that the firm's hiring procedures discriminate against women. But the employer has a stereotype of women as being hypersensitive about gender-related issues and of black women as being aggressive and combative and invested in identity politics.[17] Thus the employer may interpret her criticism as more of the usual sensitivity or as a confirmation that black women are uncooperative and think primarily in terms of their racial identity. These interpretations confirm the stereotype about the employee and can lead the employer to disregard the criticisms.

At the same time, how the employee perceives her employer's judgment of her may affect her ability to shape her criticisms. If she believes that the employer sees her as sensitive about gender-related issues or overly committed to identity politics, she may remain silent when her colleagues ask her to comment on the firm's hiring practices. In this scenario, her speech is constrained, and her workplace identity undermined. She is unable to register her concerns about a problem that matters to her and that, if remedied, would benefit her. Nor is she able to show that she is institutionally engaged and committed to the firm.

The inability to show that one is institutionally engaged and committed is further complicated by the "double bind" female employees often find themselves in. As we noted in chapter 1, the problem is that the negation of one stereotype can lead to the activation of another. Race shapes the operation of this "double bind." If our hypothetical black female employee elects not to comment when asked about hiring practices, so as to avoid being stereotyped as sensitive about gender issues, she could activate the stereotype of black women as lacking both intellect and leadership skills. If she speaks up, she could activate the stereotype of black women as aggressive, loud, or angry.

Assuming that the black woman decides to speak, she might work her identity to mitigate the risk that her employer will misinterpret or discount what she says. She may dress herself up—that is, literally try to appear more conventionally female in her choice of makeup, clothing, and overall self-presentation—to "soften" her criticisms and reduce the likelihood that she will be read as "the angry black woman." She may believe, moreover, that, to get her colleagues to listen to her, and not dismiss her as intellectually "soft" or self-interested, she has to back her statements up with "objective" research. But doing extra research is no guarantee that her colleagues will take her concerns seriously. It may backfire.[18] Her colleagues may view her extra work, not as good citizenship or institutional commitment, but as a confirmation of excessive sensitivity about, or deep investment in, a personal issue: See, she did extra work only because of her preoccupation with gender politics. In other words, her colleagues might see her research as political, rather than institutional, work. The bottom line is this: whenever an employer or co-worker interprets an employee's words through the prism of negative stereotypes, or whenever an employee perceives that this is taking place, the employee's ability to engage in discussions about institutional policy is circumscribed by the risk that she will be misinterpreted.

Saying Yes to the Right and the Wrong Kinds of Work

Concerns about being misinterpreted and about the negative signals one's communication can send can also lead Outsiders to say yes to both the right and the wrong kinds of work. To understand why, it's helpful to distinguish between two forms of work: advancement tasks (the "right" kind of work) and citizenship tasks (often the "wrong" kind of work). Advancement tasks are directly linked to promotions. An employee has to perform enough of these tasks to advance within the institution. A key feature of advancement tasks is that performance is relatively easy to measure, compensate, and verify. For example, scholars at most academic institutions must meet publication requirements as a precondition for promotion. These publications can be evaluated by other faculty members, and those evaluations can be verified by members of other faculties. In a corporate law firm, the number of large transactions an associate has successfully managed is an important factor in the partners' decision to promote him to a partnership. On both law faculties and at law firms, there are hierarchies among advancement tasks. Some are more connected to promotions and pay increases than others. For example, running large deals and writing influential articles are considered more important than hours billed and teaching.

Citizenship tasks, on the other hand, are indirectly related to advancement and are difficult to measure and verify. Often they are intended to show whether an employee is loyal, a teamplayer, or collegial. Yet even if the employer thinks it can measure those qualities, the evaluations do not lend themselves to easy verification. The problems with measurement and verification, and the resulting room they leave for bias, mean that promotions and pay increases cannot be directly tied to the performance of these tasks.[19]

But both law school faculties and law firms need employees to perform citizenship tasks. Some can be particularly "lumpy," meaning that they take up so much time and effort that they significantly detract from the employee's ability to perform advancement tasks. At a large law firm, a citizenship task might be due diligence or document-production that involves months of tedious work in a warehouse in rural Oklahoma. On a law school faculty, it could be teaching a course that is unrelated to the employee's scholarship (colloquially known as a "service" course). In either case, the citizenship task reduces the employee's ability to advance.[20] Even if an employee assigned such a task were to sacrifice all her leisure time, she would still not have time to do enough advancement tasks. Given the nature of these lumpy citizenship tasks, employees want to avoid them. Avoidance strategies are likely to be especially appealing to outsiders, who distrust the institution and are seeking to protect their value on the external labor market. The following example illustrates how these dynamics can play themselves out in very ordinary workplace interactions.

Imagine a traditional corporate law firm in which Matt Ramond, a white man, is a partner and Stephanie, a black woman, is a first-year associate. It is 7:30 on a Friday evening and the associate is about to head home. The senior partner, whom the associate has never met, approaches her by the elevator.

"Hi, you're Stephanie Johnson, right?"
"Yes," responds Stephanie.

"I'm Matt Ramond, head of the real estate division." Matt and Stephanie
   shake hands.

"I understand that you are interested in real estate," Matt continues.

"Yes. I was a real estate broker for several years before going to law school,"
   Stephanie answers enthusiastically. "I just love the business."

"Great," Matt replies. "I was wondering whether you might have time to
   do a quick real estate research assignment for me this evening. It should
   take no more than a couple of hours, especially for someone with your
   experience. And please do not hesitate to tell me if you have plans and
   need to leave, in which case I will shuffle things around."

For the new associate, responding to this request is complicated. Stephanie
could just say no. Presumably, the partner would understand that Stephanie
has declined the assignment. Such a response would be clear but would fail to
explain why Stephanie cannot take the assignment.

Alternatively, Stephanie could thank Matt for the opportunity, but indicate that she is unable to take the assignment because she has plans and has to
leave the office early. She may be confident that Matt will not misinterpret her
response. That is to say, he will hear the response and understand that she cannot
take the assignment because she has other plans.

Yet, Stephanie might be reluctant to offer this more detailed reason. It might
send a signal that she is not hard working enough, does not have her priorities
in order, or is not loyal to the institution. To the extent that her response fosters
these impressions, she may worry that the senior partner in her practice area might
not offer her a more desirable and important advancement task the next time one
comes around. Whether, and to what extent, Stephanie actually perceives this cost
will turn on whether she believes that Matt will interpret her response through
a stereotype lens. Because Stephanie is black, she may believe that declining the
assignment would comport with a pervasive stereotype of black women as having
a poor work ethic.[21] In other words, Stephanie may believe that her decision to say
no would confirm the stereotype by signaling laziness. The fact that Matt makes it
clear that she should not hesitate to tell him if she has plans may not allay her fears.
She may believe that the "exit option" Matt presents is a professional courtesy or a
test of both her loyalty and work ethic. Stephanie may believe that if she fails this
test, Matt or the other partners in the firm will burden her with lumpy citizenship
tasks. These concerns create an incentive for Stephanie to say yes.

To complicate the hypothetical, imagine that Stephanie is a single mother with
a four-year-old child and needs to leave work to get home before the babysitter
leaves. Assume that Stephanie perceives the partners at her firm to be concerned
that she will not be able to pull her weight because of her commitments to her

child. In this scenario, refusing the partner's assignment becomes even more difficult. Although Stephanie is unlikely to be worried about being misinterpreted in the literal sense, here again, she may be concerned about negative signaling. Specifically, she may worry that declining the assignment would confirm the partners' preconceived notion about her level of commitment.

Indeed, Stephanie may perceive that the male partners (perhaps unconsciously)[22] sort the female associates into one of two broad categories: those who are "committed to work" and those who are "committed to family."[23] Her thinking may be that the partners know that she has a young son and should know that it is unlikely that she will be able to make last-minute arrangements for a babysitter on a Friday evening. So the fact that she is being asked to stay late might suggest to her that the request is a screening device. That is, if she says no, she faces a high risk of confirming the preconception that she falls into the committed-to-family category. Being stuck in that category would increase the likelihood that the partners would assign her lumpy citizenship tasks (though presumably not ones that involve travel) based on the idea that to assign her advancement tasks would be a waste, since she lacks the requisite level of commitment to warrant promotion.

For black women, the committed-to-family category is particularly fraught with stereotypes about race, gender, and reproduction. Declining the work assignment could lead Matt to think of Stephanie as a black woman who wants the firm to subsidize or accommodate her poor (and morally suspect) reproductive choices. This would be the corporate version of the "Welfare Queen" stereotype, the image of black women as welfare cheats who expect the government to support them and the children they have out of wedlock. If Stephanie perceives that Matt is (even implicitly) screening her in this way, she will feel additional pressure to say yes to the assignment.[24] Doing so decreases, or at least does not increase, the salience of her identity as a black woman. Saying yes in this context, then, is tantamount to not talking "like a black woman" in the sense of not triggering stereotypes about that social category. In the next chapter, we take up in more detail the problem of "acting like a black woman" in a corporate context. Here, it is enough to understand there is an incentive for Stephanie to take the assignment if she is concerned that saying no would trigger stereotypes about black women.

Stephanie would not be vulnerable in this way if she were a man. The partner would probably not interpret a male associate's isolated decision to decline an assignment because of childcare obligations as an indication of lack of commitment. Given the assumption that men privilege work over family,[25] the partner may conclude that the associate must be in a bind to be invoking family obligations. This is not to say that men are not punished for being overly committed to family. Though social norms about men and family work have shifted, it remains the case that, by and large, childcare responsibilities are considered "women's work," a characterization that suggests that men should not be responsible for childcare. Thus, it is not hard to imagine a corporate culture in which men, and not just women, are punished for being overly committed to family. Our point is that because of the assumption that men will not be overly committed to family, a particular decision to leave work to attend to childcare is less likely to be read as a lack of commitment to work on the part of the male employee.

One might agree with the above analysis and nevertheless conclude that, after all is said and done, it's not a big deal for Stephanie to take on the assignment. She should suck it up, particularly because the assignment is an advancement task, a relatively minor one, to be sure, but an advancement task nonetheless. Giving up one evening to create the possibility of getting future and more significant advancements tasks seems like a reasonable quid pro quo.

But the quid pro quo is more burdensome than a single event. An employee in Stephanie's position could conceivably have multiple experiences of the sort we describe. She is likely to be a repeat player in this work negotiation game. So, more than one evening is at stake. Moreover, this dynamic applies not only to advancement tasks but to lumpy citizenship tasks as well. Given the nature of these tasks, all employees will want to avoid them. This avoidance strategy is likely to be especially appealing to Outsiders like Stephanie who may distrust their institution or believe that their opportunity for advancement within it turns on the value they have on the external labor market. On this view, the more citizenship tasks Stephanie performs, the less time and energy she will have to work on advancement tasks. In short, as an Outsider, Stephanie will have a greater-than-normal incentive to avoid citizenship tasks.

But Stephanie will also have a greater-than-normal incentive to perform citizenship tasks. Stereotypes about race and work ethic (black people don't pull their weight) and race and citizenship (black people shirk responsibilities) increases the likelihood that Stephanie will say yes to citizenship tasks.

There is a second set of pressures that may operate on Outsiders to perform citizenship tasks. These derive from being a "token" and they come in two forms. First, the Outsider may believe that the employer hired her with the expectation that she would perform the role of the "good" Outsider who will help fill the need for Outsider presence on committees, such as the hiring and recruiting or the promotions committees. She may believe that the employer expects to extract a diversity profit from her presence. Recall our discussion in the prologue that employers often engage in what Nancy Leong calls "racial capitalism"—the use of a person's race to enhance the value of the institution.[26] An all-white hiring committee sends a message that there are no, or no respected, racial minorities at the firm. This is a message the firm does not want to send; hence, the request to the racial minority or Outsider to serve. If the Outsider says no, she risks sending the message that she is the "wrong" type of Outsider, one who refuses to allow the employer to capitalize on her racial identity.

Second, the Outsider might feel an obligation to her Outsider group (or to other Outsider groups), not only to ensure that Outsiders are treated fairly in the recruiting and hiring process, but also to increase the representation of Outsiders within the firm. A version of this dynamic extends to the mentoring of junior Outsiders or Outsider; the absence of mentoring leaves junior Outsiders adrift within their institutions and renders them even more vulnerable to being treated unfairly. Lila Coleburn and Julia Spring explain:

> The professor who is different in any way—a woman, a minority, disabled, gay—is likely to be particularly anxious about burdens of being conspicuous. How can she do her writing, out-Kingsfield Kingsfield, as she knows she must be respected, and still have time to attend to the special care students will expect of her? Those students who identify with her, those who surround her after class or call her in distress, will be bitterly disappointed if she shields herself from their needs to attend to her own.[27]

This Outsider constituency concern is another pressure on Outsiders to say yes to citizenship tasks.

Compounding all this is the fact that decision-makers typically create asking mechanisms that make it costly for employees to say no. For example, a partner who needs a junior associate to work on the firm's self-study committee (no rational associate would want this job) would probably not send out a broad e-mail request for volunteers. No one is likely to respond, in part because all the junior associates will calculate that the overwhelming majority of their colleagues are also going to ignore the request, and therefore the cost of not responding (in terms of being perceived as a bad citizen) is small.

To induce someone to say yes to a citizenship task, the cost of saying no has to be large. The senior decision-maker can create this penalty through the use of a personal request—where the decision-maker goes to the junior employee's office and says, "We really need you to do X." Here, the costs are high because saying no can easily be interpreted as an affirmative anti-citizenship statement. This dynamic is exacerbated if the employee is, like Stephanie, an Outsider. Stereotypes about her identity increase the likelihood that she will say yes if a partner asks her to perform citizenship tasks.

Things for Stephanie are potentially even worse. If the employer perceives that she is vulnerable to the stereotypes and thus likely to say yes to requests for her to perform citizenship tasks, there is an incentive for the employer to exploit that vulnerability. This saves the decision-maker time and resources. Not only does the decision-maker expend less on search costs (finding people who will say yes), but also, because of stereotypes, the Outsider is less likely than an Insider to ask for favors in return for performing the citizenship task.[28] Selecting Outsiders for lumpy citizenship tasks also helps the firm manage a scarce resource—advancement tasks (there are never enough to go around)—and enables the firm to funnel that resource to the employees it thinks are most likely to succeed: Insiders. Finally, even if an employer over-allocates citizenship tasks to an Outsider employee, that employee might nevertheless succeed. In that circumstance, the institution ends up with the kind of Outsider it wants—an Outsider superstar. Outsiders who succeed in this way have likely repudiated the employer's negative stereotypes about work ethic, intellectual capacity, and institutional fit. Under this frame, singling out Outsiders to perform lumpy tasks is efficient (Outsiders are likely to say yes), cost-effective (there's no quid pro quo), mindful of human capital constraints (diminishing the demand for advancement tasks), resource-sensitive (allocating a limited resource to "favored" employees), and racially selective (separating the bad Outsiders, those who say no, from the good Outsiders, those who say yes, and the superstar Outsiders from the rest).

Saying No to Squeaking the Wheel

If stereotyping increases the likelihood that Outsiders will say yes to citizenship tasks, it also diminishes the likelihood that Outsiders will request extra resources—institutional "goodies"—from their employer. Employees typically have to request a number of resources from their employers, including expense accounts for trips to seminars, exemptions from unpleasant work and/or citizenship tasks, access to good work, good administrative assistance, extra administrative assistance, updated equipment, and even bonuses. Employers give each employee a basic level of support, but anything above that level is provided on a "who asks" or "who complains" basis. If employees do not ask, they do not receive. The employer has only a limited number of extra goodies, and if everyone asked there would not be enough to go around. However, the system works because not everyone asks for their additional resources.

Presumably, some people do not ask because they do not need or do not want the extra resources. However, many people who do not ask are deterred by the social cost of asking—being perceived as greedy, selfish, and uncollegial. The squeaky-wheel system works best in low-information environments with risk-averse employees. Employees who know what goodies others are receiving will not be shy about asking for favors; this is especially true if it turns out that they have been receiving fewer resources than the others. For example, if an employee knows that all her colleagues have had their seminar trips funded, she likely will not hesitate to ask for a trip for herself. Conversely, she is less likely to ask when she does not know how much funding the others received. She could ask, but she is not sure that her colleagues will give her accurate information (keep in mind that her receiving more means less for them).

Outsiders lose out in such a system in two ways. First, the system works best for those who have inside information about what to demand. If an employee has a list of high-cost and low-cost requests, she is already in a good position. However, this information is not readily available in low-information environments. As such, the problem for Outsiders is obtaining this information.

Of course, access to information is a potential problem for Insiders as well. Any employee who seeks information about high-cost and low-cost resources risks creating the impression that she is trying to game the system. But, as a general matter, Insiders do not need to seek out this information as often as Outsiders. This is because of the identity-based ways in which informal workplace networks get established[29] and because of identity demographics of law firms and law faculties.[30] Junior Insiders are more likely than junior Outsiders to benefit from their interactions with senior Insiders because of the informal, Insider networks that exist in those institutions. When a senior Insider and a junior Insider interact, there is a greater chance that the senior will do something like pull the junior into the senior's office and, without being asked, something like: "This is how things work here, and X is what you should ask for. And, by the way, whatever you do, don't ask for Y." In low-information environments, Outsiders typically have to request this sort of information. Thus, the first difficulty for an Outside employee in a squeaky-wheel system is obtaining information about low-cost and high-cost requests.

The second difficulty is requesting the goodies. Outsiders might fear that the employer will not only interpret their request as a sign of greed or a lack of collegiality but also as an indication that she needs "extra" or "special" help—a thumb on the scale—to succeed. Note how this easily fits into the affirmative action frame, which suggests that Outsiders who benefit from affirmative action receive preferential treatment.

Outsiders might also worry, rightly or wrongly, that if they ask for additional goodies, the decision-maker is likely to say no because of bias. A final concern Outsiders might have is that requesting goodies will make them vulnerable to getting extra lumpy citizenship tasks. The employer may respond to an Outsider's request with an implicit quid pro quo: "You need extra goodies; we need more people to perform lumpy citizenship tasks." And the Outsider may feel pressured to accept the terms of the bargain. She may worry that if she responds with a "no, thank you," she will be perceived as selfish and anti-institutional—a person who wants resources from the institution, but is unwilling to give back. An Outsider's awareness of this dynamic, combined with her general concern that squeaking the wheel will confirm stereotypes, creates a disincentive for her to ask for additional resources.

Holding One's Tongue in the Interview

Thus far, we have focused on how stereotyping constrains what an Outsider employee thinks she can say, and fosters worry that a simple yes or no can make her Outsider identity more salient. This creates an incentive for Outsiders to avoid communications that have the potential to trigger negative stereotypes about their identity. Sometimes this will mean saying nothing at all (for example, refraining from criticizing a firm's institutional governance practices or from asking the institution for additional resources). Sometimes it will mean saying yes to assignments when they would really like to say no. All of this ends up affecting the Outsider's capacity to shape the institutional culture of the workplace, the kind of work she ends up doing, and her career trajectory.

A similar dynamic is at play at the hiring stage. Here, too, an Outsider might police what she says, or even hold her tongue, for fear of triggering negative stereotypes. Consider law firm hiring practices. Depending on the economy, large law firms typically hire from five to twenty first- and second-year law students to work for roughly two months as summer associates. Student summer associates are already part of the pool from which the firm will hire permanent associates. Imagine that a firm has organized an end-of-the-summer dinner in honor of the summer-associate class. Five permanent associates are present: four white men and one white woman. The summer associate, Debra, is a black woman who has just been extended a permanent offer to join the firm upon graduation from law school. Debra is excited. But her excitement is cautious, for she realizes that if she accepts the offer, she will be one of only two black women and five black people in a firm of two hundred attorneys.

As the evening progresses, there are many celebratory toasts. This firm prides itself on getting summer associates to accept its offers by the end of these dinners. Molly, the white female associate, wants to know if Debra has been to a Knicks game lately. She tells Debra that the firm has lots of tickets and continues: "It is great fun. Even if you don't care for basketball, it is fun to watch all the famous people. When I went to the Knicks versus San Antonio game, I got to see Woody Allen and John McEnroe close up." The conversation then turns to the National Basketball Association's dress policy for its players. Debra has strong views about race and the NBA. She recalls that she has read about the NBA's dress code. She thinks about the fact that the dress code policy was part of a larger movement to reform the NBA's image after a number of unsavory incidents involving players during prior seasons, including the Kobe Bryant sexual assault case in 2003[31] and the Pacers-Pistons brawl that spilled into the stands in 2004.[32] The NBA was worried that it was acquiring a hip-hop image and that this was driving away white fans.[33] The dress code, along with a public-service initiative known as NBA Cares, was an effort to overhaul the image of NBA players—and the image of the NBA writ large.

Debra also remembers that some of the earliest and most vocal critics of the dress code were the players themselves. The consensus was that the NBA wanted to steer away from hip-hop culture and that this discriminated against black players. The policy was seen as racist because hip-hop culture is predominantly associated with young black men.[34] Despite the fact that all NBA policies disproportionately affect young black men (because the NBA is roughly 70% to 80% young black men), Debra felt this rule was aimed specifically at black players. Debra's thoughts turned to comments then-Lakers head coach, Phil Jackson, who is white, made in an ESPN.com interview: "The players have been dressing in prison garb the last five or six years . . . all the stuff that goes on, it's like gangsta, thuggery stuff."[35]

Debra's view of the NBA's policy is that it was, at least implicitly, racially motivated. But she worries that should she make her views known to the four white men and one white woman at the table, she will be vulnerable to being seen as overly race conscious, that is, as the overly sensitive person who sees race when it "isn't" there, the person who likely will be resistant to the conformity requirements of firm life. Accordingly, Debra compromises her identity and responds:

> The result of this policy seems to be that things calmed down and fans do not have to be as worried about some crazy player like Ron Artest jumping into the stands and a melee breaking out. It sends a positive message to young black boys to pull up their pants and walk tall. I am sure President Obama, if asked, would not say that the policy was racially discriminatory. After his foray into the Henry Louis Gates affair, I am sure he is going to be much more cautious about invoking race. In fact, I don't think he mentioned race when commenting on the Trayvon Martin case. And that makes sense. In some ways, all of us need to be less vigilant about race; we need to stop seeing it in everything, particularly given that so much racial progress has been made.

The other associates agree and invite Debra to the next Knicks game. Debra says yes, even though she believes that that next encounter, too, will require her to work her identity.

As with the earlier examples, this one, too, is exaggerated. But we find it easy to imagine a black woman both holding her tongue about her racial views and employing her conversations to signal that she is not overly committed to racial politics. It is conceivable that a woman in Debra's position would experience the entire event as a test that she had to (racially) pass.

A version of the foregoing dynamic applies to everyone. Presumably, no associate is free to say whatever crosses his mind at an official dinner. Assume that, instead of Debra, the summer associate, Phil, is white and male. Assume further that Phil has strong views about race and sports. Phil would have to both hold his tongue and work his conversations as well. There are two ways to explain why.

First, no summer associate at an official dinner would feel free to speak his mind. Everyone feels the pressure to fit in; everyone works identity. However, the general pressure to conform is compounded by whether and to what extent one's identity (e.g., being black) and assumptions about what it represents (e.g., being overly racially sensitive and committed to racial politics) are at odds with values the institution wants to promote (e.g., colorblindness). When this is the case, talking back to one's colleagues—especially disagreeing with them about identity-related issues—is tantamount to "talking black."

This brings us to the second, more racially specific way in which Phil might feel pressured to compromise his identity. If Phil is in agreement with the policy, he might worry that expressing that view would render him vulnerable to being perceived as a racist. Being labeled as racist is serious business. Moreover, Phil's sense of vulnerability would be heightened if one of the lawyers around the table were black. This is just one example of how a white man might feel pressured to compromise his sense of identity.

That said, lawyers within majority-white law firms are unlikely to harbor the stereotype that white men are racists. Moreover, at every employment decision-making point within a law firm—hiring, pay increases, partnership deliberations—Phil can be confident that most of the decision-makers will be white and male. Thus, while race-specific performance demands are at play for people who are white, those demands exert greater pressures on the Debras of the world than the Phils.

Finally, even if Phil, like Debra, believes that the NBA policy is racially motivated, the fact that he is white and male gives him greater freedom to express that view. This is because white men are not stereotyped as being overly racially sensitive or overly committed to identity politics that favor people of color. This is not to say that that there are no potential costs to Phil arguing that the

NBA's policy is racist. Expressing that view could cause the white attorneys to worry that Phil will be too sympathetic to allegations of racism on the part of one of the few people of color at the firm. There have been cases involving white plaintiffs who argued that their employers retaliated against them for supporting discrimination claims asserted by people of color.[36] While Phil is not yet an employee of the firm, the attorneys representing the firm could take his views about the NBA as a proxy for whether he is likely to identify with the Outsiders already at the firm. Put crudely, there might be performance demands on Phil—namely, that he work his identity to signal white racial solidarity. To what extent is hard to say. Still, assuming Phil and Debra articulate precisely the same racial critique of the NBA's policy, the risk that the attorneys at the dinner will view Debra as a race-baiter is likely greater than the risk that they will view Phil as a race-traitor or, at least, as someone who overly identifies with people of color. There is a nasty historical term that captures this race-traitor idea— "Nigger Lover." Few people today would use that term. But the phenomenon of whites punishing other whites for perceived racial disloyalty remains a part of the racial landscape, as the cases we mention above attest.

Legal Intervention

The problems we describe do not fit easily within current law, which bars intentional discrimination in the workplace. Outsiders' extra burden often appears to have been taken on voluntarily. For example, requests that an Outsider take on lumpy tasks are probably made with the caveat, "we really need you, but you should feel free to say no." Similarly, an Outsider's failure to receive goodies in the squeaky-wheel system can be attributed to the fact that they did not ask for them.

Accordingly, we are skeptical that a court would pay attention to how stereotypes structure the interactional dynamics of the workplace such that Outsiders are likely to say yes to lumpy tasks and unlikely to squeak the wheel for extra resources. Nor do we think courts will take note of the employer's incentives to exploit these vulnerabilities. Likely, a judge would conclude that the Outsider employee simply exercised bad judgment in taking on more than she was capable of handling and in not asking for help. Ironically, this finding would reinforce stereotypes that the Outsider was more likely to fail anyway. Making matters worse, because the story we told about stereotypes and conversations at work is not a story about animus, the threat of sanction under the current anti-discrimination law is unlikely to induce employers to institute structural changes aimed at addressing the problems we have identified.[37]

What's the Problem, Anyway?

Quite apart from questions about legal intervention, one might argue that we haven't identified a real problem. After all, we concede that our models are stylized and that our examples are exaggerated. A skeptic might assert that the existence of affirmative action/diversity initiatives and anti-discrimination law protections turns the "talking white" dynamic on its head in reality. The thinking is that management inevitably worries about asking Outsider employees to perform such tasks for fear that those requests might result in claims of discrimination (which would hurt the career prospects of the managers in question). A skeptic might also argue that a similar dynamic applies to squeaking the wheel, that Outsiders are comfortable squeaking the wheel, perhaps because of the protections of anti-discrimination law and the backdrop of affirmative action and diversity mandates. The question is an empirical one; people's perceptions are bound to differ. While we think we have made the theoretical case for our conclusions, we have no attachment to them. Our goal is to get people to think about race as a "talking" and not just a "looking" phenomenon. This "talking" phenomenon is not just about accents but more fundamentally about the relationship between what we say and the salience of our identities.

A bigger objection to our thesis might be that our project was misguided from the start. The very definition of an Outsider, one might argue, is someone who has to prove his or her loyalty before being allowed into the fold. As one of our colleagues explained, "Guests to my home don't get to start rearranging the furniture right away. They have to stay long enough to become members of the family before they can do that." Under this view, everyone, in a way, is an Outsider; everyone has to prove that he or she belongs; everyone has to fit in; and everyone has to, well, "talk white" in the sense of engaging in speech that the institution favors and avoiding speech that the institution disfavors.

Surely that is right. We would respond, however, that, because of stereotypes, people interact with institutions with different "identity priors." People who are vulnerable to stereotypes have a heavier burden proving that they belong than people who are not so burdened. Consequently, people who are burdened with stereotypes are likely to hold their tongue to a greater extent than others. The cumulative effect of doing so—day in and day out—can be significant over the course of a person's career. We have already hinted that we do not think this is a problem anti-discrimination law can fix. But the question of legal intervention is a matter we take up more in later chapters, in the context of a broader discussion about Working Identity and the law. Putting the law to one side for purposes of this discussion, and assuming that there is some empirical basis for our theoretical claims, surely we should recognize the "talking white" phenomenon as a potential problem. Perhaps the answer is, we should not. Perhaps Outsiders should do the extra work to fit into the contemporary workplace. Perhaps Outsiders should be encouraged to "talk white." If that is what we think, let us be transparent about it; let's say so explicitly.

This brings us back to Senator Harry Reid. Wittingly or not, Reid broadened our understanding about racial dynamics. His comments suggesting that Obama does not speak in a "Negro dialect" highlighted the fact that, to have crossover appeal, blacks might have to "talk white." In this sense, rather than criticize Reid, we should have asked ourselves whether in fact the success of Obama's presidential bid was contingent upon his "talking white"—and, more generally, whether Outsiders have to "talk white" to succeed within the workplace.

But this is a difficult conversation for Americans to have. No politician or public figure is going to say that blacks should act or talk less black. Meanwhile, blacks know that this is exactly the racial expectation of not only the political world but the corporate world as well. It is part of a broader set of expectations about how a black person should self-present. In the next chapter we explore how these expectations play themselves out in the context of a case not about speech but, ostensibly, about hair. As will become clear, hair can be a signal for Working Identity and, more specifically, for racial palatability and racial salience. In the corporate context, black women who wear their hair in braids or dreadlocks are less palatable and more racially salient than black women who do not. Does this explain why American Airlines adopted a policy prohibiting its employees from wearing braids? In adopting this policy, was American Airlines forcing black women to "act white"—or denying them the right to "act black"? Is there any way we can even know? These are the questions we now turn to in chapter 3, employing *Rogers v. American Airlines* to do so.

Acting Like a Black Woman

When white actress and sex symbol Bo Derek made headline news in 1979 for appearing in the movie *10* with beaded and braided hair, she could not have known that her choice to style her hair in that way would have legal significance in an anti-discrimination case two years later. (See figure 3.1.) The case, *Rogers v. American Airlines*, centered around an American Airlines policy that prohibited its employees from wearing all-braided hairstyles.[1] Renee Rogers, a black female

Figure 3.1 Bo Derek in *10*.
Source: © Bettmann/CORBIS.

employee, challenged the policy. She argued that it discriminated against her based on race and gender, in violation of the Civil Rights Act of 1964.

The court disagreed. It reasoned that the grooming policy did not reflect sex discrimination because it applied to both women and men. The court further noted that because the policy restricted braided hair, irrespective of race, the policy was race neutral. In reaching this conclusion, the court invoked Bo Derek's braided hairstyle in *10*. The court credited American Airlines' argument that Renee Rogers "first appeared at work in the all-braided hairstyle on or about September 25, 1980, soon after the style had been popularized by a white actress in the film '10'."[2] The court rejected Rogers's claim that braided hair "has been, historically, a fashion and style adopted by Black American women, reflective of the cultural, historical essence of Black women in American society."[3] For the court, from an anti-discrimination perspective, braided hair had no significance. Consequently, it concluded that American Airlines' prohibition on braided hairstyles had "at most a negligible effect on employment opportunity."[4]

Both Paulette Caldwell and Angela Onwuachi-Willig have critiqued the court's approach for failing to consider the constitutive role hair plays in shaping black women's identity. As Onwuachi-Willig puts it, "[a]lthough the *Rogers* court clearly understood that there were significant differences in the structures and textures of black and white hair—Afros and non-Afros—its ultimate conclusion was rooted in an incomplete or flawed understanding of black hair, especially as it relates to black women."[5]

A more general way to critique the court's analysis is to say that the court separately analyzes Rogers's racial discrimination and sex discrimination claims. The court failed to adopt an intersectional approach. Caldwell and Onwuachi-Willig advance this critique as well. According to Caldwell, "In a case such as *Rogers*, an intersectional analysis would necessarily examine the issue at the core of the plaintiff's complaint: that race and gender discrimination operated together to affect her [Rogers] as a black woman in a way that was not experienced by either white women or black men."[6]

Central to Intersectionality Theory is the idea that all of us have multiple identities—race, gender, class, sexual orientation, and so on—and these multiple social identities intersect in ways that shape the form and extent of discrimination we experience.[7] Under this view, because of the gender difference, black women and black men are not equally vulnerable to the same forms or extent of racial discrimination; and, because of the race difference, black women and white women are not equally vulnerable to the same forms of gender discrimination. Thus, Intersectionality Theory suggests that when courts adjudicate discrimination claims, they should utilize the plaintiff's intersectional identity to determine whether the person was subject to discrimination in relation to her identity as a whole, as compared to utilizing one identity (e.g., race) separate and apart from another (e.g., gender).

Part of the significance of paying attention to the plaintiff's intersectional identity is that it allows courts to consider evidence on the question of whether the plaintiff experienced discrimination based on a sub-group status (for example, being an Asian American woman) within a larger identity group (Asian Americans). Informing this sub-group approach to discrimination is the idea that it is plausible that an employer would not discriminate against all Asian Americans, but would discriminate against Asian American women. Under such a scenario, the employer would be making an intra-racial distinction—a distinction between people in the *same* racial group.

The standard discrimination claim involves people from different identity groups—for example, a company discriminating against Asian Americans in favor of whites. This approach requires an Asian American plaintiff to demonstrate that she was treated differently from a similarly situated non–Asian American (usually a white) employee.[8] But our hypothetical plaintiff might not be the victim of this standard form of discrimination. As noted in the prior paragraph, it is possible that her firm prefers Asian American men to Asian American women, discriminating against the latter but not the former. Framing the discrimination question solely in terms of the plaintiff's Asian American identity ignores the fact that the plaintiff's discrimination could be based on her intersectional identity as an Asian American female.

This chapter demonstrates how the Working Identity concept we advance further develops one of Intersectionality Theory's insights that discrimination is based both on perceived and real inter-group differences (differences among people from different identity groups), in addition to intra-group differences (differences among people in the same identity group). Central to Working Identity is the idea that to appreciate a person's vulnerability to an intra-group distinction, one must take into account how a person works or is perceived to work their identity. While a firm might prefer Asian American men to Asian American women, it is also true that a firm might utilize stereotypes to prefer one Asian American woman over another. This chapter builds on Intersectionality Theory to capture the latter form of discrimination, a form of discrimination that current anti-discrimination law largely does not reach.

***

Over two decades ago, Kimberlé Crenshaw published *Demarginalizing the Intersection of Race and Sex: A Black Feminist Critique of Antidiscrimination Doctrine, Feminist Theory, and Antiracist Politics.*[9] The article is a classic in anti-discrimination theory.[10] In it, Crenshaw identifies an anti-discrimination problem that derives from the employment of "single axis frameworks"[11] to adjudicate discrimination claims

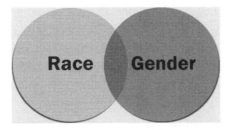

Figure 3.2 Race/Gender intersection.

brought by black women. These frameworks typically focus on just race or just sex, failing to consider that these two identities interact and intersect in ways that materially shape a person's vulnerability to and experiences of discrimination.

One can read intersectionality to mean that personhood (or identity) can be separated out into discrete social parts. For example, race can be separated from gender. This is because the notion that two things "intersect" brings readily to mind a Venn diagram within which each thing exists both inside and outside of the intersection. Indeed, this is the conception of intersectionality that our students often articulate. This understanding is schematically captured in figure 3.2.

The diagram invites us to imagine social circumstances in which race and gender exist apart from each other as "pure" identities. Although the metaphor of intersectionality conveys this idea, the fuller theory of intersectionality, and Crenshaw's conceptualization of this theory, rejects it. Fundamental to Intersectionality Theory is the understanding that race and gender are interconnected, and as a result, they do not exist as disaggregated identities. In other words, there are no nonintersecting areas in the diagram. In this sense, there might be a tension between the conception of identity that the intersectional metaphor invites and the substantive theory that intersectionality articulates. Perhaps because of this tension, scholars have employed other terms—*cosynthesis*,[12] *multidimensionality*,[13] *multiple consciousness*,[14] *compoundedness*,[15] *interconnectivity*,[16] and *multiplicity*[17]—to discuss the "single axis" problem (or some variation of it) that Crenshaw identified. It is arguable whether these terms are better metaphors, since each seems to be predicated on the idea of separate identity categories coming together in some way. Moreover, none of the terms, at least one of which Crenshaw herself employs in her original articulation of the theory, alters the core insight—namely, that the overlapping nature of identities affects whether and how we experience discrimination.

To better understand how intersectionality implicates anti-discrimination law, consider the following hypothetical. Tyisha, a black woman, is interviewing with an elite corporate law firm. There are eighty attorneys at the firm, twenty of whom are partners. Only two of the partners are black, and both are men.

The firm has three female partners, and all three are white. There are no Asian American, Native American, or Latina/o partners. The firm is more diverse at the associate rank. There are fifteen female associates: three are black, two are Asian American, and one is Latina. The remaining female associates are white. Of the forty-five male associates, two are black, two are Latino, three are Asian American, and the rest are white.

Stipulate that four other recent law school graduates are interviewing for the job along with Tyisha: a black man, an Asian American man, one white man, and one white woman. The firm does not hire Tyisha or the white male applicant. Tyisha brings a disparate treatment discrimination suit under Title VII.[18] She advances three separate theories: race discrimination, sex discrimination, and race and sex discrimination combined. She does not have any direct evidence that her employer intentionally discriminated against her. That is, Tyisha can point to no explicit statements, such as "We don't like you because you are a woman" or "We think that you are incompetent; all blacks are." The evidence is circumstantial: Tyisha was qualified, but was rejected for a position that was arguably open.

The court rejects all three of Tyisha's claims. With respect to the race discrimination claim, the court reasons that the claim is not supported by evidence of intentional racial discrimination or hostility. According to the court, there is no evidence that the firm dislikes (or has a taste for discrimination against) blacks. In fact, argues the court, the evidence points in the other direction. The very year the firm denied employment to Tyisha, it offered an associate position to another African American. Moreover, the court points to the fact that the firm had, in the past, promoted African Americans to the rank of partnership. The court concludes that the simple act of not hiring one black person, especially when other blacks have been hired and promoted, is insufficient to establish racial discrimination.

The court disposes of Tyisha's gender discrimination claim in a similar way. That is, it concludes that the fact that the firm hired a white woman the same year it did not hire Tyisha, and the fact that it has promoted white women to the rank of partnership, suggests that the firm did not engage in intentional sex-based discrimination against Tyisha.

The court concludes its dismissal of Tyisha's compound discrimination claim (the allegation of discrimination based on her race and sex) with an argument that such claims are beyond the reach of anti-discrimination law. More particularly, the court explains that while Tyisha may argue that the firm discriminated against her based on her race *or* based on sex, she may not argue that the firm discriminated against her based on her race *and* sex concurrently. According to the court, "there is no indication in the legislative history of Title VII that the statute intended "to create a new classification of 'black women' who would have greater standing than, for example, a black male."[19] Further, "[t]he prospect of the creation of new classes of protected minorities, governed only by mathematical principles of permutation and combination, clearly raises the prospect of opening the hackneyed Pandora's Box."[20]

The foregoing articulates the classic intersectionality problem wherein black women fall through an anti-discrimination gap constituted by black male and white female experiences.[21] The problem can also be framed in terms of essentialism. Consider first the court's response to Tyisha's race discrimination claim. In determining whether Tyisha experienced race discrimination, the court assumes that there is an essential black experience that is unmodified by gender. This approach paints a totalizing picture of racism—namely, that racism affects black men and black women in exactly the same way. In other words, racism is totally about race. Thus, this formulation implicitly suggests that it is unlikely that a person who holds negative racial views will distinguish between black men and black women.[22]

Yet this is precisely what Tyisha is arguing. Her intra-racial distinction argument is that the firm distinguishes between black women and black men, that it prefers the latter, and that this preference is discriminatory. However, to the extent that a court essentializes race (by, for example, conceptualizing race without taking gender differences into account), it makes it likely that the court will not view Tyisha's identification of the firm's preference for black men as racially discriminatory. Put another way, if, as in our hypothetical case, a court's anti-discrimination starting point is based upon an essential conception of race, that court may have difficulty understanding how a racist firm might promote some black people (e.g., men) but not others (e.g., women).

Consider now the court's adjudication of Tyisha's sex discrimination claim. Here, too, the court's analysis reflects essentialism—namely, that women's experiences are unmodified by race. The court assumes that if a firm engages in sex discrimination, such discrimination will negatively affect all women in the same way. The court fails to consider that an institution might make an intra-gender distinction between black women and white women. Yet this is the crux of Tyisha's gender discrimination claim—that intra-gender distinctions constitute actionable gender discrimination. But because the court essentializes gender, it does not view the employer's preference for white women as gender discrimination. Under an essential conception of gender, it is difficult to understand that a sexist firm might promote some women (e.g., whites) and not others (e.g., blacks).

Finally, consider the court's rejection of Tyisha's compound discrimination claim. Here, the court erases black women's intersectional identity as *black-women*. In effect, the court is saying that, for purposes of Title VII, black women exist only to the extent that their experiences comport with the experiences of black men or white women. The contrary view recognizes that blackness is not gender neutral (it is shaped by and experienced through gender) and gender is not race neutral (it is shaped by and experienced through race).

Assume now that a court is sympathetic to Intersectionality Theory or at least recognizes discrimination claims based on both race and sex.[23] This stipulation helps to introduce the Working Identity issue. To appreciate how, assume again that Tyisha is an African American female seeking employment with a predominantly white elite corporate law firm. Stipulate now that four other black women are interviewing with the same firm. The firm hires the first four black women, but it does not hire Tyisha, the fifth black woman.

This hiring decision creates a buzz around the firm. The firm had never hired so many nonwhite attorneys at once. Moreover, the firm has never hired a class within which all the associates were nonwhite attorneys. Prior to 1980, the firm had never hired a single black female associate. Further, most of those who were hired after that date left within two to three years of their arrival. Given the history of black women at the firm—low hiring rate, high attrition rate, low promotion rate—associates at the firm dubbed this the "year of the black woman."

Tyisha, however, is not happy with her rejection by the firm. She files a Title VII discrimination suit, alleging (1) race and sex compound discrimination, that is, discrimination against her on account of her being a black woman, and (2) discrimination based on Working Identity. The firm moves for summary judgment, the dismissal of the case without a full trial, on two theories. First, it argues that Tyisha may not ground her discrimination claim on her race and sex. According to the firm, Tyisha may separately assert a race discrimination claim and a sex discrimination claim. She may not, under Title VII, advance a discrimination claim combining race and sex. Second, the firm contends that whatever identity Tyisha invokes to ground her claim, there is no evidence of intentional discrimination.

With respect to the first issue, the court agrees with Tyisha that anti-discrimination law does recognize compound discrimination claims based on both race and sex. The court has read, understood, and agrees with the literature on intersectionality. Under the judge's view, black women should be permitted to ground their discrimination claims on their specific intersectional identity as black women. According to the judge, failing to do so would be to ignore the complex ways in which race and gender interact to create social disadvantage: a result inconsistent with the goals of Title VII.[24]

Turning now to the second issue, the court agrees with the firm. The judge reasons that recognizing Tyisha's intersectional identity alone does not prove that the firm discriminated against her because of that identity. The judge specifically notes that the firm hired four associates with Tyisha's precise intersectional identity—that is, four black women. Why, the judge rhetorically asks, would a racist/sexist firm hire, not one or two of these women, but four, if the firm held discriminatory views against black women? The judge reasons that when there is clear evidence of non-discrimination against members of the same identity category at issue, this evidence produces an inference that the plaintiff was not the victim of discrimination.

The judge rejects Tyisha's arguments that Title VII itself and the Supreme Court's interpretation of Title VII focuses on protecting individuals, not groups, from discrimination.[25] Tyisha had argued that a black applicant who is not promoted may bring a discrimination claim even if other black people are promoted or represented in the position for which the plaintiff is applying, or are represented in the workplace more generally. Central to Tyisha's argument is the idea that an employer cannot escape liability for having a group represented in the workplace; there is no "bottom line" defense to discrimination.[26]

The judge acknowledges that, as a "theoretical matter," Tyisha is right. The firm's non-discrimination against the four black women is not proof positive that it did not discriminate against the fifth. The judge insists, however, that such evidence is persuasive. It explains that

> [p]roof that [the employer's] work force was racially balanced or that it contained a disproportionately high percentage of minority employees is not wholly irrelevant on the issue of intent when that issue is yet to be decided. We cannot say that such proof would have absolutely no probative value in determining whether the otherwise unexplained rejection of the minority applicants was discriminatorily motivated. Thus, although we agree that such proof neither was nor could have been sufficient to conclusively demonstrate that [the employer's] actions were not discriminatorily motivated, [it is proper] to consider the racial mix of the work force when trying to make the determination as to motivation.[27]

The court also rejects Tyisha's Working Identity argument. It reasons that Title VII protects against discrimination based on immutable characteristics. The judge explains that, because Title VII provides no protection for an employee's choices relating to appearance,[28] there is no need to engage the question of whether Tyisha's means of self-presentation (e.g., her hair style and manner of dress) caused discomfort to the lawyers who interviewed Tyisha for the job.

What's wrong with the judge's approach? After all, the court explicitly invoked and took intersectionality into account. What more should the court have done? We argue that the court should have considered whether Tyisha was the victim of an intra-racial (and intra-gender) distinction based not simply on her intersectional identity as a black woman, but also on how she worked or was perceived to work her identity. Whereas in the previous hypothetical, the court essentialized race by not taking gender differences into account, and vice versa, the problem here is that the judge essentializes all "black female" experiences without taking into account Working Identity differences among and between the five black women. In this respect, the court assumes that Tyisha and the other four black women are equally vulnerable to discrimination. However, this might not be the case. How black women work or how others perceive them to work their identity affects whether and how they are discriminated against.

Consider the extent to which the following Working Identity issues might help to explain why Tyisha was not hired, but the other black women were. Stipulate that the following information was visually apparent, disclosed on the resume, or revealed in the context of the interview.

> *Name.* Each of the four black women has a name that is perceived to be mainstream, read: white (Mary, Susan, Tiffany, and Sarah). Tyisha's name has a black racial signification.
>
> *Hair.* Tyisha wears her hair in dreadlocks; the other black women relax their hair.
>
> *Dress.* Tyisha does not wear makeup and wore a trousers suit with a Kente cloth scarf to the interview. Each of the four black women wear makeup and each wore a skirt suit with a white cotton blouse.
>
> *Political Identity.* Tyisha's resume revealed that, as a law student, she was a student activist and served on, among other committees, the Black Student Solidarity Committee and the Students for Faculty Diversity Committee. Only one of four black women participated on an identity-related committee—Students for Interracial Cooperation. One was a member of the Federalist Society, a conservative law student association.
>
> *Social Identity.* All four of the black women play tennis and two of them play golf; Tyisha appears disinterested in sports.
>
> *Marital Status.* All four of the black women are married. Two are married to white men and each of them is married to a professional.
>
> *Motherhood.* Tyisha is the only single mother.
>
> *Residence.* Each of the other black women lives in predominantly white neighborhoods. Tyisha lives in the inner city, which is predominantly black.
>
> *Religious Affiliation.* Tyisha is a member of the Nation of Islam. The religious identities of the other four black women are unknown.

Because the court conceptualizes Tyisha's discrimination case solely in terms of her intersectional identity as a black female, it does not consider any of the foregoing Working Identity dynamics. Yet any one of them could (and all of them together likely would) explain the firm's decision not to hire Tyisha. In other words, it is possible that the firm's hiring decisions reflect an identity preference based on Working Identity.

Note that in this hypothetical, we purposefully exaggerated the Working Identity dimensions of Tyisha's identity. We do not mean to suggest that Tyisha can stand in for most or even a significant number of black women, as we are not advancing an empirical claim. Our argument is theoretical in that it strives to critically examine the relationship between a person's vulnerability to discrimination in the workplace, on the one hand, and their Working Identity, on the other.

But let's assume now that, as an empirical matter, the foregoing Working Identity dynamics are indeed at play in Tyisha's case, such that the firm disfavors Tyisha's Working Identity and prefers the Working Identity of the other four black women. It's not obvious that this preference constitutes discrimination. Perhaps the partners' preference for the four black women is based on their sense that, unlike Tyisha, each of the other black women is likely to fit comfortably within the law firm.

This is not far-fetched. After all, working in an organization is not only about doing work in the literal sense of completing one's assignments. It is also about getting along and establishing relationships with one's colleagues, essentially getting them to like, trust, and feel comfortable around you. This kind of work is particularly important in the context of law firms, where there is a strong expectation that associates complete at least some of their work in teams. Perhaps not surprisingly, then, there is now an entire genre of books that stresses the importance of getting along in the workplace—and fitting in. Dale Carnegie's now-classic *How to Win Friends & Influence People*[29] is an early iteration of this genre.

With concerns about institutional fit and collegiality in mind, one could take the position that the firm did not discriminate against Tyisha when it refused to hire her. Instead, the firm was simply attempting to hire the associates most likely to get along with each other and work collegially and collaboratively in teams. By that yardstick, Tyisha looks decidedly less promising than the other four black women—and some may argue that this has nothing to do with the salience of her Working Identity as a black woman who is "too black."

One could also argue that none of the performative factors that constitute Tyisha's Working Identity—her hairstyle and dress, place of residence, religious affiliation, among other factors—implicate race per se. At best, they are proxies for race—but not race itself. This argument brings us back to the *Rogers* case. Part of the reason the court rejected Renee Rogers's claim was that, from the court's perspective, race was an "immutable characteristic"[30] but a braided hairstyle was not. "An all-braided hairstyle is an 'easily changed characteristic,' and, even if socio-culturally associated with a particular race or nationality, it is not an impermissible basis for distinctions in the application of employment practices."[31] The court went a step further by distinguishing braided hair from an "Afro/bush," the latter being "a natural hairstyle" that "would implicate the policies underlying prohibition of discrimination on the basis of immutable characteristics."[32] In concluding this much, the court left open the possibility that a grooming policy disallowing an Afro hairstyle "might offend" anti-discrimination law.[33] In effect, the court's argument was that while braided hair was not race per se, an "Afro/bush" might be.

It is beyond what we want to do in this chapter to pursue philosophical arguments about what is and isn't race. But as we argued in the prologue, race is not immutable in the sense of being fixed and biologically determined. We agree with most scholars who write about race that race is a social construction. But even if one rejects that conceptualization of race, and even if one is of the view that the list of performative or Working Identity factors we outline above are not race per se, it remains plausible that an employer could draw upon any one of those Working Identity factors, and certainly all of them together, to conclude that Tyisha is "more black" or "too black" as compared to the other black women. Such a conclusion would make Tyisha more vulnerable than the other black women to implicit or explicit negative racial stereotypes.

One can restate this point employing a concept from social psychology: priming. Tyisha's Working Identity is a stronger racial prime, that is, a stronger catalyst, for the triggering of negative racial stereotypes, than the working identities of the other four black women. As such, race could be (though is not necessarily) implicated in the employer's decision not to hire Tyisha, notwithstanding that the employer hired four other black women.

But can the law intervene to manage this Working Identity problem? And assuming it can, should judges push anti-discrimination doctrine in that direction? These are questions we take up later (chapter 7). In the next chapter, we note a set of cases in which courts grapple with at least a part of the Working Identity phenomenon. In these cases, plaintiffs assert sex discrimination without referencing race or any other social category. In adjudicating these claims, courts draw a distinction between sex (which they denote in terms of whether someone is "male" or "female") and gender (which they denote in terms of whether someone is "masculine" or "feminine").

The judges deciding these sex discrimination cases do not employ the language of Working Identity. They rely heavily on gender role, arguing, for example, that it is impermissible for an employer to refuse to promote a woman because that woman is insufficiently feminine. Similarly, it is impermissible for a firm to terminate a man because that man is insufficiently masculine. In effect, this body of law prohibits employers not only from requiring women to work their identities as feminine but also from requiring men to work their identities as masculine. Cumulatively, these sex discrimination cases suggest that courts are now sensitive to the fact that men and women are vulnerable to discrimination when they refuse or fail to embody or enact traditional gender stereotypes. We refer to this area of law as the anti–sex-stereotyping or gender non-conformity cases. Because these cases have implications for whether courts should recognize Working Identity claims based on race, or based on race and gender, the next chapter explains the factual backdrop against which they were litigated. We do so by focusing on *Jespersen v. Harrah's Casino*, a Ninth Circuit case involving a casino that terminated one of its female bartenders because she refused to wear makeup. The bartender sued, arguing sex discrimination. Describing the nature of this case, explaining how it implicates sex discrimination, and revealing how the law responds to Working Identity claims that are framed solely with respect to gender puts us in a better position to assess whether plaintiffs like Tyisha should have their day in court.

4

Acting Like a (White) Woman

Few would have expected Alex Kozinski, the conservative chief justice of the United States Court of Appeals for the Ninth Circuit, and a Reagan appointee, to lead the charge supporting a gender discrimination claim about makeup and self-presentation—that is to say, a case about Working Identity. Nor would many have predicted that a prominent liberal woman and former chief judge of the Ninth Circuit, Mary Schroeder, and a Carter appointee, would lead the charge against the plaintiff. (See figure 4.1.) To ask the Marvin Gaye question, "What's going on?"

The case, *Darlene Jespersen v. Harrah's Casino*, involved a white woman named Darlene Jespersen. In August 2000, after having worked at Harrah's Casino in Reno for over two decades, Jespersen found herself out of a job. Harrah's had

Figure 4.1 Judges Alex Kozinski and Mary Schroeder (Ninth Circuit).
Source: Courtesy of Paul Sakuma/Pool/Getty Images.

fired her, despite performance evaluations that indicated that she was both successful and well liked, because she refused to comply with the company's grooming policy. Instituted in February 2000 as a part of Harrah's Beverage Department Image Transformation Program, the policy mandated that Harrah's female employees wear makeup. When Jespersen refused, Harrah's terminated her. Subsequently, Jespersen sued.[1] This chapter tells the story of the case.

One might ask, why a story about a white woman and her makeup in a book about race and Working Identity? The reason is that cases involving race and identity performance rarely come up in the courts. We know of no case in which a black male employee alleged that he was terminated because he refused to comply with an employer's request that he "act white." More generally, there is little in the way of race-based anti-discrimination precedent for the theory the preceding chapters have advanced. Partly, this stems from the difficulty of proving such claims. But it may result from the failure to identify the Working Identity problem as a form of employment discrimination. There is virtually no legal consciousness about Working Identity, race, and discrimination. A discourse about the phenomenon might change that. In the meantime, if one wants to examine how courts might respond to racial performance claims, one has to turn to the context in which lawyers and litigants actually bring such claims and judges treat them seriously: gender discrimination.[2] The *Jespersen* lawsuit is a part of a broader area of law on gender discrimination where courts explicitly grapple with gender in performative, or Working Identity, terms.

Though not framed in this way, the question the gender performance cases such as *Jespersen* present is whether an employer can require its female employees to act more feminine, particularly when they are also competing for jobs for which the norms of behavior are distinctly male. While the outcome of *Jespersen* is discouraging in terms of what it portends for how courts might grapple with racial Working Identity dynamics, the broader body of law upon which the *Jespersen* litigation draws reveals that judges and employers understand well that the problem of discrimination in the contemporary workplace is about intra- and not just inter-group differences. They understand that sex discrimination at work can take the form of employers preferring men over women (inter-group discrimination) or take the form of employers preferring some women over others based, roughly, on how women work their identities in relation to gender norms of masculinity and femininity (intra-group discrimination).

A starting point for thinking about the Jespersen litigation is to imagine the standard image of a Vegas cocktail waitress. Better yet, take out your smart phone and google images for Vegas cocktail waitresses; you will find no shortage of them. Next, google images of Darlene Jespersen from her days at Harrah's

Casino.[3] There is a disjunction; Jespersen looks nothing like the standard image of a casino cocktail server. Her self-presentation at work was decidedly less feminine—from the way she styled her hair (very short) to the uniform she wore (trousers and a waistcoat) to the fact that she wore no makeup. Jespersen's self-presentation was butch, to use a normatively charged term. The disjuncture between our description of Jespersen and the typical image of a Vegas cocktail waitress is a clue to why Darlene Jespersen lost her case. An en banc panel of the Ninth Circuit decided in a 7–4 vote that requiring her to wear makeup was not unlawful sex discrimination.[4] The rationale was that the burden the makeup regimen imposed on her was not necessarily discriminatory because it was not a heavier burden than the burden the company's grooming policy imposed on men.[5] Nor, from the court's perspective, did the grooming policy constitute illegal sex stereotyping.[6]

This chapter fleshes out the *Jespersen* Court's reasoning. The Ninth Circuit's reasoning is a window on how courts might react to Working Identity claims that a plaintiff frames in terms of race. We begin our discussion describing the line courts have historically drawn between biological sex and the perceived choices women (and men) make about their gender self-presentation. This line is rooted in a narrow understanding of Title VII and formed the legal background against which the *Jespersen* case was litigated.

Before *Jespersen*: Sex as Biology, Working Identity as Choice

Title VII prohibits employers from discriminating on the basis of sex, among other aspects of identity. Historically, Title VII sex discrimination jurisprudence has rested on a biological conception of sex. Three ideas inform this conception: (1) there are biological differences between men and women; (2) these differences are not a result of personal choice; they are immutable; and (3) because these differences are immutable, employers should accommodate them, except when doing so compromises job performance. The theory was aimed at employers who denied women employment opportunities simply because they were women. Judges looked for evidence that the employer treated all its female employees or job applicants worse than it treated all their male counterparts. Evidence that demonstrated this inter-gender disparate treatment created a colorable claim of discrimination on the basis of sex.[7]

But gender discrimination does not always take this inter-gender form. In the 1970s, courts began to grapple with discrimination claims brought by women that did not fit comfortably within an inter-gender frame. In these cases, the employer neither excluded nor penalized all women in favor of men but rather subcategorized women, preferring certain "types" over others. Consider the early round of pregnancy discrimination cases. Central to these cases was the question of whether it was permissible for employers to exclude *pregnant* women from particular jobs or deny them benefits. Employers argued that they had not violated Title VII because they were not discriminating against women *per se*, only some women; those who were pregnant. To the extent the employers had jobs that were predominantly or exclusively female (for example, flight attendant jobs in the 1960s and 1970s), the argument had additional purchase. In those contexts, this was even more clearly a matter of intra-gender discrimination. Rhetorically, these employers asked various versions of the following two questions: How could companies that hire and promote mostly women be liable for sex discrimination? How does choosing some women over others become discrimination on the basis of sex? In 1976, the issue reached the Supreme Court. In a 6–3 vote, the Court, per Justice Rehnquist, concluded that pregnancy-based discrimination, or screening out pregnant women in favor of women who were not pregnant, did not violate the prohibition on sex discrimination.[8]

The victory for employers was short-lived; the reaction from Congress was swift. In 1978, Congress passed the Pregnancy Discrimination Act, which prohibits employers from discriminating on the basis of pregnancy. In hindsight, the view that employers could legally discriminate against pregnant women was never likely to have legs. Pregnancy is perceived to be an integral part of being female. For many, becoming pregnant is one of the quintessential ways to both perform femininity and transition into womanhood. Further, protecting pregnancy would not necessarily require courts to move away from a biological understanding of sex discrimination because the capacity to become pregnant is biologically determined: women, but not men, give birth. With this in mind, congressional action prohibiting pregnancy discrimination was hardly radical—and, in hindsight, not surprising.[9]

The pregnancy lawsuits were not the only intra-gender discrimination cases courts were forced to deal with. In the 1980s, questions emerged as to whether it was legal for employers to discriminate on the basis of gender plus some other identity characteristic, such as race, marital status, or religion. These cases established the "sex-plus" regime—namely, that it is impermissible for the employer to discriminate against women based on sex plus some other aspect of identity,[10] the caveat being that this other identity characteristic had to be either a fundamental right (for example, the right to get married) or a supposedly immutable characteristic (for example, race). While this body of law moved anti-discrimination doctrine beyond the inter-gender frame, it did little to disrupt the biological conception of sex discrimination, a conception that another body of case law further entrenched—the cross-dressing cases.

Litigated roughly during the same period as the sex-plus cases, were cross-dressing cases that, for the most part, involved men who came to work dressed in what most people would describe as "women's clothing." When their employers terminated them, they filed suit, alleging sex discrimination. Courts rejected their claims, often with little more than the assertion that Title VII protects biological sex, not gender performance. The notion was that sartorial practices were not immutable; unlike one's sex, people could make choices about how to dress. It was not impermissible, therefore, for employers to discriminate based on dress, which judges perceived to be a mutable (and non-fundamental rights) aspect of identity.[11]

The sex discrimination landscape changed in 1989. In that year, the Court decided *Price Waterhouse v. Hopkins*. The facts of the case are these: after being denied partnership at the accounting firm of Price Waterhouse, Ann Hopkins was informed that, to improve her chances the following year, she should "walk more femininely, talk more femininely, dress more femininely, wear make-up, have her hair styled, and wear jewelry."[12] While neither standards of dress nor makeup are biologically determined, the Court concluded that Hopkins stated a case of actionable discrimination under Title VII. In so holding, the Court departed from earlier cases that rendered immutability a precondition for establishing a case of sex discrimination.

But how far does *Price Waterhouse* extend? Should judges apply the *Price Waterhouse* doctrine to *Jespersen*? Upon hearing Jespersen's claim, and in light of *Price Waterhouse*, wouldn't a court conclude that Harrah's Casino, via its grooming policy, was in effect asking Jespersen to do precisely what the partners at Price Waterhouse were asking Hopkins to do—"dress more feminine, wear makeup [and] have her hair styled"? But at no point in the *Jespersen* litigation did a court so conclude. Remember, Jespersen lost her case. We will not, in the remainder of this chapter, offer descriptions of what the various judges said at the different stages of the *Jespersen* litigation. Suffice it to say that Darlene Jespersen lost at every stage, starting in the state courts and going all the way to an en banc panel of the Ninth Circuit. Although the analysis of the case increased in sophistication as it traveled up the judicial hierarchy, the bottom line at each point was the same: Based on the evidence, Harrah's grooming policy did not constitute sex discrimination. We focus on the last stage of the litigation, the decision by the Ninth Circuit's en banc panel. In the wake of *Price Waterhouse*, this is the highest federal court to have decided a grooming case. The Court's conclusion, analysis, and the cases upon which it draws, provide an indication of how future courts might respond to the racial Working Identity dynamics of the sort we describe in this book.

Ann Hopkins and Darlene Jespersen:
Separated by Law

The Ninth Circuit could have employed *Price Waterhouse's* anti-sex-stereotyping theory to find in Jespersen's favor. Harrah's grooming policy required women to act like women, and men to act like men. The claim would be that this is precisely what *Price Waterhouse* maintains employers may not do. To determine whether this is a fair characterization of the policy, we reproduce the grooming requirements the policy imposes below.[13]

Beverage Bartenders and Barbacks will adhere to these additional guidelines:

Overall Guidelines (applied equally to male/female):
* Appearance: Must maintain personal best image portrayed at time of hire.
* Jewelry, if issued, must be worn. Otherwise, tasteful and simple jewelry is permitted; no large chokers, chains, or bracelets.
* No faddish hairstyles or unnatural colors are permitted.

Males:
* Hair must not extend below top of shirt collar. Ponytails are prohibited.
* Hands and fingernails must be clean and nails neatly trimmed at all times. No colored polish is permitted.
* Eye and facial makeup is not permitted.
* Shoes will be solid black leather or leather type with rubber (non skid) soles.

Females:
* Hair must be teased, curled, or styled every day you work. Hair must be worn down at all times, no exceptions.
* Stockings are to be made of nude or natural color consistent with employee's skin tone. No runs.
* Nail polish can be clear, white, pink or red color only. No exotic nail art or length.
* Shoes will be solid black leather or leather type with rubber (non skid) soles.
* Makeup (face powder, blush and mascara) must be worn and applied neatly in complementary colors. Lip color must be worn at all times.

The anti-sex-stereotyping argument, again, is that Harrah's was employing the foregoing grooming standards to ensure that men look and act like men and women look and act like women. Women must wear makeup. Men are prohibited from doing so. Women may wear colored nail polish. "No colored polish is allowed" for men. Men are not permitted to have ponytails. Women's hair must be "teased, curled, or styled." These grooming differences align with a particular image of how men and women should make themselves up. Under this view, the policy reflects both descriptive sex stereotyping (as a descriptive matter, women *are* people who wear makeup, polish their nails, and style their hair; people who do not groom themselves in this way *are not* women) and normative sex stereotyping (as a normative matter, people who are women *should* wear makeup, polish their nails, and style their hair; people who do not groom themselves in this way *should not* be viewed as women).

The Ninth Circuit rejected Jespersen's anti-sex-stereotyping argument. In the context of doing so, the court distinguished this case from *Price Waterhouse*, noting that in *Price Waterhouse*, the partners specifically singled out Hopkins; their grooming suggestions were directed solely at her.[14] Not so with respect to Darlene Jespersen. Harrah's grooming policy applied to every employee—not just Jespersen and not just women. Men were regulated as well. Furthermore, the court noted, there was no evidence that Harrah's promulgated its policy to stereotype women, or for that matter, men. According to the Ninth Circuit, Jespersen's subjective experience of sex stereotyping was not enough to sustain a sex discrimination claim. To go in that direction, the court reasoned, would "come perilously close to holding that every grooming, apparel, or appearance requirement that an individual finds personally offensive, or in conflict with his or her own self-image, can create a triable issue of sex discrimination."[15]

Still another factor that seemed to have motivated the Ninth Circuit's rejection of Jespersen's anti-sex-stereotyping claim was the court's sense that Harrah's grooming policy was distinguishable from those that require women to be sexually provocative. Darlene Jespersen did not have to wear shorts or high heels. Her uniform was not revealing. Her body parts were not exposed. It is hard to make the argument, based on what she looked like in her uniform, that she was being stereotyped as a sex object. In interviews with the media, representatives for Harrah's Casino claimed that friendliness and a smile were more important at Harrah's casinos than looks. This is somewhat at odds with the guidelines for Harrah's grooming policy, which included the express expectation that Harrah's employees would be "appealing to the eye, be firm and body toned, and be comfortable with maintaining this look." Nevertheless, one could argue that, to the extent that Harrah's was interested in projecting employees who were "appealing to the eye," the company had professional and not sexual appeal in mind. And, indeed, this was precisely the argument that Harrah's advanced in the litigation.

The Ninth Circuit bought this argument, perhaps because, as we have indicated, Darlene's employment photographs show her in a bow tie, black jacket and pants, and low-heeled shoes. This attire is hardly sexually provocative. Again we ask you to compare this picture with the standard image of a Vegas cocktail waitress. This difference did not escape the attention of the court. The court reasoned that Harrah's uniform was "for the most part unisex, from the black tie to the non-skid shoes." The court seemed to be saying that if Harrah's policy required Jespersen to dress like the cocktail server (sexy, not unisex) she would have had a better sex-stereotyping argument. This was not, for the court, "a case in which the dress or appearance requirement is intended to be sexually provocative, and tending to stereotype women as sex objects."[16]

This is a narrow way of conceptualizing sex stereotyping, particularly in the context of a case about makeup. At no point in the Court's analysis does it address the history of makeup and the extent to which it has been employed to regulate women's entry into the public sphere generally (from the private sphere of family) and the workplace specifically. Judge Harry Pregerson hinted at the role of makeup in this regard in his dissent. According to Pregerson, the makeup requirement was based on "a cultural assumption—and gender-based stereotype—that women's faces are incomplete, unattractive, or unprofessional without full makeup."[17] This social meaning of makeup derives from the historical role cosmetics have played facilitating women's entrance into the workplace.

By the middle of the twentieth century, women increasingly participated in formerly male spheres—in politics, in economic activities, and in the labor market. Makeup served to appease an anxiety concerning this intrusion and integration. While some employers were troubled by the use of makeup on the job (for both safety and cultural reasons),[18] others welcomed it. Makeup functioned as a means of maintaining separate spheres and roles for men and women—separate masculine and female identities—in the face of gender integration. Advertisers, employers, and the women laborers themselves used "appeals to femininity" to "diffuse some of this unease around the role of women."[19] By using makeup at work, the consciousness of women as women was reinforced, in contrast to the consciousness of women as workers.[20] Tangee cosmetics, for instance, used an advertisement that "encouraged the use of lipstick, even though the world was at war, and congratulated women on 'keeping your femininity—even though you are doing a man's work.'"[21] Lockheed and Sperry, Boeing, and the Seattle Navy Yard formally encouraged this gender signaling by offering beauty salons, cosmetics stations, charm classes, and beauty advice respectively.[22] "[T]he All-American Girls Professional Baseball League, organized during the war, ordered women ballplayers to take makeup lessons from Helena Rubinstein and to appear ladylike on the field."[23] Although cosmetics were temporarily banned from the market in an attempt to conserve essential materials in the United States, the ban only lasted four months, as cosmetics had "come to be seen as essential to the war effort in terms of the role it played in securing women's commitment."[24] Makeup was even described as essential to women's mental health during the war.[25]

In short, makeup and women's entrance into the modern workplace have gone hand-in-hand. Employers have used makeup to both screen women into the workplace and to screen them out. Through makeup, women could signify not only femininity but also gender difference. Makeup was a means by which women could transform themselves into gender-role types expected in particular jobs, such as saleswoman, secretary, or waitress. More generally, the presence of makeup on the faces of women inscribed their bodies to convey something like the following assurance to employers: "The fact that we are in the same workplace as men, and doing the same work as men, does not mean that we are in fact the same as men." Through makeup, women could perform gender palatability and gender comfort. Makeup signified that gender integration would not mean the disruption of gender hierarchy. Because of the social continuities of makeup—namely, that women wore makeup across the public/private distinction—men could be assured that, at the end of the day (at home), and during the day (at work), women were going to be women. Rosie the Riveter always wore makeup—at home and at work.[26]

The grooming policy in *Jespersen* is best understood in light of the preceding history of makeup. That is to say, the imposition of grooming standards on women is less about whether grooming policies require women to be sexually provocative and much more about whether such policies require women and men to work their identities in gender-conventional ways. Think about the grooming policies in *Jespersen* with the norms of gender conventionality in mind. Conventionally, we expect women to wear makeup, not men. Conventionally, we expect men to have short hair, not women. Conventionally, we expect women to wear colored nail polish, not men. These conventions about self-presentation do not exist in a vacuum. They reflect and help entrench other conventions— roughly, that women are and should be feminine and that men are and should be masculine.

Framing sex stereotyping solely about sex-object stereotyping (where the question is whether the grooming policy "on its face indicate[s] any...sexually stereotypical intent" or is likely to lead to sexual harassment) obscures the more general ways an employer might impose gender norms on its employees: hiring and promoting those employees who comply with these norms and firing those who do not. This framing also limits a court's ability to grapple with instances in which an employer utilizes formal grooming standards to make intra-gender distinctions, preferring some female (or male) employees over other female (or male) employees based on whether their Working Identity aligns with conventional notions of gender.

As we have been arguing with respect to race, and given the current nature of anti-discrimination law, it is unlikely that modern employers are going to be engaging in blanket identity exclusion, refusing to hire any women. Moreover, market pressures militate against male exclusivity. Not only are women an important and significant part of the labor force, but many companies face the danger that too few women within the company might limit that company's market reach. Plus, the presence of at least some female employees offers employers a kind of litigation protection against sex discrimination claims. In sum, there are incentives for the contemporary employer to hire at least some women. Those whose Working Identity a firm perceives to be appropriately female. Different institutions will reach different conclusions about what "appropriately female" means. For Harrah's it meant that, at a minimum, its female bartenders had to wear makeup.

In sum, employing grooming policies to produce gender appropriate self-presentation is inconsistent with one reading of *Price Waterhouse*. Under this reading, the Supreme Court ruled that partners at that firm could not deny Hopkins partnership because Hopkins's working identity was not within the boundaries of what Price Waterhouse perceived to be gender-appropriate expressions of female identity. In theory, Hopkins could have altered her behavior to be more feminine. Clearly the partners thought so. That is why they suggested to Hopkins that she could improve her chances for making partner if she changed her working identity and acted more feminine. The Supreme Court ruled that Hopkins did not have to alter her behavior in this way. By implication, no employer should be permitted to pressure an employee to change her gender identity, or punish her for refusing to do so.

Gay plaintiffs used precisely this argument in a series of cases in which their co-workers harassed them. In none of these cases was there a dispute about whether the plaintiffs were actually harassed. Nor was there any dispute about whether these plaintiffs could assert that they were entitled to a remedy based on their sexual orientation. Title VII, as of this writing, does not protect against discrimination on the basis of sexual orientation. Thus, if a black lesbian experienced discrimination in the workplace, she could not frame her claim in terms of sexual orientation. Moreover, if she asserted that the firm discriminated against her based on her race, the employer could well assert that it discriminated against her not on the basis of race but on the basis of the fact that she was a lesbian—that is to say, on the basis of her sexual orientation. Under Title VII, that form of discrimination is legal.

Given this state of the law, the gay plaintiffs explicitly stated that their claim was not about sexual orientation but about sex discrimination. Their theory was that they were being punished for being effeminate, not for being gay per se.

Underlying that punishment were stereotypical expectations about how men and women should work their identities—women were expected to be feminine and men were expected to be masculine. The plaintiffs' failure to perform masculinity invoked the displeasure of their male colleagues. Some of these plaintiffs won on this theory of *Price Waterhouse*, and others lost on the grounds that their claim boiled down to a claim of sexual orientation discrimination.

Constraining the Stereotyping Doctrine

So, why didn't *Price Waterhouse* plus the effeminacy cases produce a victory for Darlene Jespersen? Why did the Ninth Circuit constrain the reach of the anti-sex-stereotyping doctrine? One answer, as discussed earlier, is that the court framed sex stereotyping largely in terms of whether Jespersen was being asked to be a sex object and concluded that she was not being stereotyped in this way. The difficulty with this explanation is that *Price Waterhouse* itself did not involve either sexual harassment or sexy dress. The partners were not asking Ann Hopkins to come to work as a sex object. They were asking her to come to work "professionally female," where professionally female includes wearing makeup. The partners were not asking Hopkins to wear body-revealing and tightly clad clothing. They wanted her to look and act less masculine. The notion that the stereotyping theory is only available to plaintiffs who are subject to sexy dress requirements or vulnerable to sexual harassment makes the sex-stereotyping argument inapplicable to the very case in which the Supreme Court first articulated the theory: *Price Waterhouse*. Yet, that is exactly what the *Jespersen* majority seems to do— limit the sex-stereotype theory to cases involving sexy dress or harassment, a limitation that denied Darlene Jespersen a remedy.

A second possible reason that Jespersen lost her case, even with *Price Waterhouse* and the effeminacy cases as part of the legal landscape, is that the judges might have understood the effeminacy cases as primarily implicating sexual orientation, rather than gender. One can read these cases as reflecting the recognition on the part of judges that gays and lesbians would be vulnerable to incredibly hostile work environments if there was no remedy for the facts that gave rise to the effeminacy lawsuits. Because the plaintiffs in these cases could not argue that they were being discriminated against on the basis of sexual orientation, a theory of sex discrimination was the only viable doctrinal route available to judges and litigants alike.

If this reading of the cases is correct, the effeminacy cases reflect a kind of doctrinal maneuvering. Because sexual orientation as such cannot be employed to support a claim of discrimination, the courts grounded their finding of discrimination on the *Price Waterhouse* theory of sex stereotyping. It is less than clear to us, then, that by invoking Title VII in the effeminacy cases, those judges were articulating a general theory of sex stereotyping. Possibly, they were engaging in subversive judging—enacting a minor rebellion against refusal by Congress to provide any protection against sexual orientation discrimination. If Congress would not provide protection, the judges would use *Price Waterhouse* to carve out a minimal amount of protection for the worst cases.

A third possible reason that, in spite of the anti-stereotyping theory attributed to *Price Waterhouse*, Jespersen lost her case relates to the double bind under-standing of *Price Waterhouse*. In concluding that Price Waterhouse discriminated against Ann Hopkins, the Court made reference to the "catch-22," what others have termed the "double bind." The notion is that Hopkins was in a double bind because her employer's demand that she act feminine came into conflict with another institutional demand of many corporate environments: to act mascu-line and aggressive in order to excel in a historically all-male occupation. These two pressures produced a scenario in which women were in trouble if they acted masculine and also in trouble if they acted feminine. The Court claimed that "Title VII lifts women out of this bind."

There is no language in *Price Waterhouse* clearly indicating that being subject to a catch-22 was necessary to the finding that Hopkins had a cause of action under Title VII. Rather, the majority and concurring opinions emphasize sex-stereotyping language, as we discussed earlier. Nevertheless, a few commen-tators and courts have read the result in the case as hinging on the presence of a catch-22. Their claim is that sex stereotyping, including demands for stereotypi-cal or gender-appropriate grooming practices, only presents a problem under Title VII when an employee proves that it comes into conflict with attributes and behaviors that help an employee perform a job well, creating a catch-22, or "double bind." The logic of this interpretation of Title VII is that the catch-22 can function to exclude all women from the workplace—no matter whether they act feminine or masculine. It is, in other words, an impossible standard to meet.

The problem with this theory is that it neither applies to the facts of *Price Waterhouse*, nor is it generally plausible. Although Ann Hopkins was denied partnership at Price Waterhouse, another woman had made partner the preced-ing year. Thus, even assuming the firm was screening women in terms of a catch 22, that screen did not operate as a group-based barrier to all women. Plus, the fact that there are conflicting pressures in operation does not mean that we can-not satisfy them; most of us deal with conflicting pressures all the time (work/ family, work/leisure, job satisfaction/income, and so on). Think back to our discussion of the conflicting pressures on President Obama. At every moment, he has to negotiate the competing demands of acting both white and black. He performed this negotiation so well—racially sensitive, but not too sensitive; racially understanding and tolerant, but not racially angry—that the country elected him president. Along those lines, many women professionals find the catch-22 described by the Court familiar, not because it barred their promotion, but because it describes their daily realities; ones that they negotiate with success. Similarly, one can imagine a woman like Darlene both complying with Harrah's makeup rules while maintaining other more unconventional aspects of her Working Identity.

Nevertheless, we should be concerned about the catch-22 precisely because it requires women to meet a set of contradictory demands. The Court in *Price Waterhouse* rightly reasoned that it is especially unfair for an employer to screen its female employees for femininity in the context of a historically male occupation where aggression and other masculine traits are prized. Darlene's counsel, LAMBDA Legal, the leading gay rights advocacy group, made essentially this argument in their brief—namely, that Harrah's grooming policy placed Darlene Jespersen in an untenable catch-22. Requiring her to act feminine by wearing makeup was in tension with the job requirement that bartenders deal with rowdy patrons.

This catch-22 argument had no traction. Perhaps the judges simply did not find it plausible that the level of feminization in this case made it difficult for Darlene Jespersen to do her job. Perhaps the judges had encountered more than a few female bartenders who were both feminine and in full control of their bars. Perhaps the judges could not imagine Darlene in particular having difficulty managing rowdy customers, mandatory makeup or not. Or perhaps the judges simply wanted more evidence. That, after all, was the formal explanation the court offered for rejecting Darlene's catch-22 argument—namely, that there wasn't enough evidence to show that makeup limited Jespersen's ability to do her job.

A final reason neither *Price Waterhouse* nor the effeminacy cases resulted in a victory for Jespersen is that in addition to inheriting the antistereotyping jurisprudence, Jespersen inherited another body of law: the dress and appearance or grooming standards case law that sets forth the so-called unequal burdens test. Recall from the previous chapter that Renee Rogers challenged an American Airlines grooming policy that prohibited women from wearing braided hair. At the time that case was litigated, courts had not yet adopted the "unequal burdens" doctrine,[27] a doctrine that was front and center in the *Jespersen* case.

Under the "unequal burdens" doctrine, the question of whether a particular grooming policy regulating, for example, body weight, piercings, tattoos, and clothing constitutes impermissible sex discrimination turns on whether the policy unequally burdens one sex—that is, whether the standard imposes greater burdens on, for example, women than it does on men. Putting to one side the gender issue Judge Kozinski paints, he is right to assert that "even those of us who don't wear makeup know how long it can take from the hundreds of hours we've spent over the years frantically tapping our toes and pointing to our wrists."[28] For him, Harrah's grooming policy imposed an undue burden on women. The majority of the Ninth Circuit disagreed. According to the court, "all bartenders wore the same uniform. The policy only differentiated as to grooming standards."[29] The court concluded that Jespersen presented no evidence that the grooming requirements burdened women more than they burdened men. From the court's perspective, the grooming standards "appropriately differentiate[d] between the genders."[30] Another way to pen that sentence would be to say that Harrah's policy was not discriminatory because it merely required its male and female employees to enter the workplace "appropriately" marked as men and women.

Screening, Cultural Norms, and "Good" and "Bad" Women

We are not saying that Harrah's termination of Jespersen was therefore legitimate. Reaching that conclusion is tantamount to saying that firms should be allowed to incorporate social norms and background cultural assumptions about gender into their hiring and promotion decisions. At one level, the incorporation of social and cultural norms by employers and judges is inevitable; all of us draw on social norms, albeit often only implicitly, when we make judgments. Moreover, the law sometimes expressly requires judges to look to tradition and custom to guide their interpretation and application of legal doctrine. The tension is that anti-discrimination law typically bucks social and cultural norms.[31] For example, when Congress passed Title VII, racial discrimination in the workplace was both routine and rampant; it was a ubiquitous social and cultural norm. Title VII was promulgated to repudiate those social norms, not incorporate them into law. In this respect, the fact that an organization might run more smoothly if its female employees exhibit gender identities that are consistent with our current social norms about gender does not mean that the law should permit employers to instantiate those norms as a workplace practice. It might well be the case that (1) it is impossible for judges to interpret the law without using the lens of culture and social norms, and (2) that employers will inevitably draw on culture and social norms in deciding which employees to hire. Neither of those realities means that the law should allow employers to assert—explicitly or implicitly—something like a "culture of gender stereotyping" defense under which employers can prefer women who work their identities by wearing makeup ("good" women) over those who do not ("bad" women).

Grooming requirements such as makeup for women and short hair for men help to constitute gender. They shape what it means to be a man and what it means to be a woman. The gender-constitutive role grooming standards perform is one explanation for why courts allow employers to impose these differential requirements. This differentiation helps to preserve the very gender differences that some judges—even female judges—think are normal, natural, and normative. It is also one reason employers adopt gendered grooming standards; because they help separate the women (and men) who are willing to conform to societal definitions from those who are unwilling to do so.

This brings us to some questions that come primarily from our female law students when we teach the *Jespersen* case. They invoke a set of concerns about the case that relate to their sense of their future careers as lawyers. Most of them are outraged that an employer might be able to mandate makeup. However, they find claims in the literature about the sexualizing aspects of makeup also wrong and too simplistic to boot. A question that comes up frequently, in the context of discussing *Jespersen*, is whether it would be permissible for an employer to bar makeup altogether, for both men and women. Makeup, as one of them put it, is a tool that women have long used to construct their workplace identities. Women, she went on to claim, would be disadvantaged if they were not allowed to use it. Some other students pointed to the history of informal dress codes for women at elite law firms. Not long ago, when women were entering the ranks of lawyers at these firms, men and women thought that it made sense for women to dress "gender neutral"—which is to say, dress as much like men as possible, but not wear trousers. Women embodied this view by donning boxy suits, avoiding makeup, and sporting big bow ties that supposedly simulated men's neckties. This sartorial regimen changed, not simply for reasons of aesthetics but also because this simulation of male styles did not help to integrate women into law firms, let alone the partnership ranks of those organizations. At least some women in these same law firms today succeed by wearing makeup and appearing feminine, at least in terms of dress. Big bow ties and boxy suits are gone, and makeup is in. For many, the moral of the story is that it is better for women to have these informal dress requirements be gendered rather than gender neutral. Gender neutrality produces gender anxieties, which inevitably disadvantage women.

That might well be true. It might also be true that women who wear makeup have an easier time in the workplace than those who do not—and that some women strategically employ makeup as a tool for both access to and integration into the workplace. Still, we remain concerned about grooming standards that inscribe gender roles in terms of traditional notions of masculinity and femininity. Without getting into a debate about agency, free will, and choices under constraints, there is a difference between women choosing to make themselves up, on the one hand, and employers mandating that they do so, on the other. Formalized grooming policies of the sort Harrah's promulgated can create double binds, harden sex stereotyping, and encourage women to work their identities conventionally.

What does any of this have to do with race? Assuming that we are right about the gender-inscribing role of Harrah's grooming policy—assuming that the policy does indeed "make up" both men and women to exhibit gender normative working identities—how does this implicate the "acting white" phenomenon this book describes? The answer is that if judges are unwilling to extend *Price Waterhouse* to a case in which the employer requires its female employees to wear makeup, it is unlikely that they will extend the doctrine to adjudicate a claim by a black employee that his employer required him to "act white." We elaborate on this point in chapter 7. For now, it is enough to understand that, with respect to gender, plaintiffs have brought a number of Working Identity claims. Some, like *Price Waterhouse*, mark victories. Others, like *Jespersen*, mark losses. If nothing else, these cases suggest that gender Working Identity claims are cognizable. In other words, courts have been willing to entertain them. There is no conceptual reason why they cannot do so with respect to race.

5

(Not) Acting Criminal

One might conclude from the preceding chapters that the Working Identity problem we have described is limited to the professional workplace. The parameters of the problem are broader than that. This chapter takes the Working Identity idea to the streets. On the streets, every day, African Americans feel pressured to work their identities to reduce the likelihood that they will be involved in interactions with the police. Functioning as coping mechanisms, these performances are intended to signal racial respectability ("I am a good black"), law abidingness ("therefore, I am not a criminal"), and racial obedience ("so tell me what I must do to prove this to you"). These performances constitute a form of racial labor

Figure 5.1 Sergeant James Crowley.
Source: © Steven Senne/AP/Corbis.

Figure 5.2 Henry Louis Gates's mugshot.
Source: AP Photo/Cambridge Police Dept. © 2012 The Associated Press.

that is potentially stigmatizing, dignity destroying, and privacy compromising. The pressure to perform this work, like the pressure to work one's identity in the workplace, exists because of racial stereotypes. Specifically, the stereotype of black criminality creates an incentive for African Americans to work their identities to demonstrate that they are what police officers might not presume them to be—law abiding. We begin with an episode that made headlines. The episode involved Sergeant James Crowley (see figure 5.1) of the Cambridge Police Department and the renowned black Harvard professor, Dr. Henry Louis (Skip) Gates. (See figure 5.2.)

Sergeant Crowley is now one of the most famous US police officers. Crowley catapulted into the public arena after he arrested Professor Gates in his own home. Gates had just returned to his Cambridge, Massachusetts, home from a trip to China. After attempting to enter his front door with his key, he realized the door was damaged. He then entered his rear door with his key, turned off his alarm, and again attempted to open the front door. With the help of his driver, who also happened to be black, they were able to force the front door open. The driver then carried Professor Gates's luggage into his home.[1] While this was happening, a neighbor saw these two individuals with suitcases forcing themselves into the home. She called the police and said, "I don't know what's happening. I don't know if they live there and they just had a hard time with their key, but I did notice they had to use their shoulders to try to barge in."[2]

Enter Sergeant Crowley, a white, male, 11-year veteran of the force[3] who teaches the Anti-Racial Profiling class in the department.[4] Professor Gates and

Sergeant Crowley have since disagreed about what happened next. Suffice it to say, their altercation made news—especially for President Barack Obama. Less than a week after Gates's arrest, and at the end of the president's primetime press conference on health care, the *Chicago Sun-Times*'s Lynn Sweet asked President Obama, "What [did the] incident [with Gates] say to you? And what does it say about race relations in America?"[5] Obama responded by acknowledging his friendship with Professor Gates, referring to him as Skip, and noted that he did not know all of the facts. He went on to say: "I think it's fair to say, number one, any of us would be pretty angry; number two, that the Cambridge police acted stupidly in arresting somebody when there was already proof that they were in their own home; and, number three, what I think we know separate and apart from this incident is that there's a long history in this country of African Americans and Latinos being stopped by law enforcement disproportionately. That's just a fact."[6]

Obama's comments set off a firestorm of controversy. Some people derided the president for being disrespectful of police officers; others went further, suggesting that President Obama acted "stupidly" when he made the comments. Surprised by the media blitz his comments generated, Obama held a press conference to clarify his statement. He first explained that he had called Sergeant Crowley to discuss his comments and to invite him to share a beer with him and Professor Gates. Obama then conceded that he should have better "calibrated" his words, but maintained "there was an overreaction in pulling Professor Gates out of his home." Crowley made a public statement, saying: "It is clear to us from this conversation that the president respects police officers and the often difficult and dangerous situations we face on a daily basis. We appreciate his sincere interest and willingness to reconsider his remarks about the Cambridge Police Department."[7]

The controversy caught Obama off guard. Perhaps he assumed that it was politically safe to challenge aggressive police behavior, particularly when directed at an older and distinguished African American man. At least since the 1990s, police abuse of blacks whom the public perceives to be respectable and law-abiding is almost always condemned. Surely, this would apply to one of the most distinguished African American academics, a 58-year-old public intellectual and Harvard University professor? Obama could have believed that most people would consider Officer Crowley's conduct excessive.

It is also possible that rather than catching Obama off guard, the episode placed him in a no-win situation. If he kept quiet, he risked both angering the black community and providing ammunition to those who had accused him of being "too white." If he spoke out, as he did, he risked reminding others of his blackness and perhaps of the reasons they were wary of having a black president.

While Obama never framed Gates's arrest expressly in terms of what it signaled for black Americans, that was the way in which Gates discussed the episode. In an interview with CNN reporter, Soledad O'Brien, Gates was emphatic that "this is not about me, this is about the black man in America. If it can happen to me, it can happen to anyone in the United States."[8]

Implicit in Gates's claim is the idea that the encounter he experienced wasn't supposed to happen to *him*. By this, Gates is not suggesting that the encounter should have happened to someone else. His point is a subtle one and might be restated: "Typically, only a certain kind of black person is vulnerable to the level of abuse I experienced; black people like me just don't experience this stuff. If a black person like me has to endure this kind of indignity, then no black person is safe." What happens to Gates portends what will happen to everyone else. Note that the reverse is not necessarily true: What happens to everyone else does not portend what will happen to Gates. Gates is familiar with the problem of race and policing. His assumption was that the problem resided outside of the domain of his particular black experience.

Gates's sense that "if it can happen to me, it can happen to anyone" is part of a broader prism through which allegations of racially motivated police conduct are viewed. As a general matter, the public views racial profiling as a problem only to the extent that the racial profiling claim is made by African Americans who most people believe were not supposed to be racially profiled, that is, innocent or respectable blacks who don't deserve to be racially profiled. African Americans like Gates, who the public views as "good blacks." When blacks who are perceived to be "bad" allege racial profiling, they get less sympathy.

Part of what determines whether a black person has a "good" or "bad" black Working Identity is criminal conduct. If an officer racially profiles a black person, searches that person, and finds incriminating evidence, that person will have a difficult time airing his racial profiling claim. The fact that the police found drugs on him renders the person "bad" and therefore a poor icon for racial victimization.

However, let's suppose that upon executing the search, the officer does not find any drugs and there is no other evidence of criminal wrongdoing. Even under these circumstances, a black person can be viewed as "bad." This is because the line between "good blacks" and "bad blacks" is not solely about actual criminality. It is about perceived criminality as well. How a black person speaks, dresses, and comports himself generally—that is, that person's Working Identity—provides viewers with information that they can utilize to evaluate whether negative stereotypes about African Americans as a group should apply to that particular individual. To proceed with the example above, assuming again that the police officer stops and searches the individual and finds no drugs, that person can still be deemed to be "bad" if his self-presentation makes him "look like" or "sound like" what we perceive criminals to look like and sound like.

The principal argument this chapter makes is that whether a person's racial profiling story has traction turns on whether that person is perceived to be a "good" black. There is a perversity to this: blacks who are the most vulnerable to incarceration because their experience with racial profiling provided the police with evidence of criminality ("bad blacks") are the least likely to engender public sympathy when they assert that they have been racially profiled. They are unlikely to ever have either an opportunity or platform to complain. By contrast, Gates was able to mobilize attention around his sense of victimization, notwithstanding that he was less vulnerable than most African Americans to both experience racial profiling and to be incarcerated. His ability to do so was partially a function of his celebrity. But it was also because the public perceived him to have a "good" black Working Identity.

This chapter focuses mostly, though not entirely, on black men. It begins by drawing attention to a particular police practice that is often a manifestation of racial profiling—*stop-and-ask*. By *stop-and-ask* we mean instances in which a police officer engages an individual, whom the officer has no objective reason to believe did anything wrong, and seeks permission to search that individual's person or belonging. African Americans with a "bad" black Working Identity are more likely to experience stop-and-ask than those with a "good" black Working Identity—and they are more likely to consent to the officer's request for a search. Saying yes to a police officer's request to conduct a search, even and perhaps especially when one has a right to say no, is one way to prove that one is not a criminal, notwithstanding racial stereotypes to the contrary.

We move from a discussion of stop-and-ask to a discussion of the law's approach to traffic stops or the driving while black/brown (DWB) problem. Here, we demonstrate that DWB is also based on this "good" black/"bad" black dichotomy. We also show how civil rights responses to racial profiling sometimes explicitly draw upon the figure of the "good" black in order to generate support for anti–racial profiling initiatives.

Stop-and-Ask

The legal doctrine of consent is one body of law that is applicable to the practice of stop-and-ask. The doctrine permits police officers to approach any person and seek permission to search that person's body or belongings without any objective reason to believe that the individual committed a crime. Officers are not required to inform the person of their right to refuse consent, and the fact that the person lacks knowledge of this right does not, standing alone, make the consent invalid. This body of law makes blacks, and Outsiders more generally, vulnerable to police encounters. There are two reasons for this. First, consenting to searches is one way for blacks to prove that they have done nothing wrong and have nothing to hide, particularly against background assumptions that they are criminally inclined. This means that, on average, blacks will have to give up more of their privacy—by consenting to more intrusive searches—than whites to erase any police suspicions about their criminality. The more one is perceived to be black, the greater the incentive to give up rights to prove innocence.

Second, blacks are less likely than whites to assert their constitutional rights. Part of their socialization will include the idea that, in the context of encounters with the police, they should comport themselves to make the officers racially comfortable.[9] The assertion of rights undermines that comfort strategy. Specifically, it can racially aggravate or intensify the encounter. The blacker one thinks the officer perceives one to be, the stronger the disincentive to assert one's rights.

Think back to the episode involving the Skip Gates's arrest. In response to criticism that he acted excessively, Officer Crowley explained that he arrested Gates for disorderly conduct because Gates was engaging in "loud and tumultuous behavior in a public space."[10] Crowley maintained that Gates was "combative" from the moment he arrived at Gates's house.[11] Moreover, Crowley stated that he gave Gates two warnings, which included showing Gates his set of handcuffs, before arresting him. According to Crowley, he "really didn't want to" arrest Gates but was eventually "forced" to do so after Gates refused to de-escalate the situation.[12] Note that Crowley's threat of arrest occurred *after* Gates had already established that he was not engaged in a robbery but was inside of his own home.[13] In this sense, it was Gates's assertion of his rights (from Crowley's perspective, Gates's questioning of Crowley's authority) that caused Crowley to arrest him.

A case that illustrates how the law's treatment of stop-and-ask obscures the incentive for blacks and other outsiders to give up their rights to prove that they are "good" is *Schneckloth v. Bustamonte*.[14] While virtually every textbook on constitutional criminal procedures includes this case, none frames the case to highlight the incentive problem we describe below.

The facts are these: A police officer, Officer Rand, stopped a car after observing two burned-out lights.[15] Robert Bustamonte was a passenger, and five other men were in the car. Only one of the men, passenger Joe Alcala, had identification.[16] Officer Rand asked each man to exit the car.[17] By this time, two other officers had arrived.[18] Subsequent to their arrival, Officer Rand requested permission to search the car.[19] To this request Alcala responded, "Sure, go ahead."[20] While there was no indication that Officer Rand or the other two officers employed force to elicit Alcala's consent, none of the officers informed Alcala that he had the right to refuse consent.[21] Upon searching the car, the officers found three stolen checks under one of the seats.[22] Bustamonte challenged the legality of the search, and lost.

Part of the Court's analysis is premised on the productive role that consent searches perform in police investigations. The Court explains that "[i]f the search is conducted and proves fruitless, that itself may convince the police that an arrest with its possible stigma and embarrassment is unnecessary."[23] Fair enough? Perhaps. But let us think about the racial upside and downside of the Court's analysis. The upside: stop-and-ask is racially friendly and costless in the sense that the practice provides blacks with a quick and easy means to prove to police officers that they have done nothing wrong. The downside: because of stereotypes about black criminality, it is more likely that blacks will feel added pressure to say yes to consent searches. Whites in a similar position are unlikely to feel this added pressure because they are not confronted with a similar stereotype about white criminality.

The problem is compounded by the fact that whites and blacks are not similarly situated in terms of their interest in terminating a police encounter. Blacks, as a general matter, are going to be less trusting of the police and less comfortable in their presence than whites. They may fear that their rights will not be respected even when asserted and will simply result in encouraging police violence. These fears, whether justified or not, add pressure on blacks to terminate police encounters by giving up their rights, consenting to searches, and otherwise being overly cooperative. In fact, as a matter of both socialization and formal or informal political advice, African Americans are encouraged to signal cooperation by giving up their privacy. Consider Robert Johnson's and Steven Simring's *The Race Trap: Smart Strategies for Effective Racial Communication in Business and in Life.*[24] In it, Johnson and Simring offer the following strategies for people who are racially profiled:

- Don't display anger—even if justified. Most police officers resent challenges to their authority, and may overreact to any real or perceived affront.
- Don't argue the Fourth Amendment.... [A]t the point you are stopped, it is important to maintain control of your emotions and your behavior.
- Don't be sarcastic or condescending to the officer. Always be cooperative and polite.
- Don't lose sight of your goal. The objective in most racial profiling scenarios is to end the encounter as quickly as possible with a minimum risk of potential trauma. Getting stopped for no good reason is inconvenient. But being jacked up against your car and searched is an experience that can stay with you for years. Getting handcuffed and taken into custody escalates the nightmare.[25]

Johnson and Simring conclude their discussion with the suggestion that "[r]acial profiling by the police is a reality in a system that often treats minorities unfairly. However, the immediate issue isn't fairness. Rather, it's your ability to negotiate the encounter you are facing at the time."[26] The negotiation to which Johnson and Simring refer is between a suspect's sense of self as a rights-bearing person of worth and dignity and the suspect's sense of what he needs to do to manage the police encounter and to establish that he is neither a criminal nor otherwise dangerous. Engaging in conduct to demonstrate that one is neither dangerous nor a criminal will often compromise one's rights.

African Americans make this compromise all the time. Parents, family members, and community leaders teach children and fresh immigrants how—and when, if at all—to speak, when and how to say "Sir,"[27] "Officer," or "Trooper,"[28] on how to refrain from making sudden movements,[29] and basically, when, if at all, to assert one's rights.[30] Blacks often grow up with the expectation that they will be called upon to negotiate their dignity and privacy in the context of police encounters. They are taught to immediately demonstrate subservience and respect, when confronted by a law enforcement official. That is the key to ending the episode and avoiding a possibly violent encounter. If blacks were socially assumed to be "good" they would have to perform less of this work.

Whites are subject to pressures to comply with requests from the police as well. One can construct scenarios in which subsets of whites also feel stereotyped as "bad" by the police. However, the pressures on whites to comply with police orders are nowhere near as high as the pressures for blacks to comply. Because of stereotypes, black people are subject to a kind of surplus compliance. They are more vulnerable to compliance requests, more likely to comply, and have to give up more privacy to do so.

As many have learned the hard way, performing consent to counter stereotypes will not always prevent an unpleasant police encounter. Saying yes to an officer's request to conduct a consent search will not always be enough to establish innocence. While exposing the interior of one's bag to a police officer is one way of saying, "I am not carrying drugs," this innocence-signaling strategy, like the speech-signaling strategies we discussed in chapter 2, are not always enough to dissipate stereotypes. Imagine, for example, that a police officer perceives, but does not have any objective reason to believe, that Tony, a black man, is a drug dealer. Assume that Tony is carrying a bag and that the officer requests permission to search it. Stipulate that Tony says yes, and the officer searches the bag but does not find any drugs. The officer's suspicions of Tony's criminality will not necessarily disappear. Tony's consent to the search of his bag will not necessarily terminate the interaction. In fact, his consent may prolong it. The officer may believe that Tony granted him permission to search his bag because Tony is carrying drugs elsewhere on his person; the officer may further assume that Tony strategically consented in order to conceal his criminality.

Alternatively, the officer may believe that Tony's consent reflects vulnerability. This vulnerability could derive from Tony's awareness that the officer may be employing stereotypes to judge him, for example, stereotypes that reflect the assumption that Tony is a criminal. Plus, the officer knows that Tony probably fears a violent encounter and perhaps jail. If the officer believes that Tony has this fear, he may also believe that Tony will want to prove to him (the officer) that he (Tony) is not the stereotypical black man—that is, a drug dealer. To the extent that the officer interprets Tony's consent in either of these ways, he is likely to request permission to conduct another, more intrusive search: a search of Tony's clothing. If Tony does not consent to this second search, the officer's suspicions will intensify. Why would a person who is not carrying drugs grant permission to search his bag but not his person? This hypothetical suggests that it is less than clear that "fruitless" consent searches—consent searches that do not produce incriminating evidence—will be enough to terminate an encounter between an individual and the police, particularly when racial stereotypes are taken into consideration.

By contrast, imagine an encounter between the police and a white male professional on New York's Upper East Side. If this man refuses to grant consent, the police will not necessarily conclude that he is hiding something. Instead, this assertion is likely just an assertion of rights by a man of privilege—the man knows that he does not have to consent and perhaps wants to assert that he is not intimidated. If the police want to search him, they will need a real basis to do so.

The facts of a Supreme Court case, *United States v. Drayton*,[31] help make our point. In *Drayton*, three members of the Tallahassee police department—one black and two white—boarded a bus just as it was about to depart. Working from the back of the bus forward, the officers asked passengers questions about their travel destinations, identity, and personal belongings. The "[d]efendants Drayton and Brown (both of whom are black) were seated next to each other a few rows from the rear." One of the officers identified himself as a police officer, informed them that he was part of a drug interdiction team, and asked Drayton and Brown whether they had any luggage. Both responded in the affirmative. The officer then asked for permission to search the bag, to which Brown responded, "Go ahead." Another officer searched the bag but no illegal substances were found.

If Brown's consent was a privacy-compromising performance strategy to disconfirm the assumption of his criminality and to end the encounter, the strategy did not work. The strategy had the opposite effect. Upon learning that Brown's bag did not contain any illegal drugs, the officer requested permission to conduct a pat down. The officer's reasoning, which he supplied in his testimony defending his search as constitutional, was that the two men "were overly cooperative during the search [of the bag]." In short, the fact that Brown and Drayton consented to the search of their bag created, rather than eliminated, the officer's suspicion and prolonged, rather than terminated, the encounter. In this case, the officer's suspicions were confirmed: The pat down of Brown produced incriminating evidence, as did the subsequent pat down of Drayton.[32]

As is the case with anti-discrimination law, the relationship among race, Working Identity, and cooperation does not inform the law's approach to stop-and-ask and is absent from the Supreme Court's analysis in *Bustamonte*. There, the Court ignores how race—and particularly, racial stereotypes—can constrain one's choice, one's will, and one's capacity to say no to consent searches. Had the *Bustamonte* Court engaged the stereotype-disconfirming performance strategies especially African Americans and Latinas/os regularly employ in the context of police encounters, it could not so easily have concluded that the consent search in that case was constitutional. Central to the Court's thinking in this regard was the notion that there were no obvious signs of coercion. (Remember that Alcala's response to the officer's request to search was, "Sure, go ahead.") The officers did not physically or verbally abuse any of the six men. As the Court indicates, "[p]rior to the search no one was threatened with arrest,"[33] and, according to the uncontradicted testimony of one of the officers, the situation "was all very congenial."[34]

Rather than signaling a lack of coercion, the congeniality of the encounter was likely a function of coercion. The encounter occurred at 2:40 a.m. in the morning in Sunnyvale, California, a predominately white community in the San Francisco Bay Area.[35] The officers were all white and at least three of the car's occupants were Latinos.[36] In the early 1970s, the relationship between police and the Latino community in California was marked by distrust and hostility, with many Latino leaders decrying instances of police brutality against their constituents.[37] Given stereotypes about Latinos—that they are illegal immigrants and criminally inclined—the occupants of the car undoubtedly would have been concerned about how the officers were going to treat them. They might have believed that fully cooperating with the police officers would decrease the likelihood that the police officers would physically abuse or otherwise mistreat them. They were negotiating their interaction in the shadow of potential violence and abuse.[38] This potential for violence both chills and shapes communication between police officers and people of color. As one commentator put it: "If, say, during a twenty-five-dollar traffic stop, an officer should decide that my manners are not good enough, he can summarily end my life. If my wife and daughter are lucky, an official might issue a tepid apology—with raised shoulders and thrown-up hands. It would be a mistake, albeit a fatal one. And I would be faulted for disobedience, for resistance, for unlawful breathing."[39]

All of this is to say that the congeniality between the officers and the Latinos could have derived from a strategy on the part of the Latinos to signal racial obedience. This would explain not only why Alcala consented to the search, but also why he helped the officer conduct it. Because the Court does not pay attention to the nexus among race, Working Identity, and cooperation, it avoids having to address this problem.

Driving While Black/Brown

Traffic stops are another context in which racial performance, police investigation, and racial stereotypes converge. Three aspects of traffic stops make them particularly worrisome: (1) all of us commit traffic infractions some the time; (2) police officers have almost unbridled discretion with respect to deciding whom to stop; and (3) the police have neither the resources nor the inclination to stop everyone. Under these conditions, the question becomes, who are the police most likely to stop? Unsurprisingly, they are more likely to stop blacks and Latinas/os than whites.[40] This evidence confirms what blacks and Latinas/os have been saying for a long time: DWB is a crime. Many of us find ourselves committing this crime every day. We try not to get caught. Some strategies (e.g., avoiding certain neighborhoods, driving low-profile cars, driving within particular speed ranges) work better than others (e.g., dressing "respectably" and employing vanity license plates that signal a professional identity).[41] None of these strategies, however, is one hundred percent effective, and all of them are costly.

Few people publicly would take the position that it is legitimate for police officers to target black and brown motorists for traffic stops. That practice, the most vivid example of racial profiling, is almost universally condemned. Yet, racial profiling remains a social problem. What then explains the disjunction between the rhetoric and practice?

Part of the answer returns us to the episode involving Professor Gates; our discussion of racial profiling has focused on "bad" cops who racially profile "good blacks" and Latinas/os—doctors, lawyers, students, athletes, teachers, and so on.[42] These "good blacks" and Latinas/os are "people with good jobs and families." The only reason one could possibly believe that they did anything wrong is if one assumed, based solely on their race, that they were somehow criminally inclined.[43] The focus on "good blacks" suggests that the public is not condemning racial profiling per se, but rather profiling as it is deployed against certain blacks and Latinas/os. These blacks and Latinas/os, like Skip Gates—but unlike "bad blacks" and Latinas/os—are not supposed to be racially profiled.

Put another way, the public campaign against racial profiling invariably calls upon notions of innocence. If, for example, a police officer racially profiles a black person who is not in possession of drugs or any other incriminating evidence, that person is perceived to be innocent. He becomes a "good" black, and the officer who racially profiled him becomes a "bad" cop. As a "good" black, this person can be employed as an icon of racial victimization to challenge the conduct of the "bad" cop. This is how the public has come to view racial profiling—as a "bad" law-enforcement practice that affects "good" or innocent blacks, Latinas/os, and other nonwhites.

Consider, for example, part of the ACLU's campaign against racial profiling. (See figure 5.3)

The caption for figure 5.3 asks: What do these men have in common? One answer, perhaps the easiest, is that they were both racially profiled. But at least

Figure 5.3 American Civil Liberties Union pamphlet from an anti–racial profiling campaign.
Source: Courtesy of the ACLU.

two other similarities between these two men explains their racial appearance on the cover of an ACLU pamphlet.

First, the visual economy of each image disconfirms stereotypes. They are not thugs, gangsters, or drug dealers. They are ordinary men. Their suits and ties, polished shoes, and manicured faces exude middle-class respectability. To the extent that we perceive either of these men to be suspicious, it must be because of their race. In every other way, both men seem innocent and law abiding.

Second, the text of the pamphlet narrates a story about both men in which their innocence and respectability are explicit. Carlos Gonzalez, for example, "is a junior high math teacher" in the community in which he grew up: South Central Los Angeles. He appears to be a responsible family man: a father who plays and communicates with his sons. His experience with racial profiling "humiliated" him. According to Gonzalez, he was made to endure that humiliation "all because two LAPD officers thought I was a hoodlum or a criminal because of the way I looked." To the extent that Gonzalez appears respectable—in suit and tie—the "look" to which he refers is, of course, his race. If we were to control for Gonzalez's race, he would be utterly unimaginable as a hoodlum. The ACLU pamphlet tells a similar story of respectability for the other man who is pictured, Timothy Campbell.

The message the ACLU hoped to convey with this pamphlet is clear: racial profiling "results in the persecution of innocent people based on their skin color."[44] The political pragmatism behind this idea is also clear: to the extent that (white) people understand that racial profiling harms innocent blacks or Latinas/os, they are more likely to condemn racial profiling and the police officers who practice it.

This strategy is similar to the strategy the NAACP (National Association for the Advancement of Colored People) employed in the 1930s and 1940s to determine which criminal procedure cases to litigate. The association specifically sought out cases in which it perceived the defendants to be innocent.[45] The notion was that, in the Jim Crow era, white Americans were not going to be sympathetic to arguments about due process or racial inequality in the context of cases involving "bad Negroes." This approach to litigation was part of a broader civil rights strategy to represent black people as civil and civilized.[46] Litigating cases within which the defendants were not innocent would have undermined this project of racial respectability.[47]

According to Randall Kennedy, the politics of respectability reflects two basic, if controversial, ideas:

> The principal tenet of the politics of respectability is that, freed of the crippling invidious racial discriminations, blacks are capable of meeting

the established moral standards of white middle-class Americans.... One of its strategies is to distance blacks as far as possible from negative stereotypes used to justify racial discrimination against all Negroes.[48]

The second idea that buttresses the politics of respectability is that a "stigmatized minority" individual must make every effort to present one's self as being a "good" Black or Latino/a, so as to enhance the "reputation of the group" and "avoid the derogatory charges lying in wait in a hostile environment."[49]

To the extent that either of these ideas structure how we think about racial profiling, only reputation-enhancing or stereotype-disconfirming Outsiders like Carlos Gonzalez and Timothy Campbell can figure as representative victims.

Not everyone who is racially profiled, however, has the innocent identities of Gonzalez or Campbell. Some are less respectable. When they are, their capacity to challenge the practice of racial profiling both legally and politically is severely restricted. To appreciate this point, consider a key Supreme Court case on racial profiling, *Whren v. United States*.[50] Although *Whren* is not the first case in which the Supreme Court has addressed the constitutionality of race-based policing, it is the case to which scholars most often refer to discuss the Supreme Court's response to racial profiling. In *Whren*, plainclothes officers in an unmarked car observed a Nissan Pathfinder at a stop sign in a "high drug area."[51] According to the officers, they became suspicious because the car's occupants were young, the driver seemed to be looking toward the lap of the passenger, and the car had a temporary license plate.[52]

The officers' suspicions intensified after the vehicle remained at a stop sign for an "unusually long time" and subsequently drove off in excess of the speed limit.[53] The officers followed the vehicle, which came to a stop at a traffic light.[54] Upon approaching the vehicle, one of the officers observed that Whren, the passenger, was holding two plastic bags.[55] On the assumption that the bags contained cocaine, the officers arrested both men.[56]

One could argue that the officers racially profiled Whren. The claim would be that, but for Whren's racial identity as black, the officers' suspicions would not have been aroused, and they would not have stopped the vehicle. Put another way, if Whren had been white, the police likely would not have noticed the Pathfinder and Whren would have escaped the encounter altogether.

It is not easy to prove the foregoing. After all, the officers had an "objective" reason for stopping the vehicle: the driver had committed a traffic infraction. To the extent this underlying justification is established, it becomes difficult to prove that the police officers racially profiled Whren. The Supreme Court is right, then, to worry about the difficulties of proving that a particular police activity is race motivated.[57] This is so even though it turns out that the officers in *Whren* were not exactly good cops. Almost four years after the case was decided, a report broke that two of Wren's arresting officers, as well as other members of the vice squad the officers were assigned to, "had engaged in excessive use of force, planted evidence, and perjured themselves to secure drug convictions."[58]

But quite apart from the evidentiary difficulty of establishing whether or not the officer engaged in racial profiling, is the question of whether such a claim should be theoretically available to litigants like Whren. In *Whren*, the Court made clear that when police officers have probable cause to stop a car, under the Fourth Amendment, racial profiling claims based on such a stop are not constitutionally cognizable. One cannot help but wonder whether or not the fact that Whren was not "guilty" (he was found with drugs) played some role in the Court's analysis. At best, one can estimate that Whren's inability to claim he was an "innocent" victim of racial profiling shaped the way the Court discussed the issue, and at worst, negatively impacted the Court's inclination to address racial profiling as it applies to all people of color, regardless of their guilt or innocence. Note that this case was decided at the height of public discussions about racial profiling. Yet, despite the public attention directed at this issue, the Court showed little concern for the problem. The opinion was unanimous.

Five years after *Whren*, Justice O'Connor, who was part of the unanimous opinion in *Whren*, specifically invoked racial profiling in *Atwater v. City of Lago Vista*.[59] Why she does so is potentially instructive to the point we are making about innocence, "good blacks" and racial profiling. In *Atwater*, Gail Atwater was arrested and transported to the station for failing to wear her seat belt, failing to fasten her children in seat belts, and failing to provide her driver's license and proof of insurance.[60] The legal question was whether the arrest was unreasonable.[61] Atwater argued that it was.[62] Her claim was that a simple misdemeanor crime could not serve as a basis for a full custodial arrest.[63] The Court disagreed, and Justice O'Connor dissented.[64]

Justice O'Connor's dissent is revealing in the way it describes the encounter and the parties involved—particularly Atwater and her children. Notwithstanding that Atwater committed a crime—several, in fact—she remains, throughout Justice O'Connor's dissent, innocent. While Atwater's innocence is clearly a function of the specific crimes she committed (again, they were all misdemeanors), it also appears to be a function of her identity as a (white) mother.[65] Consider the following from Justice O'Connor's dissent:

> Officer Turek handcuffed Ms. Atwater with her hands behind her back, placed her in the police car, and drove her to the police station.

Ironically, Turek did not secure Atwater in a seat belt for the drive. At the station, Atwater was forced to remove her shoes, relinquish her possessions, and wait in a holding cell for about an hour. A judge finally informed Atwater of her rights and the charges against her, and released her when she posted bond. Atwater returned to the scene of the arrest, only to find that her car had been towed....

[T]he decision to arrest Atwater was nothing short of counterproductive. Atwater's children witnessed Officer Turek yell at their mother and threaten to take them into custody. Ultimately, they were forced to leave her behind with Turek, knowing that she was being taken to jail. Understandably, the 3-year-old-boy was "very, very, very, traumatized." After the incident, he had to see a child psychologist regularly, who reported that the boy "felt very guilty that he couldn't stop this horrible thing...he was powerless to help his mother or sister." Both of Atwater's children are now terrified at the sight of any police car. According to Atwater, the arrest "just never leaves us. It's a conversation we have every other day, once a week, and it's—it raises its head constantly in our lives."[66]

The above passages convey the message that Atwater and her children were not supposed to experience that kind of encounter. They were not supposed to be traumatized by, or become terrified of, the police. Officer Turek should not have humiliated Atwater. Nor should he have rendered the family a public spectacle. Implicit in Justice O'Connor's concern for Atwater is the notion that Turek's treatment of Atwater sent a public message about who Atwater is—that is, she is a criminal. As we read Justice O'Connor, she was making the point that neither the misdemeanors Atwater committed nor her identity as a (white) mother invited or justified the dissemination of that message.[67]

Toward the end of her dissent, Justice O'Connor writes: "[A]s the recent debate over racial profiling demonstrates all too clearly, a relatively minor traffic infraction may often serve as an excuse for stopping and harassing an individual."[68] This concern for racial profiling was absent in *Whren*—a case in which the litigant specifically argued that the officer racially profiled him. Our guess is that Justice O'Connor felt comfortable engaging race because Atwater's encounter occurred in a context in which neither "bad blacks" nor drugs were a part of the case.

The ACLU also marginalized *Whren* in its campaign against racial profiling. In its "Driving While Black" pamphlet, the ACLU's analysis of the case is almost entirely doctrinal.[69] The pamphlet features no images of *Whren*. Nor does the booklet narrate a story about Whren's life, his family, education, upbringing, and community membership. Even the racial facts of *Whren* are conspicuously absent from the ACLU's description of the case, much as they are absent from the Court's recitation of the facts.

The obfuscation of the circumstances under which Whren was arrested, we suspect, relate to the fact that, unlike Campbell and Gonzalez, he was not innocent. He was a drug possessor, if not a dealer. He confirmed rather than disconfirmed stereotypes about black criminality. The good black trope is not available to him. Presumably, the ACLU understood that their ability to employ Whren as a representative icon for racial profiling victimization was circumscribed by the fact that many people would perceive him to be a "bad" black. The ACLU may have surmised that, to the extent that people perceive Whren as "bad," they would likely perceive the police officers who arrested him as "good"; as officers whose racial suspicions were confirmed.

None of this is to suggest that the ACLU's campaign against racial profiling has been unhelpful. Because of the ACLU's efforts, one can say that there is "[s]ome cautious optimism about the problem of racial profiling"[70] at least in the context of everyday policing on the ground. This claim is more difficult to sustain with respect to the racial profiling of people who are racialized as Muslim, particularly subsequent to September 11, 2001. Here, too, there is a good/bad dichotomy at play. As a result, there are pressures on people who are vulnerable to being racialized as "Muslim-looking"[71]—and thus terrorists—to work their identities so as to negate or preempt the activation of that stereotype. As John Tehranian put it, "In the post-9/11 world, I do not go to the airport without shaving first. It is covering, plain and simple, and a rational survival strategy. I prefer the close shave to the close full-body-cavity search."[72]

But even outside the context of the "war on terror" our racial profiling engagements are still framed in terms of innocence, or the notion that "bad" cops are racially profiling "good blacks". The problem is that this good black/bad cop framework does not fully capture cases like *Whren*. Moreover, the framework renders such cases difficult to challenge publicly. Yet, the public must come to care about cases involving "bad blacks", like *Whren*, where the victim of racial profiling is vulnerable to incarceration.[73]

And, moreover, there is a pragmatic reason for being concerned about racial profiling claims involving "bad blacks": Any approach to racial profiling that reflects the idea that there are "good" and "bad" blacks, further entrenches stereotypes of black criminality. The notion that there are "good" and "bad" black people has political currency and makes sense only because there is already a presumption of blackness as "bad." For example, few, in the context of thinking about crime, would conceptualize whiteness, or the category "white people," in terms of "good" and "bad."

The application of this dichotomy to the black community makes sense to us because people understand it to mean that "not all black people are bad. There are exceptions. Some of them are good."[74] This understanding encourages surveillance of the entire group, even as it purports to be concerned only with "bad blacks." Consider again Randall Kennedy's endorsement of respectability:

> It should be clear by now that I am recommending a politics of respectability, albeit a version that steers clear of excesses.... Some readers will undoubtedly object on the grounds that, however modified, the politics of respectability smells of Uncle Tomism. It may have been a necessary concession earlier, they concede, but championing the politics of respectability today, they charge, is an anachronistic error. Obviously, I disagree. In American political culture, the reputation of groups, be they religious denominations, labor unions, or racial groups, matters greatly. For that reason alone, those dedicated to advancing the interests of African Americans ought to urge them to conduct themselves in a fashion that, without sacrificing rights or dignity, elicits respect and sympathy rather than fear and anger from colleagues of other races.[75]

The problem with Kennedy's approach is that he does not seem to perceive that there are material costs to a politics of respectability, so long as this ideology "steers clear of excesses."[76] But these material costs are inherent to the politics of respectability. For these performances of respectability to work, they have to involve costs—and specifically, costs that help distinguish the "good" from the "bad." It is not clear to us that blacks can—and Kennedy's analysis does not supply a methodology for how blacks might—"conduct themselves in a fashion that, without sacrificing rights or dignity, elicits respect and sympathy rather than fear and anger from colleagues of other races."[77] Working Identity performances, particularly when they are intended to alter how "others see us," are *always* compromising, and not just in terms of one's sense of self but in terms of rights. One need only refer back to the point we made about consent searches at the beginning of this chapter for an indication of how both one's sense of self and one's rights are implicated when performing racial respectability.

***

The ACLU pamphlet's story of Carlos Gonzalez was effective, in part, because it lacked nuance. Outrage at his humiliation comes easy. The problem with such sharp examples of racial injustice, however, is that they obscure the harder cases where the victims of profiling are "bad." This obfuscation is a problem. So long as police officers are searching for the "bad," the "good" will have to prove that they are "good." In other words, the good/bad dichotomy makes all black people vulnerable to being racially profiled. Think back to the episode with which we began this chapter: Officer Crowley's arrest of Professor Gates. One way to understand the episode is to say that Gates was insufficiently deferential to Crowley; he refused to provide enough of the "good." More than that, he asserted rights and questioned Crowley's authority. This made him "bad." In this respect, Gates miscalculated the tenuous nature of his "good black" status. International academic stature, Harvard professorship, fancy home in Cambridge, friendship with the president of the United States, and other factors, notwithstanding, even Gates was not allowed to assert his rights. Even he was required to perform "surplus compliance."

This does not mean that Working Identity is irrelevant. If it was, so many of us would not strategically perform our identity. At bottom, "good" black Working Identity probably does reduce both the likelihood that one will be stopped by the police and the likelihood of arrest or violence when the police perform such stops. The problem for Gates was not simply that he is black but that he was insufficiently "good." To borrow from the Dave Chappelle "When Keeping It Real Goes Wrong" skit with which we began chapter 1, Gates might have thought that in asserting his rights he was "keeping it real." But that is why the encounter went wrong.

Police interactions and the employment arena are not the only contexts in which "keeping it real" can go wrong. University admissions are another. Here, too, people of color have to decide how to work their identities—or, to put the point more specifically, work their diversity. This is because most colleges and universities justify their utilization of affirmative action on diversity grounds; admitting students of color renders their campuses more racially diverse. This creates an incentive for students of color to work their identities as diverse, even if doing so is not "keeping it real."

The dominant way of thinking about diversity admissions, more generally, is to say that it results in schools selecting students of color over whites, thus the charge that affirmative action constitutes "reverse discrimination." This "reverse discrimination" claim is predicated on an inter-group (typically black over white) framing of affirmative action as a racial preference. But as we discuss in the next chapter, just as employers can intra-racially select which African Americans to hire and promote, and just as police officers can intra-racially select which African Americans to stop, search, or arrest, university admissions officers can intra-racially select which African Americans to admit. How this can happen, why we should care, and what the law might say about it are the subjects to which we now turn. Our analysis begins outside of the admissions context with a discussion of President Obama's nomination of Sonia Sotomayor to the United

States Supreme Court. While everybody was talking about the diversity implications of the nomination, what really was at stake was Sotomayor's Working
Identity—how racially salient a Supreme Court justice was she going to be? We
highlight this aspect of the controversy around Sotomayor's nomination as a
point of departure to discuss how diversity and Working Identity function with
respect to university admissions.

Acting Diverse

On May 26, 2009, President Obama nominated Sonia Sotomayor, of the Second Circuit, to replace the retiring justice, David Souter. Never before had a president nominated a Latina to the Court. Central to the debate over her nomination was whether she was the right kind of Latina to join the Court. How would she work her identity as a Supreme Court justice? Would she be a "wise Latina"? Would she "whitewash" her race?

Figure 6.1 Justice Sonia Sotomayor on the cover of the magazine *Latina*.
Source: Courtesy of Latina Media Ventures.

Consider these questions with respect to the photograph with which this chapter begins. The image appeared on the cover of *Latina* magazine. (See figure 6.1.) A blog entry created something of a furor by asking: "Why did they wash out her skin like that? What's going on with our beloved Justice's hair?"[1] The entry also referenced an Associated Press article that commented on Sotomayor's hoop earrings and red nail polish: "Why did the AP article announcing Sotomayor's [nomination] lead with a story about her hoop earrings and red nail polish?" According to the AP article, "Sotomayor heeded White House advice to paint her fingernails a neutral shade during her Supreme Court confirmation process—up to a point. At a White House reception after her confirmation, Sotomayor showed her freshly painted red nails to President Barack Obama, along with her red-and-black semi-hoop earrings."[2] At the reception, "Obama joked that Sotomayor had been briefed on proper nail color and earring size."[3]

Joking aside, both Sotomayor's detractors and her supporters were paying attention to her Working Identity. But nail color and earring size was the tip of the iceberg. The real debate over Sotomayor's Working Identity was triggered by comments she had made some years prior suggesting that "a wise Latina" judge might view a case differently than one of her white male counterparts and that this different perspective might be useful—perhaps even better.[4] The critics hammered her. What did she mean by her "wise Latina" comment? Did it mean that she would engage in identity politics while on the Court?

Sotomayor's supporters, such as President Obama, tried to re-characterize her remarks. They suggested that Sotomayor had been sloppy in her "wise Latina" comments and that what she said was insignificant. They tried to assure Sotomayor's critics that she was going to be just as neutral as other members of the Court.

This defense of Sotomayor strikes us as disingenuous. Surely, something more was at stake vis-à-vis her nomination than simply having the Court "look" more diverse in its official photographs. And something more was at stake than having a person with humble beginnings on the Court. Plausibly, Obama might have thought that: "There are no Latinas on the Supreme Court. It's high time that we change that. I am going to pick a Latina who is qualified and who best advances my particular diversity interests." We do not presume to know what diversity benefits, over and above the fact that Sotomayor is Latina, Obama sought to advance. Perhaps he wanted a "Latina voice" on the Court—that is, a Latina justice who would not be afraid to speak explicitly from her experiences as a Latina (notwithstanding that he distanced himself from her "wise Latina" comment, as did Sotomayor herself). Perhaps, instead, Obama wanted a Latina who would be palatably racially conscious. Such a person would promote racial remediation efforts in a way that produced racial comfort and solidarity, on and off the Court, rather than racial division and animosity. Perhaps he wanted a Latina who would work her identity on the Court the way Justice Marshall did, someone who would not be afraid to be racially salient when the moment called for it. We do not know which, if any, of the foregoing diversity interests informed Obama's decision to nominate Sotomayor. We simply mean to note that different potential Latina Supreme Court nominees would appear more or less *racially* attractive to Obama based on the diversity benefits he was interested in advancing.

A similar dynamic is potentially at play when colleges and universities express an interest in diversifying their institutions. Just as Sotomayor was evaluated in terms of the diversity benefits she might bring to the Supreme Court, admissions officials can evaluate prospective students in terms of the diversity benefits they might bring to the school. Specifically, officials can intra-racially select some African Americans over others based on whether their perceived "degrees of blackness" advance some diversity interest the school seeks to promote. Note how this intra-racial selection process functions like the intra-racial selection processes in the contexts of employment and police encounters. This chapter describes how intra-racial selections can occur in the domain of admissions and suggests that we might wish to be concerned about the phenomenon.

Harvard law professor Lani Guinier brought a version of the issue to the fore some years ago, pointing out that many top US universities were pursuing black racial diversity primarily by admitting first-generation immigrants of African and Caribbean descent.[5] Other scholars, including Angela Onwuachi-Willig and co-authors Kevin Brown and Jeannine Bell have made similar observations, exploring whether African Americans who trace their ancestry to American slavery are disadvantaged in admissions processes vis-à-vis other blacks.[6] This might well be the case. But intra-racial selection mechanisms are likely broader than university officials preferring African or Caribbean black ethnicity over American black ethnicity. Intra-racial selections in the domain of admissions likely will depend on the performances of blackness that institutions find palatable, which would include but not be limited to inquiries about black ethnicity or even class. To develop our argument, we begin with an analysis of the legal parameters of affirmative action in admissions since that is the policy through which most universities effectuate their commitment to diversity.

Diversity through Affirmative Action

The legal basis for pursuing diversity in education harkens back to Justice Powell's opinion in *University of California v. Bakke.*[7] In that case, the Court had to determine the constitutionality of the affirmative action plan of the medical school of the University of California, Davis. The Court applies different standards of review to determine whether a particular governmental decision violates equal protection. Race-based classifications receive the highest level of scrutiny. Concluding that Davis's affirmative action plan was a race-based classification, Justice Powell argued that the medical school was required to demonstrate that there was a compelling justification for its plan and that the school did not overly rely on race in implementing the policy. Although Justice Powell concluded that the affirmative action plan was unconstitutional because the school set quotas, he suggested that the "attainment of a diverse student body" constituted a compelling interest that could justify the consideration of race as a positive decision-making factor.[8] In everyday language, UC Davis had a good reason for putting in place its affirmative action policy, but utilized a bad mechanism for implementing it; a mechanism that relied too crudely on race (quotas).

But what did Powell mean by diversity—and what constitutes a good mechanism? While Powell did not articulate a definitive definition of diversity, he explained that the value of diversity in a student body largely derived from the "discourse benefits"[9] that flow from placing individuals with different social and cultural perspectives together in a shared educational environment.[10] As to the mechanisms schools could use to realize this diversity benefit, Powell was less clear. Quotas, we know, are bad; but what is good? Powell's answer seemed to be: individualized review—officials must evaluate candidates as individuals, and not as part of a group.

Roughly twenty-five years later, in a pair of cases, *Grutter v. Bollinger* and *Gratz v. Bollinger*, the Supreme Court revisited the question of whether diversity can be a legitimate basis upon which universities implement affirmative action programs. Writing for a majority of the Court, Justice O'Connor answered that question in the affirmative, stating that the pursuit of diversity advanced compelling governmental interests:

> [T]he [University of Michigan] Law School's admissions policy promotes "cross-racial understanding," helps to break down racial stereotypes, "enables [students] to better understand persons of different races." These benefits are "important and laudable," because "classroom discussion is livelier, more spirited, and simply more enlightening and interesting" when the students have "the greatest possible variety of backgrounds."[11]

O'Connor also observed that the law school's policy "reaffirm[s] the Law School's longstanding commitment to...'racial and ethnic diversity with special reference to the inclusion of students from groups which have been historically discriminated against, like African-Americans, Hispanics and Native

Americans, who without this commitment might not be represented...in meaningful numbers.'"[12] Finally, O'Connor endorsed the law school's argument that it was important to admit a "critical mass" of underrepresented students to "ensur[e] their ability to make a unique contribution to the character of the Law School."[13]

O'Connor's opinion suggests that, in addition to Justice Powell's discourse benefits, there are at least seven other values that the pursuit of diversity might achieve. Each of those values, in theory, helps ground her conclusion that diversity can be a justification for affirmative action.

- Diversity to promote speech and the robust exchange of ideas (Justice Powell's discourse benefit)
- Diversity to effectuate the inclusion of underrepresented students
- Diversity to change the character of the school
- Diversity to disrupt and negate racial stereotypes
- Diversity to facilitate racial cooperation and understanding
- Diversity to create pathways to leadership
- Diversity to ensure democratic legitimacy
- Diversity to prevent racial isolation and alienation

In suggesting that diversity might advance any of these values, O'Connor expanded upon Powell's rationale for why diversity was a goal that educational institutions are permitted to pursue. However, as in *Bakke*, the Court made clear that admissions officers did not have a blank check with respect to the techniques they could employ to pursue diversity. At the same time, nor would the Court second-guess a university's articulation of the benefits it sought to achieve. The caveat, as in *Bakke*, was that whatever diversity benefits the university endeavored to realize, the mechanism it employed to do so had to entail an individualized analysis of the admissions candidates. Our interest is in how admissions officers are likely implementing this law. Below, we sketch out some possibilities.

Imagine that a university's general counsel, seeking to ensure that the school's diversity policy for admissions survives constitutional challenge, issues the following two instructions to an admissions team: "First, when you consider race as a factor in admissions, the analysis must be individualized. In other words, a precise *plus* value cannot be put on the value of a candidate's race. The analysis has to be a multifactor subjective analysis." In *Gratz*, the companion case to *Grutter*, the Court declared the University of Michigan's undergraduate admissions plan unconstitutional because it assigned points to applicants depending on their membership in particular racial groups.

The second instruction the university's general counsel issues is: "In performing the individualized analysis, your employment of race should be narrowly tailored to achieve one or more of the specific diversity goals outlined above." These two instructions can lead admissions officers to make intra-racial distinctions that neither Powell nor O'Connor might have contemplated. Below, we work through two hypothetical scenarios.

In scenario one, we assume that the admissions officer is screening applicants on the basis of whether they will provide the benefits of diversity that the Court mentioned in *Bakke* and *Grutter*. We further assume that the admissions officer is screening on the basis of the paper record that the applicant submits. While most admissions decisions are made by committees, our sense is that the individuals reading files do so in a disaggregated way—meaning, that there won't often be group-based conversations about which candidates to admit. This is why we frame our hypothetical around a single decision-maker. For simplicity, we limit our discussion to two of the eight types of diversity benefits Justice O'Connor mentions in *Grutter*: countering racial stereotypes and enhancing racial cooperation. In positing that the admissions officer can choose which diversity benefit he wishes to pursue, we are assuming that he has considerable discretion.

In scenario two, our starting point is that the institution takes a greater interest in shaping diversity decisions. To achieve more effective screening, the institution authorizes the resources for its admissions officer to interview candidates. As with the previous scenario, in this one the prospective students have a range of diversity attributes, including racial diversity, geography, academic background and interests, work experience, and extracurricular activities. With respect to racial diversity, the university instructs the admissions officer to focus on pursuing one particular benefit—enhancing racial cooperation. Motivating this mandate is the view that more cooperation on the racial front reduces racial conflict on campus, and therefore produces a direct benefit to the institution. In this scenario, the admissions officer is screening for racial palatability. Consistent with our prior chapters, we employ African Americans as exemplars.

Scenario One: From the Paper Record

Scenario one has three basic assumptions. First, among the list of eight diversity values outlined above, the admissions officers are only interested in pursuing diversity to counter racial stereotypes and enhance racial cooperation. Second, in any given admission cycle, the officer will seek to promote only one of those values. Third, we assume that while institutions are prohibited from employing quotas and separate admissions tracks, they nevertheless engage in comparative racial assessments about the diversity benefits particular individuals might deliver. In this scenario, our admissions officer is performing that comparative analysis with respect to three black female applicants: Kimberly, Tanisha, and Rachel.

Kimberly grew up in the inner city, attended a predominantly black high school, and was parented by a single mother, who is a nurse. In high school, Kimberly founded the Sisters Reading Group, a book club for teenage African American girls, and led an organized effort at the school to hire more black teachers. Her personal statement suggests interests in Ethnic Studies and Women's Studies.

Tanisha also grew up in the inner city, but was bused to a school in the suburbs. Her father is a policeman and her mother is a stay-at-home mom. Her extracurricular activities include tennis and the Environment Club. Tanisha is interested in environmental justice, with a particular focus on clean-air policy.

Finally, *Rachel* grew up in a largely white neighborhood and attended an elite private high school. Her parents are professionals—her mother a lawyer, her father a dentist. She was on the lacrosse team in high school. Her parents immigrated to the United States from the Caribbean to attend university. Rachel's interest is in finance and corporate law.

Consider now how an admissions officer might select among these "diversity" candidates. The vagueness of diversity as a concept, administrative discretion, and behind-doors decision-making combine to give admissions officers wide latitude to make intra-racial choices.

Diversity Justifications and Resulting Choices

Negating Stereotypes

Diversity in a student body might help disrupt negative stereotypes about race. Imagine that our hypothetical admissions officer believes that inter-racial interactions among the students can alter white students' previously held negative perceptions of black intellectual capacity. His sense is that white students whose past experiences included little interaction with blacks will now be able to see that their black student counterparts are no different than they are. Conversely, the absence of black students does little to disrupt existing stereotypes about black intellectual inferiority: they are not present at this university because they are not smart enough to get in.

All three of the students could perform this particular stereotype-disconfirmation function. But they might not do so to the same extent. Based on the instructions he received, the admissions officer knows that he has to perform an individualized consideration of each applicant and decide which of them is the best candidate in terms of what her race brings to the table, assuming that all other factors are the same (high school grades, references, and so on). The question is whether one candidate stands out on the basis of the diversity benefits she can deliver.

The admissions officer could decide that because Kimberly has an interest in majoring in Ethnic Studies and Women's Studies, and few white male students and a small number of white women major in those areas, she would have limited interactions with white students and thus have few opportunities to negate racial stereotypes. The admissions officer might also reach a similar conclusion with respect to Tanisha—that her background and interests also indicate that she will spend her time primarily interacting with other black students.

The admissions officer might also view Kimberly as the least attractive candidate to negate racial stereotypes. After all, she confirms certain stereotypes of blackness (e.g., overly committed to racial politics and community organization). The same, albeit to a lesser extent, could be said for Tanisha. Rachel, the first-generation immigrant who plays lacrosse, by contrast, might be the ideal candidate to disrupt traditional notions of blackness.

The admissions officer's decision-making could get more granular if he decides to take seriously his casual reading of press accounts of social psychology research on de-biasing. A feature of this research focuses on the characteristics that make a person a good de-biasing agent. In order to serve as a de-biasing agent, one has to be perceived as belonging to the group to which the bias or stereotype attaches. Rachel is black—but she is of West Indian descent. Would her interactions with white students change their perspectives of African Americans? To some extent, blacks of Caribbean descent are treated differently than blacks who trace their ancestry to American slavery. Whether Rachel could serve as a de-biasing agent might turn on the salience of her Caribbean background. If it is not generally known that her parents are Caribbean immigrants and she does not conspicuously identify as a Caribbean, she might be in a better position to perform de-biasing work than if her Caribbean identity is salient. Given the foregoing, our admissions official might decide that he needs to investigate in detail the nature of Rachel's Caribbean heritage.

The officer's interest in the de-biasing research would have implications for Kimberly and Tanisha as well. He might read the research to suggest that likable Outsiders are probably better de-biasing agents than unlikable Outsider. Thus, while images of Martin Luther King might de-bias people with respect to their assumptions about blacks, images of Malcolm X might not. Here, our admissions officer might engage in a comparative analysis of the candidates' likability.

Of course, it is hard to say precisely how any particular admissions officer would decide these cases. Our point is to demonstrate how easy it is for an admissions officer to slip into intra-racial thinking. We reiterate this point with respect to one other diversity objective.

Promoting a Racially Cooperative Citizenry

Diversity can help to facilitate the formation of a racially cooperative society. To the extent that universities are crucibles in which social identities are shaped, an admissions officer could believe that students perform in society the racial interactions they learn and rehearse in school.

At first blush, it might seem that Kimberly, Tanisha, and Rachel would equally advance this function of diversity. But some admissions officials might reason that Kimberly is likely to be something of a racial separatist—or a race and gender separatist—given her black girls' reading group. An admissions committee might also conclude that Kimberly probably will not be as good at socializing across the colorline as Tanisha and Rachel, both of whom attended predominantly white schools and presumably have had many white friends. Under this view, Tanisha's and Rachel's past experiences with integration suggest that they would facilitate, rather than undermine, social integration at the school and this, over the long run, would lead to integration benefits in society more generally. On the other hand, a different admissions officer might decide that the maximal cooperative benefits will be realized if they force white students to learn to work with black students like Kimberly, rather than her less radical counterparts, Tanisha and Rachel.

Our hypothetical admissions officer could also engage the issue of racial cooperation through the prism of colorblindness. The notion would be that the students who are most likely to facilitate cooperation are the ones who take the colorblind perspective. Under this frame, the officer might decide that, of the three students, Rachel is the most likely to advance the colorblindness goal. She has no expressed interest in racially oriented activities and showed her ability to fit in with her classmates, including on sports teams, at a predominantly white high school. She is the one most likely to view herself in nonracial terms. By contrast, the admissions officer might predict that Tanisha and Kimberly are more likely to view themselves in racial terms.

A different admissions officer, however, might worry about a candidate being unduly colorblind. This officer might be looking for an applicant who would express a "soft" commitment to colorblindness. Such a student would neither deny that race still matters nor completely elide racial consciousness. The admissions officer could believe that, in order to facilitate racial cooperation, the black person with whom whites interact must be "credibly" black. The officer could believe that at least some existing black students could perceive admitted black students who are too colorblind as sellouts and conclude that white students who associate with such students are only interested in interacting with black students who disidentify with or disassociate from other blacks. This would result in racial distrust and animosity, not cooperation and understanding. The point, again, is to show the ease with which an admissions officer can engage in intra-racial thinking.

Scenario Two: Interviewing Diversity

Thus far, we have assumed that the admissions officers will evaluate the applicants' written materials—resume, personal statements, and essays—to screen each applicant's potential diversity benefit to the school. But, given the discretion that the Court has given educational institutions in structuring their application process, an institution might decide that to ascertain whether any given applicant would contribute to the diversity of the school, it needs to do interviews. And given the Court's instruction that the consideration of race has to be individualized, subjective, and granular, interviews should fit the mandate.

An admissions officer interested in pursuing the interview option could ferret out information about diversity in subtle ways. To demonstrate how, we assume that our hypothetical admissions officer will want students who are diverse in terms of how they look, but not diverse in terms of how they act. We also assume, for purposes of this discussion, that the university's mandate to the admissions officer is that he should use the interview to screen for one specific diversity value: racial cooperation. The thinking is that people who look "different" (not white) but act the "same" (as whites) are more likely to facilitate racial cooperation than people who look and act "different."

The admissions officer's screening in this respect is designed in part to minimize two perceived costs of diversity that the institution is concerned about. First, the admissions officer believes that diversity can create friction and conflict not only among students but also between students and the administration. A concrete example of this, from the perspective of the admissions officer, is students pushing for greater diversity on the faculty or a more robust affirmative action policy. Second, students who are "too" diverse might not fit into the institution. The hypothetical admissions officer might believe that the presence of black students who are alienated and under-performing might not only exacerbate tensions but also create the impression that the school is hostile to underrepresented students. Moreover, poor academic performance on the part of enough students of color could affect the reputation of the school. The result of such outcomes is an incentive for the admissions officer to screen minority candidates to reduce the "friction costs" he believes diversity potentially produces. One way he can do so is by getting as much sameness from the diversity buck as possible. The higher the level of sameness, the higher the level of grease (rather than grit) and the lower the level of friction.[14] In the discussion that follows, we demonstrate how an admissions officer can use the interviewing process to intra-racially screen applicants in light of the foregoing concerns.

Greasing the Admissions Process

The officer can employ at least the following three profiles in the context of the interview to screen minority applicants for their grease rather than grit: similarity, comfort, and differentiation. Assume that our hypothetical black applicant is applying for admission to an elite business school. The school has asked him to come in for an interview, in part to ascertain the diversity contribution he might make.

Similarity

The similarity question is whether the individual exhibits personal characteristics suggesting he is similar to the other students who are likely to be admitted in his class. The more a minority applicant appears similar to other students, the more likely the admissions committee is to conclude that the individual has the potential to be assimilated. The prospective student's response to standard interview questions can help signal his potential for assimilation. Consider Johnny, a black candidate being considered for admission at our fictional business school. An admissions officer has asked Johnny to "tell me a little bit about yourself; what do you do when you are not studying?" Johnny responds:

> I like reading...I'm rereading Gore Vidal's *Julian*. I'm not a huge sports fan, but I do love watching the Tour de France. The internal politics, with all the doping, and the weird social conventions, such as the one where everyone waits to see if the leaders need to take a leak or if one of the leaders has a crash, are fascinating. I spent a year in Europe after college and I got to watch a couple of the stages of Le Tour. I fell in love with it. I hope to take advantage of the school's summer program in Belgium. Maybe I will be able to go back to the Tour. And then, of course, there is the wonderful food and wine that one inevitably consumes while following the Tour.

This response provides the admissions officer with signals about Johnny's socialized identity, information that the officer can use to make a determination as to whether Johnny is sufficiently like the school's other students. Johnny likes cycling. Cycling is not a mainstream sport in the United States, but Johnny's interest in it, and in European food and drink, suggests that he wants to develop the international aspect of his identity. He may make friends with the European and Latin American students who form an important part of the modern business school's class.

Johnny is not an avid sports fan. But his interest in cycling signals respectable (but not hyper-) masculinity and a willingness to participate in group-based spectator sport rituals. He also appears to be cultured (he reads Gore Vidal). Finally, the fact that he likes to travel, drink wine, and eat exotic foods suggests that he will socialize with others.

Not every institution will select for the foregoing characteristics: Screens for similarity will vary as a function of the characteristics of the institution. The point is that most admissions officials will have a set of characteristics that they perceive to define their institution's culture. Without much difficulty, they can screen for these characteristics through some combination of the application essay, interview, and background information.

Comfort

A second dimension upon which an admissions officer can screen applicants is comfort—hoping to assess how comfortable the applicant will be interacting with fellow students inside and outside of the classroom. The officer can select for comfort by considering a prospective student's response to standard interview questions. Remember, Johnny is interviewing for a spot at an elite business school. The admissions officer asks: "What kind of school you are looking for." Johnny responds:

> I am looking for a business school with a strong finance department that is associated with a strong law school because I am hoping to enroll in the JD-MBA program. I don't want to attend an institution where I have to feel embarrassed about wanting to work for a hedge fund focusing on distressed debt. You know, a vulture fund.
>
> I'd like that to be a place where students have a voice. I'd like the opportunity to be part of the student government process—especially in terms of helping attract a wider range of employers. Many business schools seem to focus only on the big investment banks like Goldman or Morgan. But there are many good boutique firms that provide much better training than the big banks. At any rate, given the downturn in

the economy, students cannot put all their eggs in the big I-bank basket. Those days are over.

The admissions officer could interpret Johnny's response in a number of ways. Assuming that it is screening for comfort and fit, the committee might focus on Johnny's desire to work in distressed debt financing. He appears to have a single-minded focus on that area. While that does suggest that he will likely not be a student activist, it also might not quite fit the business school ethos. Most business schools profess a commitment to ethics and public service, despite the large numbers of students who go into the private sector. Johnny's interest in finance could thus be a negative or simply not enhance his application in terms of diversity. Conversely, it may be that Johnny's vulture-fund orientation is precisely what enriches his diversity profile. The officer could believe that minority students who are focused on the corporate sector are more likely to exert effort to fit in.

Differentiation

Schools are likely to utilize the differentiation mechanism when they perceive themselves to be bringing in "risky candidates." In this scenario, Johnny is risky because he did not attend an elite private college (he attended a state college that is overwhelmingly black and Latino), but his letters of recommendation are effusive.

Our hypothetical business school rarely admits students from State, in part because State is insufficiently elite and most of the students at State are from working-class backgrounds. The admissions office has determined that the students from State are likely to have difficulty fitting into the milieu at an elite business school. Given this concern, whether Johnny is selected will be a function of whether he can differentiate himself from the category within which he is situated—the category of State students. Consider the following exchange between Johnny and an admissions officer.

ADMISSIONS OFFICER: I see from your resume that you went to Andover and that you rowed crew. Do you know how we did at the race on the Charles this year? I graduated Andover in '75.

JOHNNY: Our team lost badly this year; even Concord Academy finished ahead of us. It is just embarrassing. It is one thing to be beaten by Exeter, a very different one to lose to Concord.

ADMISSIONS OFFICER: So, you did well at Andover—Magna, with a concentration in history, 3.7 GPA, member of the debating team. I suspect that you had a lot of options when you applied to college.

JOHNNY: I was fortunate to have a few. In addition to State, NYU, Chicago and Michigan said yes. Harvard and Stanford placed me on a waiting list. Duke and UCLA said no.

ADMISSIONS OFFICER: I'm curious as to how you made your decision.

JOHNNY: It was a financial decision. I couldn't bring myself to burden my parents with the guilt of not being able to financially support me. State offered me a Chancellor's scholarship. I just had to hope that I would be able to distinguish myself at State.

ADMISSIONS OFFICER: Clearly, you did distinguish yourself. I see that you published research papers in both Biology and Statistics. And then you worked in industry. But tell me about how you're thinking about business schools. You seem to have more of a research background. Finance, the subject most of our students focus on, is not for everyone; as you know, a large percentage of our students end up going to Wall Street. We are also very international.

JOHNNY: I had the good fortune of working at J. P. Morgan, in their emerging markets group, for a summer after college. I liked the work very much. But the crisis in Europe forced them to cut positions. But for that, I might have stayed on.

ADMISSIONS OFFICER: Yes, yes, an excellent firm. I worked at Lehman myself—in the good old days.

JOHNNY: I liked Morgan. People got along. They had interests similar to mine. I got the sense that the people there felt that they were part of something bigger; they were helping to create the markets of the future. I know that it is fashionable for minority students to say that they will do microfinance or some other kind of Africa- or Asia-oriented work. But the statistics, even for minorities, do not lie. Almost everyone at these schools goes to Wall Street, regardless of race. In my case, I'm interested in real finance—not microfinance—particularly in the production of new types of CDS products.

ADMISSIONS OFFICER: So you think the lifestyle at a big investment bank could make you happy?

JOHNNY: I know the reality; it is going to be a difficult life. But I also think that I will enjoy the work. And the big firms are very encouraging of pro bono work. At least Morgan was—we had multiple sessions in the summer where the firm brought in iconic figures like Bob Rubin to talk about careers in the public sector. I'd like to use my expertise in finance to work in government some day.

The foregoing might reflect enough differentiation on Johnny's part to show the admissions officer that he might well fit in at the hypothetical business school. He may have attended State, but he has a sophisticated understanding of the finance industry and his future prospects in that industry are strong. Plus, Johnny's education at Andover places him in the elite category, particularly with respect to other students at State. Most important, Johnny's ability to interact with and make the admissions officer feel comfortable suggests that Johnny will be able to do the same with his business school classmates.

The Applicant's Perspective

We assumed, in the foregoing discussion, that applicants did not know or were indifferent to the intra-racial screens admissions officers were likely to employ. But this need not be the case—and likely is not. Over the past decade, we have spent considerable time talking to minority students interested in applying to law school. Prospective students are keen to know how university officials will consider their "diverse background." Because universities generally are not forthcoming with respect to the particular diversity benefits they seek to promote, students have to guess as to how to present their diversity in their application. Some students will think that institutions want students of color who are racially distinct and who have participated in race-specific organizations and extracurricular activities. Others will think that the more they tone down their racial identity in the application, the more attractive they are in terms of diversity. All of this is to say, there is an incentive for students to work their identity in the application process to signal that they are the kind of diversity student the university wants. A student of Trinidadian descent, for example, might highlight that background in the hope that an admissions official will assume that he is a "good black" who is likely to fit into a predominantly white school and not trigger stereotypes about blackness. Alternatively, that same student might worry that highlighting his Trinidadian background could render him less authentically black from the perspective of an admissions official and thus not a good candidate for advancing that school's diversity benefit. He may choose instead to emphasize the fact that he lives in South Los Angeles, a working-class black neighborhood. In short, whether a black applicant plays up the Caribbean background or his upbringing in South Los Angeles, there is an incentive for him to cloak himself in the characteristics he thinks best mimic the diversity goals he believes an admissions officer wants to instantiate.

Why Care?

One might agree with everything we have said thus far and still ask, so what? Of course, institutions have to make intra-racial choices. Inevitably, admissions teams will select some black applicants over others, just as they will inevitably select some female students over others. Surely that is not a problem per se? It is not. What concerns us is the discretion admissions officers have to make these intra-racial choices, the extent to which these decisions are basically unchecked, and the fact that none of this enters into our discussions about race and admissions. This should worry all of us. Here are some reasons why.

First, in the context of promoting diversity, admissions officials are quite possibly using racial criteria to select among and between different black applicants. In effect, anonymous admissions committees are making decisions about whether a candidate is adequately diverse. If one takes seriously the notion of race as a social construction, then these committees are, every day, socially constructing race—literally producing a class constituted by black people who embody their blackness in a particular way. Given the importance of race in our society, it should trouble us that we know little about one of the primary sites in which bureaucrats construct race.

Second, the current regime is opaque. We have no idea which conception of diversity underwrites a university's admissions processes. Nor do we know the criteria a given university employs to select students to advance whatever diversity values it promotes. Already this should give us pause. From a social policy perspective, if we do not know what criteria is being used or what goal is being advanced, how do we know whether the system is working? Presumably, admissions programs that consider race will continue to face legal challenges. Their survival could turn on how much we know about whether schools experience the diversity values their admissions regimes seek to promote.

Third, the selection processes admissions officers employ—reading files and conducting interviews—can function like mini-trials in which admissions officers, behind closed doors, are quite literally weighing racial evidence (school activities, career interests, personal statements, community upbringing) and judging racial character (does the applicant have a race conscious or colorblind orientation?). To the best of our knowledge, no admissions committee anywhere discloses what specific goals it is pursuing when it seeks to construct a diverse class of students. Decisions are made about whether candidates are adequately diverse or not, but the candidates do not ever have an opportunity to either defend themselves or challenge the interpretations of the evidence or provide more evidence. The committees implement diversity as they see fit. And all of this occurs off the radar screen of policy makers, scholars, and judges alike.

Fourth, there is a legal question embedded in the dynamics we have described: Do the intra-racial distinctions we set out above violate the narrow tailoring analysis of the strict scrutiny regime? On the one hand, one could argue that the more racially granular the analysis, the more individualized the review. Under this view, there is no narrow tailoring problem. On the other hand, the more racially granular the analysis, the more racially salient the decision-making, which could lead one to conclude that there is a narrow tailoring problem.

Fifth, to what extent do intra-racial selections trade on biases and stereotypes? At the very least, admissions officials could be engaging in fuzzy diversity decision-making with respect to a "suspect" category—race—that university officials, among other decision-makers, historically have employed perniciously. Are clear rules the answer? If so, it's hard to know what clear rules to utilize in this context. For example, a clear decision rule that places an objective weight on the value of having a black candidate might make it more difficult for officials to practice intra-racial distinctions. But that would take us right back to the point system that the *Gratz* Court expressly rejected.

For the foregoing reasons, when a school says it is committed to diversity, it might be worth asking what that means. Few of us bother to do that. Consequently, the standard discussion about diversity admissions centers on whether a particular school admits enough black students or other students of color. Rarely is there a discussion of what goal the diversity selections are supposed to serve. Making matters worse, the Supreme Court has offered no guidance on how institutions should prioritize the various diversity benefits. Indeed, according to Justice O'Connor in *Grutter*, a university's "educational judgment that such diversity is essential to its educational mission is one to which we defer."[15] Perhaps not surprisingly, then, admissions policies are rarely challenged legally. As we explained above, so long as admissions officials review each admissions file individually, do not create separate admissions tracks for different racial groups, and eschew the utilization of quotas, they are largely free to implement diversity as they see fit. Deference to expert decision-makers is often rational. But when there isn't either accountability or monitoring, even experts will use their discretion to advance their self-interest. Shouldn't we have a better sense of what's going on behind the closed door of admissions? Do we really want to be racially blind to the intra-racial lines admissions officials likely draw?

As we write this, the Supreme Court is poised to consider a case involving affirmative action at the University of Texas.[16] And running through this case is the matter of whether admissions officers should be allowed to make discretionary decisions, using race, to determine what diversity value candidates bring to the table. The issue, roughly, is whether, given that it already has a race neutral "ten percent plan" (which guarantees admission to the top ten percent of Texan high school graduates), the University can supplement it with a traditional affirmative action policy (which employs race as one factor among many in deciding which students to admit). In legal terms, the question is whether the employment of both of these admissions regimes together runs afoul of *Grutter*? The Fifth Circuit answered that question in the negative. But not without a strong dissent from the denial of rehearing by Chief Judge Edith Jones, who, among other things, appeared incensed at the amount of deference her Fifth Circuit colleagues in the majority appeared to give to University administrators.[17]

The ligation potentially implicates the issues we discuss in this chapter. The University of Texas's utilization of both the ten percent plan and a traditional affirmative action policy arguably juxtaposes the two types of affirmative action systems that an educational institution might use. On the one hand, there is the ten percent plan that removes all discretion from the hands of the admissions officers; they have to admit blacks from inner city public schools if they fit into the ten percent. On the other hand, there is the traditional discretion-intense affirmative action system that (we would guess) will admit blacks from more elite backgrounds.

One can argue that, by combining these two approaches, the University of Texas is getting more intra-racial diversity than it otherwise would. But the university is not making this argument. More generally, the school has not articulated the diversity benefits its admissions processes are designed to realize. This is a problem. If the University of Texas is are selecting for particular types of blacks, they should be more transparent about it. Only then can we have a debate about whether certain kinds of intra-racial decision-making in this context are too messy and potentially divisive to indulge.

Acting Within the Law

Three pictures show different images of the First Lady, Michelle Obama. (See figures 7.1, 7.2, and 7.3.)The image in figure 7.2 depicts her as respectable, sophisticated, and charming, the kind of woman who could be on the cover of *Vogue*. It presents a palatable image of a black woman. She is smiling. Her hair, while not straightened, is neither in braids nor an afro. She looks conventionally feminine. She fits what we have called the "but for" racial category—*but for* the

Figure 7.1 The Obamas as depicted on the cover of the *New Yorker*, July 21, 2008.
Source: Courtesy of Barry Blitt/The New Yorker Magazine; © Condé Nast.

Figure 7.2 Michelle Obama.
Source: Courtesy of Johnny Nunez/Getty Images.

fact that, in terms of physical features and skin tone, she looks black, she is otherwise indistinguishable from other normatively feminine white women.

The image in figure 7.1 pictures Mrs. Obama as radical, conniving, and violent. In this image, she is unpalatable. Rejecting the mainstream option, her hair is afroed. Her smirk betrays both disloyalty and untrustworthiness. She is a gun-wielding separatist.[1]

The image in figure 7.3 depicts an angry, stern, and disciplinary black woman. The caption refers to Mrs. Obama as "Mrs. Grievance," a woman who complains about everything, especially race. She is unhappy, ornery, and believes that society owes her—everything. She, too, is unpalatable, notwithstanding her straight hair.

We begin with these images because, broadly framed, this chapter explores how the palatable Mrs. Obama and unpalatable Mrs. Obamas would fare as plaintiffs in an anti-discrimination lawsuit. What would their respective discrimination claims look like? Which would be the more sympathetic plaintiff? How would courts adjudicate their claims? These inquiries directly engage the extent to which judges

Figure 7.3 Michelle Obama on the cover of the *National Review*, April 21, 2008.
Source: © 2008 National Review, Inc. Reprinted by permission.

can and should employ the law to address Working Identity. Our starting point is
to imagine a small law firm that is deciding between two plaintiffs to represent—a
racially palatable plaintiff and racially unpalatable plaintiff. In thinking about the
likely success of both cases, the attorneys at the firm analyze the merits of each
plaintiff's claims through two models of discrimination: an assimilationist model
and a difference model. Both raise legal and normative questions. Conventional
wisdom would privilege the claim of the palatable Mrs. Obama to the less palatable ones. The thinking here is that only a racist firm would discriminate against
a "but for" black woman, a woman who is not stereotypically black. Such a firm
would discriminate against blacks per se—simply because they are black. The conventional wisdom holds that no jury or judge would sanction that form of discrimination. That is why the palatable Mrs. Obama would fare better in court than the
unpalatable ones. There are reasons to question this conventional wisdom.

***

Imagine that a small San Francisco law firm of self-described progressive attorneys is looking for a test case to illustrate the problems of discrimination in large

corporate law firms. The attorneys have narrowed the choice to two potential plaintiffs, both black, female senior associates at elite San Francisco law firms. While both associates received high performance ratings, both were also denied partnership. Subsequently, they filed lawsuits alleging race discrimination, and asked the attorneys at our hypothetical San Francisco firm to take their cases. For the most part, the firm accepts cases on a contingency basis—meaning, the firm's payment is contingent upon winning the case, creating an incentive for the firm to think carefully about which potential client's story will resonate with a judge or a jury. The attorneys at the firm are divided on the question of which case to pursue.

The first case involves Marlene, a graduate of Yale College, where she was on the squash team, and of Harvard Law School. Her parents are academics (one teaches at Tufts and the other at MIT), and she grew up in Concord, Massachusetts. At the firm, she was an active member of the recruiting committee and the training committee, and she could be counted on when emergency projects arose. Marlene was liked at the firm. Her senior colleagues considered her a team player. She had a reputation for professional appearance; both clients and her co-workers admired her understated but elegant Armani suits. Finally, Marlene and her husband Jeremy, an investment banker at Goldman Sachs, were frequent attendees at the firm's social functions. Most associates and many partners at the firm had assumed that Marlene would make partner. Indeed, five of the firm's three hundred or so partners sent her e-mail messages expressing disappointment with the firm's decision.

The second case involves Fay. Fay's parents are immigrants from Trinidad and Tobago. When Fay was twelve, they immigrated to New York. Fay grew up in Queens, where she spent her weekends helping at the family's roti restaurant. After completing her B.A. *summa cum laude* in ethnic studies at Hunter College, Fay attended Seton Hall Law School. There, she was an editor of the law review and a member of the moot court board. She graduated Seton Hall near the top of her class, and she was the only member of her graduating class to whom the firm extended an offer.

At the firm, Fay was an active member of the diversity committee. She was outspoken in urging the firm to hire more women, minorities, and students from less prestigious schools such as her alma mater. Fay was also known for her boisterous personality and exuberance. Her slight Caribbean accent was often commented upon as "cute," and her clothes were considered "funky." She insisted on wearing her hair in braids, despite comments from some senior women that this might be perceived as being unprofessional. She attended few of the firm's social functions, although she always played in softball games. The partners often commented on how well she got along with the predominantly "colored" support staff. "They interact like family members," was how one partner put it.

As noted, the attorneys at the Center are divided on which of the two cases to pursue.

The attorneys in favor of taking Marlene's case argue that it constitutes a perfect example of discrimination. *But for her race*, Marlene was just like the white associates the firm promoted. Based on her annual evaluations, she actually outperformed them. Moreover, she had attended the right schools, spoke with the right accent, got along with everyone, dressed in the right manner, and even laughed at the right jokes. The pro-Marlene attorneys argue that, given the foregoing, the only explanation for the negative vote on her candidacy is race: A significant number of the firm's partners were simply unwilling to vote for a black woman—any black woman, even a "really likable" and "really qualified" black woman like Marlene.[2]

The pro-Marlene attorneys argue, moreover, that there are difficulties with Fay's case that derive from the fact that law firm cultures promote assimilation of all, not just nonwhite, attorneys. That is, firms expect all their associates to make the effort to fit in. Firms harbor this expectation to promote efficiency and avoid costs; people with similar cultural practices and styles of self-presentation work better as a group and are more productive than people with dissimilar cultural and self-presentation practices. From this perspective, it makes sense for firms to establish and promote homogeneous workplace cultures.

The pro-Marlene attorneys reject the claim that cultural homogeneity is code for racism. They note the myriad race-neutral ways in which firms typically achieve homogeneity: by requiring their associates—white and nonwhite—to attend firm social events (to encourage collegiality and the building of team spirit), and, among other things, to dress and comport themselves in particular ways (to encourage professionalism). They argue that a legal decision-maker will likely conclude that this state of homogeneity is precisely what Fay's firm required of her. Framed this way, Fay's case is not about discrimination; it is about her refusal to comply with neutral workplace rules that are intended to achieve efficiency, promote professionalism, and encourage community. Fay's case presents a behavioral problem, not a racial one: Fay was not a team player. She chose to exist on the fringes, outside of the firm's culture. She chose not to fit in.

Marlene, on the other hand, is not vulnerable to this criticism, the pro-Marlene attorneys maintain. She was thoroughly integrated into the firm, fitted in, and both complied with and helped promote the cultural norms of the firm. As a result, the only possible explanation for the firm's decision to deny Marlene a promotion is her skin color. And discrimination on the basis of skin color is, in today's society, unacceptable.

The attorneys promoting Fay's case argue that Marlene's case is far from perfect. They agree that Marlene fit in well at the firm. She was "one of the boys" in the sense of practically being an Insider. The pro-Fay attorneys argue, however, that it is precisely Marlene's Insider status that makes her case a difficult one: Neither a jury nor a judge is going to want to believe that Marlene experienced discrimination. To do so, they would have to conclude that an elite San Francisco law firm is engaging in the crudest form of discrimination—one that makes no distinctions among black people, one that conflates "good" (i.e., non-stereotypical) and "bad" (i.e., stereotypical) blacks, discriminating against both. That form of discrimination is dead, particularly in the city of San Francisco, the most progressive urban center in America.

According to the pro-Fay attorneys, there is no good answer to the question of why a major metropolitan law firm would in effect discriminate against all blacks. Given the legal community's concern about the lack of racial and gender diversity at law firms—and particularly at the partnership ranks—there were strong incentives for the firm to promote Marlene. The most likely story regarding Marlene is that she just "fell through the cracks."[3] That happens all the time—to people with strong performance records and to white people as well. The pro-Fay attorneys further argue that it is simply implausible that the firm would have first embraced Marlene—that is, integrated her into the firm without regard to, or notwithstanding her race—and then denied her partnership because of her race. The incentives do not line up in Marlene's story. The pro-Fay attorneys argue that should the Center go forward with Marlene's case, the employer is likely to articulate something like the following defense:

> We never saw Marlene in racial terms. Quite the contrary. Marlene was one of us. She fit in well. She never engaged in identity politics. Unlike Jerome, another black associate at our firm, Marlene was not interested in promoting diversity; she even refused to work on the diversity committee, even though we asked her on multiple occasions. She believed in merit and we respected that. She transcended her race. To be perfectly honest, and I know this is going to sound silly, I never thought of Marlene as a black person. She was just "one of us." Everyone, as far as I can tell, liked her. Certainly, no one would have any reason to discriminate against her. The reasons she did not make partner have nothing to do with her race. Marlene simply did not build the kinds of relationships with the partners that one needs in order to make partner. She fell through the cracks. We regret what happened, but it was a function of the nature of today's large law firms and not of her race.[4]

According to the pro-Fay attorneys, precisely because Marlene fit in and became "one of us," the employer would be able to narrate a colorblind narrative in the rhetorical form we describe above.[5]

Fay, on the other hand, was not one of them. She did not fit in; she was an Outsider. Through her manner, decisions about dress, accent, hairstyle, and name,[6] Fay kept reminding the firm of her blackness. The pro-Fay attorneys hypothesize that the firm denied Fay a promotion because they perceived her to be "flaunting" her racial identity—that is, to be "out of the closet" about her non-assimilationist racial identity. Even more than her color, Fay's behavior signified blackness.

The pro-Fay attorneys are optimistic that a legal decision-maker could be persuaded that, given pervasive norms of non-discrimination and colorblindness, it is unlikely that institutions will discriminate based solely on racial phenotype. Today, to the extent that an institution wants to discriminate, they say, it will pay attention to the salience of its employees' racial identity and not simply to the phenotypic "fact" of race. Such an employer will make judgments about just how black, in a social or stereotypical sense, a phenotypically black employee appears to be based on perceived behavioral and Working Identity choices.

The pro-Fay attorneys argue that, if an employee's race is made salient by the choices the employee makes about (1) how to self-present within an institution or (2) whether to comply with the cultural norms of that institution, employers may conclude that the employee is overly committed to her race and racial identity. According to these attorneys, an employer's perception that an employee strongly identifies with being black activates negative racial stereotypes about what it means to be black. Their claim is that this happened to Fay: The firm perceived her to be too black; that perception activated negative stereotypes and made the partners uncomfortable; the firm attributed those stereotypes to Fay. Ultimately, the firm's discomfort with Fay's black Working Identity resulted in her being denied partnership.

In a sense, the debate between the attorneys about which of these two cases to take is about assimilation and homogeneity, on the one hand, and difference and heterogeneity, on the other hand. This debate invites us to think about two different models of discrimination—the assimilationist model and the difference model. From an anti-discrimination perspective, Marlene's and Fay's cases have different strengths and weaknesses depending on which of these two models a legal decision-maker employs.

The Assimilationist Model

The assimilationist model of discrimination posits race as phenotype. Under this view, a person's race is no more significant than the color of her eyes. The prototypical example of discrimination under this model is one in which (1) two employees—one white and one nonwhite—are similarly situated not only in terms of job performance, but also in terms of institutional identity (i.e., how well they fit in to the workplace culture), and (2) the institution prefers the white employee. In such a scenario, a judge or jury sees that, but for racial phenotype, the two employees are alike. That observation then becomes the basis for inferring that phenotypic difference caused the institution to prefer the white employee. The discrimination problem arises because, under the assimilationist model, that difference should not matter.

Marlene's claim of discrimination fits the assimilationist model. With respect to the schools she attended, her accent, her hair, her clothes, her social practices, and the committees on which she participated, Marlene was "just like" her white colleagues. Marlene did what she was supposed to do. She fit in. This notion of fit requires a nonwhite employee to send a signal to the employer that she will be palatably nonwhite. A judge or jury examining Marlene's case under the assimilationist model would conclude that Marlene provided that signal. She demonstrated that she was not a stereotypical black person. Through her workplace behavior and interactions, she established that she was unconventionally, and thus only phenotypically, black. Other than the color of her skin, there was no other way in which she was black. Since, under the assimilationist model, phenotypic blackness should be irrelevant to institutional decision-making, it was wrong for Marlene's law firm to discriminate against her. In effect, the assimilationist model rewards black employees who create a distance between themselves and common perceptions of blackness.

Fay's Case

With Fay, it cannot be said that, but for her phenotype, she was just like her white colleagues. Fay was different, and her workplace behavior manifested this difference. Under the assimilationist model, a judge or jury might observe that, controlling for Fay's race (that is, her phenotype), there were lots of differences between Fay and her white colleagues. Under this view, Fay and her colleagues were not similarly situated. Fay was different because she did not demonstrate a willingness to fit in. She never even tried. The judge or jury could conclude that, to the extent that one's capacity to fit in is a race-neutral criterion for promotion, it is a legitimate basis for an employment decision.

The Difference Model

The difference model of discrimination centers on a Working Identity, or performative, conception of race. Namely, that our racial understanding of people turns not only on the color of their skin but also on the perceived racial content of their self-presentation. Both Marlene and Fay could employ the difference model to advance their discrimination claims, though each would do so differently.

Under the difference model, Fay's basic argument would be that the firm draws a line between black people who do identity work to fit in at the firm and black people who do not perform such work, and that white associates are not subject to this sub-categorization and therefore are unfairly advantaged. There are three ways to make the point that this violates anti-discrimination law: (1) the sub-categorization constitutes a racial term and condition of employment; (2) it is a form of "race plus" discrimination; and (3) sub-categorizing reflects racial stereotyping. We do not present these arguments as fully worked-out doctrinal arguments. Instead, we introduce them as possible approaches courts can develop to address the discrimination reflected in Fay's case.

The terms and conditions of the employment argument is this: sub-categorizing black people based on those who do identity work and those who do not, constitutes the imposition of a race-based term and condition of employment.[7] An institution that draws such a distinction with respect to blacks would say:

> We hire only black people of a certain kind: black people who have a weak sense of racial identity and who eschew identity politics, black people who are assimilationist in political and social orientation, black people who are comfortable around, and who will not cause discomfort to, white people. In short, if you want a job at, or expect to do well within, this firm, you have to present yourself as a "good black."

The claim is that drawing intra-racial distinctions based on Working Identity is tantamount to establishing the racial terms upon which people will be hired or promoted. This alone would seem to violate anti-discrimination law. The problem is compounded if the plaintiff establishes that white people are not sub-categorized to the same degree based on the performance of their white racial identity. As such, they are not subject to racial terms and conditions of employment.

Applied to Fay, the argument would be that the employer denied Fay a promotion because she failed to perform the work of racial palatability, and that white people are not required to perform this work. To be clear: the fact that the employer might sub-categorize whites would not, without more, defeat Fay's claim. An analogy to gender discrimination is helpful. An employer probably could not defend its decision to hire only feminine women by asserting that it hires only masculine men. Although we concede that the law on stereotyping and discrimination is hardly clear—prior chapters should have demonstrated that—the foregoing strikes us as the type of argument that judges would see as too clever by half. In the same way, an employer's subcategorization of blacks doesn't escape anti-discrimination law simply because the employer also racially subcategorizes whites.

A second route Fay might take is to argue that identity performances constitute a form of "race plus" discrimination. Recall from chapter 5 that in the context of gender discrimination claims, courts have said that employers may not subcategorize women based on gender plus some "other characteristic" where the other characteristic is (a) a fundamental right, (b) an immutable characteristic, or (c) a significant burden on only one sex that deprives that sex of employment opportunities.[8]

The "sex plus" regime provides a basis for arguing that identity performances implicate Title VII. The claim would be that discrimination based on identity performance constitutes "race plus" discrimination, the "plus" here being the employee's Working Identity. One difficulty with this argument is that "performance" is neither a fundamental right nor an immutable characteristic. A phenotypically black person, for example, does not have a right to express that blackness in any manner whatsoever. Recall the *Rogers* case from earlier chapters. There, the court concluded that it was permissible for American Airlines to prohibit a black female employee from wearing a braided hairstyle to work. In reaching this conclusion, the court rejected the notion that braided hair was an important way for black women to express their identity.

Moreover, a court might conclude that expressions of identity are mutable, reflecting individual choice on the part of the employee.[9] *Rogers* is again instructive on this point in that the court made clear that a braided hairstyle was not an immutable aspect of racial identity. While it is difficult to articulate a racial performance claim that satisfies the fundamental right criterion, the immutability hurdle is surmountable if it is kept in mind that the performance is always interpreted through the lens of phenotypic race, which is considered an immutable characteristic. For a more concrete indication of how this argument might work, consider the following hypothetical.

Assume we have a firm with a number of senior partners who hold stereotypical views of racial minorities. The firm is located in Manhattan and recruits most of its attorneys from the top ten law schools. Although the firm's leaders have discriminatory views, they are also institutionally committed to hiring at least some blacks. This is because hiring no blacks would create a public relations problem for the firm. It would call into question the firm's public image as an equal-opportunity employer, send the wrong signals to prospective employees and clients, and so on.

Jelani, a black man, applies for a position as an associate at this firm. Because this firm does not have a per se rule of racial discrimination, it is possible that the firm will hire Jelani. Should the firm not hire him, it will not be because Jelani is black in a phenotypic sense. (Remember, the firm is committed to hiring some black people.) Instead, the decision will be based on the kind of black person the firm perceives Jelani to be (a "good black" or a "bad black"). That, in turn, would be based on Jelani's Working Identity. In this sense, Jelani's vulnerability to discrimination at the firm turns on his phenotypic blackness "plus" his Working Identity.

Under this theory, Jelani's phenotype constitutes the "race" of the "race plus" argument we are advancing. Recall from chapter 1 that a person can perform racial comfort (and become a "good black") or racial discomfort (and become a "bad black"). Fay would argue that while it is true that these performances are not immutable, their linkage to phenotype (which courts have said is immutable) might be enough to satisfy the immutability basis upon which one can make an identity "plus" argument.

The "race plus" argument is both normatively and theoretically problematic. Not only does this theory privilege a phenotypic conception of race, it also relies on the idea that immutability is an important factor in deciding whether a trait or a behavior receives anti-discrimination protection. These foundations of the "race plus" theory are shaky; race has never been fully determined by phenotype (think, for example, about the phenomenon of blacks passing as white) and what is and is not immutable is necessarily value-laden (think about the ways in which people employ technology to quite literally change their bodies). In settling for this "race plus" theory, then, we do not mean to endorse it. The point is to illustrate the extent to which the theory might be available to plaintiffs like Fay.

Under the difference model of discrimination, still a third theory available to Fay is stereotyping.[10] This theory is based on *Price Waterhouse*, which we discussed in chapter 5. There are a number of ways in which Fay could frame her anti-stereotyping theory. Fay could argue that, like Hopkins in the *Price Waterhouse* case, her employer was asking her to work her identity in specific ways. Price Waterhouse was asking Hopkins to act feminine; Fay's firm was in effect asking her to "act white." Additionally, she could assert that her performance of blackness made her racially salient and triggered negative stereotypes about black people that the employer attributed to her. Fay could claim that that attribution occurred at least in part because she was unwilling to work her identity to prove that those racial stereotypes did not apply to her.

There are a couple of flies in the buttermilk here. First, *Price Waterhouse* is a gender discrimination case. And the logic in gender discrimination cases does not always migrate easily to the race context. Second, assuming doctrinal migration, it is not clear that a court would read *Price Waterhouse* aggressively enough to reach racial Working Identity claims. If the Ninth Circuit was unwilling to extend *Price Waterhouse* to *Jespersen*—recall that in that case a casino required its female bartenders to wear makeup—there is little reason to think that a court would extend the theory to cover Fay's case. This is especially so if one believes that the reason *Price Waterhouse* found in Ann Hopkins's favor is because the partners at the firm held assumptions about how men and women behave and self-present, and imposed benefits and burdens based on whether female and male employees worked their identities consistent with those assumptions. Under this view, the firm fired Hopkins because she did not work her gender in line with the firm's assumption about how women should self-present. The parallel dynamic in the racial context would be that Fay's firm denied her partnership because she failed to "act black." However, in Fay's case, the firm is not expecting her to conform to the stereotypical notion of blackness. Instead, the firm wants her to do the reverse: that is, to negate the stereotypical image of blackness. If *Price Waterhouse* is understood to apply only to contexts where the plaintiff is being asked to perform a stereotypical Working Identity, then Fay loses. We think that is a rather strained reading of *Price Waterhouse*. An easier way for a judge to dispose of Fay's case would be say that *Price Waterhouse* is a gender discrimination case and that it does not apply in the race context.

Consider now Marlene's arguments under the difference model. Her claim would be that the firm required her to demonstrate racial palatability and to perform racial comfort. This theory does not turn on whether the firm promoted Marlene. Marlene's theory is that, because she is not white, she had to do extra identity work to fit in and to counter existing negative stereotypes of black women. As discussed in chapter 1, there are a number of ways a black employee might try to fit in. The employee might laugh in response to, or engage in racist humor (signaling collegiality). She might socialize with her colleagues after work (signaling that she is comfortable hanging out with and being "one of the boys"). She might avoid contact with other black employees (signaling that she is not really "one of them"). The list goes on. The point is that whatever comfort strategy Marlene employs, her aim will be to make her supervisors and colleagues comfortable with her racial identity.

Marlene might argue that because she is black, there was greater pressure for her to perform comfort strategies than her white counterparts because those colleagues do not have to worry about negative racial stereotypes about whites that would disadvantage them in the corporate context. Marlene would argue that every interaction required her to negotiate her race so as to not create racial discomfort. She would assert that this constitutes work that whites simply did not have to perform and that required her to distance herself from her sense of racial identity.[11]

Implications: Choosing a Model

With respect to race, the assimilationist model dominates in anti-discrimination law. We have not located any race discrimination cases that use the difference model. Our construction of this model is primarily based on the gender anti-stereotyping cases. The normative question is whether the approach reflected in these cases should be extended to racial discrimination claims. Asked another way, which model of discrimination should drive how courts decide race discrimination claims? One way to engage these questions is to compare the costs of choosing either model.

Assimilation Costs: Choosing Marlene's Case

There are at least three costs of choosing the assimilationist model, which we call skimming, cloning, and laboring. We can see how they play out by returning to the firm's dilemma over which case to take.

To choose Marlene's case is to construct a discrimination theory around the most-privileged members of Outsider groups—those with the most economic and cultural capital, and those who have the resources and the capacity to be the same as, or fit within, the Insider group. In this way, the assimilationist model performs a kind of racial skimming. If we assume that anti-discrimination is meant to be progressive, protecting those most in need, this outcome is anomalous.

The anomaly becomes more apparent if we think of law as a corrective tool for a particular kind of market failure—white racial preferences—which derive, at least in part, from a firm's interest in (racial) sameness or homogeneity. Against the backdrop of that interest, firms that feel pressured to pursue diversity are likely to hire and promote people like Marlene, not Fay. This is not to say that Marlene is invulnerable to discrimination. The point instead is that in a market structured by the norm of sameness, Marlene's vulnerability is less than Fay's. If the goal of anti-discrimination law is to counter the market pressures for employers to discriminate, this argues against investing scarce enforcement resources on the Marlenes rather than the Fays.

There are normative reasons why one might not want the assimilationist model. As its name suggests, the model creates incentives for people to assimilate. It requires outsiders to be, like Marlene, homogenized. Understood in this way, the assimilationist model is a means to clone racially palatable outsiders.[12] This is because homogeneity norms create both a demand for, and a supply of, Outsiders who can fit within predominantly white workplace cultures. This "market" production of palatability is not about producing Insiders. Because of the need for institutions to maintain some degree of difference to appear legitimate, employers do not want Outsiders who completely transcend their outsider identity or who pass for Insiders. They want outsiders who are palatable but who are recognizable as Outsiders.

The assimilationist model requires non-whites to engage in a form of racial labor that their white co-workers do not have to do. It requires Outsiders to work their identities to remove self-presentational and perceived (cultural) evidence of racial difference. Under this model, only phenotypic difference is allowed. In other words, non-whites are not expected to change their skin color, only the underlying content of their character.[13] The labor of identity work is ongoing and becomes more burdensome as outsiders move up the professional ladder to more homogenized environments.

Difference Costs: Choosing Fay's Case

Yet there are costs to choosing the difference model as well. We discuss four under the following rubrics: inefficiencies, (2) racial determination problems, (3) race as culture, and (4) authenticity.

Inefficiencies result from restricting managers from pursuing homogeneity. The more alike people perceive themselves to be, the more comfortable they are working together in teams. The more comfortable people are working with each other the more efficient they are inclined to be. This is the sense in which "difference" can produce inefficiency. As we discuss in the next chapter, these inefficiencies are real, even if they exist only over the short-term.[14]

Problems of racial determinacy also caution against the difference model. Race as phenotype is easy for judges and juries to understand. Few people, for example, would quarrel with the idea that Michael Jordan, the basketball great, is black. But what does it mean to say that a person has a salient black racial identity? How would we know? Is Michael Jordan "really" black, "really, really" black, or "not really" black at all? Do we want judges making these kinds of determinations? A Working Identity conception of race presents racial determination problems that are not presented by a phenotypic conception of race.[15]

Still a third cost relates to culture. Does a performative conception of race misconceive race as culture? Does it seek "to defend certain practices and expressions because they are subjectively important to an individual's or a group's sense of self?"[16] Is it the case that this defense obscures the profound and consequential ways in which race operates structurally?

Finally, there is a danger that a Working Identity understanding of race will entrench particular expressions of identity.[17] Concretely, to say that a firm discriminated against Fay because she acted black risks establishing—as a matter of law—what it means to be black based on the conduct in which Fay engaged.

At the end of the day, the choice between the assimilationist and difference models is a difficult one. The assimilationist model represents the classical notion of discrimination—two candidates, one white and one black—are equal in every respect save the color of their skin. If the black candidate is consistently disfavored, this is good evidence of discrimination. After all, blackness appears to be the only difference between the two candidates. The problem is that the model might be outdated. It does not account for the fact that most institutions today *want* to hire and promote at least some blacks. In legal terms, this suggests that the "prima facie case" in discrimination law might be misleading to the extent that it is predicated on firms hiring whites over black.

Does the foregoing mean that discrimination is a thing in the past? Not at all. Instead, discrimination is increasingly taking an intra-racial form. It behooves courts to look for intra-racial discrimination, and not just the interracial discrimination. But perhaps the answer to the problem resides outside of the courts. After all, corporate workplaces are more diverse today than they have ever been. This might suggest that we should focus our efforts on persuading people of color at the top of the corporate hierarchy to help those on the bottom. Such an approach seems less messy, less controversial, and likely more effectual than having courts weigh in on the degrees of blackness of particular plaintiffs. Our next chapter explores whether this intuition is right. It explores whether it is reasonable to expect black corporate leaders and senior employees to "lift as they climb."

Acting White to Help Other Blacks

Every year *Ebony* magazine publishes its "Power 150" edition, which includes a ranking of powerful African Americans. Immediately after Obama's 2008 presidential win, *Ebony*'s Power 150 issue featured a photograph of several prominent members of the Obama administration, including Valerie Jarrett, a senior advisor and assistant to the President for Public Engagement and Intergovernmental Affairs. (See figure 8.1.) The story accompanying the image of these high profiles African American leaders read: "Brought together by *Ebony* magazine on the White House grounds..., they are part of a team put together by the President

Figure 8.1 Valerie Jarrett
Source: Kris Connor/Getty Images.

to carry forth his vision for the country." For *Ebony*, this was a "historic collection of dynamic advisers—12, the most African Americans ever in such high
powered positions within the White House." According to the article, "no other
President has had more blacks throughout his top staff." In this sense, "it was
obvious that change has already come to the nation's capital."

Implicit in the *Ebony* article is the idea that Obama's presence at the top of
the political hierarchy produces benefits for black people further down the ladder. *Ebony's* focus on the number of African Americans within Obama's inner
circle suggests that Obama is "lifting as he climbs." Presumably, *Ebony* was also
suggesting that those in that inner circle would also transmit benefits to those
further down. They, too, would "lift" and not just "climb."

The belief that blacks should "lift as we climb" has deep roots. The expression
originated as a slogan of the National Association of Colored Women's Clubs in
the late nineteenth century to facilitate racial uplift.[1] The first president of the club,
Mary Church Terrell, expressed a version of the idea this way: "And so, lifting as we
climb, onward and upward we go, struggling and striving, and hoping that the buds
and blossoms of our desires will burst into glorious fruition."[2] Terrill employed
the expression "to refer to the commitments of club members to lift each other
socially, economically, and spiritually."[3] The idea continues to have currency today.
Organizations, like the National Association of Black Accountants, employ the "lift
as we climb" command as their institutional motto. Moreover, there is the sense
across different sectors of the black community that African Americans would be
in a better social and economic position if "each one brings one."

But how realistic is it to expect black corporate executives to "lift as they climb"?
Will senior black managers help junior black employees enter the corporate landscape and move up its corporate hierarchy? Can these managers eliminate or mitigate Working Identity problems? The question is important. As a society, and as
sub-communities within it, we make choices about where to invest our scarce
resources to enhance equal opportunity. If we believe, for example, that most African
Americans in positions of power will "lift as they climb," we should find ways to get
more African Americans on the top of various hierarchies. But if we are less san-
guine about that possibility, we should perhaps expend our resources elsewhere.

Because the notion that black people "lift as they climb" has intuitive appeal,
this chapter first sets out the basis for that intuition. We describe several benefits
that, in theory, flow from having African Americans in senior management position. We then set forth some reasons for skepticism. Although these benefits
apply to a variety of public and private sector institutions, for the sake of simplicity, we use corporations and law firms as examples.

There are a number of potential related benefits that "trickle down" from
having African Americans at the top of the corporate hierarchy. For one thing,

the success of minorities at the top could help to negate or diminish racial stereotypes that blacks are lazy or incompetent. For another, the presence of senior black executives could cause white corporate managers to monitor their racial interactions and institutional decision-making for bias. In addition, African Americans in management positions could facilitate cooperation among racial groups within the corporation and help to reduce tokenism. Finally, senior racial minorities could serve as role models for and provide mentoring to their junior minority associates. We discuss these theoretical "trickle down" benefits in turn, beginning with the negation of racial stereotypes.

To understand why one might frame the negation of racial stereotypes as a "trickle down" benefit, we should remind you that a key assumption of our book is that much discrimination today derives from stereotypes (for example, "blacks are lazy") rather than explicit racial animosity (for example, "we hate black people").[4] If that is the case, it makes sense for corporations seeking to improve the racial climate of their workplace to try to negate those stereotypes. One strategy might be to promote minorities to senior positions. The theory is that the simple fact of minority success will disrupt negative stereotypes about work ethic and competence. If Johnny, who is black and male, makes his way to the top, his success sends a message—Johnny has the capacity to lead a corporation, and so do other black men.[5] The effect of such messages is to increase the likelihood that the corporation will promote not only Johnny but other junior black men.

African American success provides another, more subtle, type of stereotype negation. Some social psychologists now believe that African Americans underperform when they perceive the risk that a negative performance will confirm racial stereotypes.[6] The standard example is black students scoring poorly on standardized tests because of the concern that their performance will confirm stereotypes about black intellectual inferiority. Claude Steele and others attribute this phenomenon to "stereotype threat." The presence of successful African Americans could reduce this threat in at least two ways. First, junior African Americans could conclude from the presence of successful black executives that the corporation is racially tolerant and that the corporate culture is not corrupted by negative racial stereotypes. Second, the success of senior African American executives could suggest that the corporate leaders, at this firm, do not interpret the mistakes of African Americans as a confirmation of racial stereotypes. To the extent that junior African Americans respond to the success of African American executives and managers in either or both of these ways, they will experience less of a stereotype threat. In this rosy portrait, the presence of successful African American employees at the top of the corporate hierarchy will make the African Americans at the bottom perform their jobs more effectively.

Consider now the monitoring benefits that potentially "trickle down" from the presence of black managers and senior executives. Imagine a law firm that has been asked to represent a conservative organization seeking to dismantle affirmative action. Theoretically, the presence of some black partners on that firm's executive committee, which decides which cases to take, produces two monitoring effects. First, white members of the executive committee will engage the issue of whether to take the case with the awareness that what they say may offend their black colleagues. The tone and substance of the conversation will be shaped by the perception that the black partners present are monitoring the conversation for evidence of racial insensitivity or intolerance. Second, the presence of black executives could also influence whether the partners ultimately accept the case. If the white partners fear that it will anger or alienate their black colleagues, they might decide that it is against their long-term institutional interests to take the case.

Monitoring effects can occur at other institutional moments as well; for example, during firm meetings about hiring and promotions. The presence of African Americans on the hiring and promotion committees might cause white members of the committee to monitor their speech so as to avoid making arguments that explicitly or implicitly reflect racial stereotypes or that are otherwise inappropriate.[7] Conduct on the part of the black managers can intensify this monitoring.[8] If a black member of the firm's executive committee explicitly speaks out against the firm taking an anti-affirmative action case, white partners may be even more careful about how they discuss the issue—and less likely to take the case.[9]

The presence of black corporate leaders might also produce racial accountability: white decision-makers having to account for institutional decisions that negatively affect nonwhites. Consider a firm that is contemplating extending offers to ten white attorneys fresh out of law school and none to minorities. The accountability costs of the firm doing so are directly related to the number of black lawyers, particularly partners, there are at the firm. The more black lawyers in leadership positions at the firm, the more difficult and costly it will be for the firm to "account" for an entering class of associates with no black attorneys. The presence of blacks, and of people of color, increases the pressure on the firm to justify a process that produces an all-white entering class. That justification could require additional meetings to discuss the matter as well as reports that describe the firm's current and historical hiring procedures and the diversity such practices have (or have) yielded. Meetings and reports of this sort take time and resources. Moreover, conversations about race are difficult to have at a firm-wide level. They can generate hurt feelings and cause fault lines within the firm. The greater the number of black people in leadership positions, and the smaller the number of African Americans hired, the more vulnerable the firm is to incurring the foregoing costs.

The presence of African American senior managers can also facilitate team-work, which is important because most corporate labor is performed in teams. Whether a team is successful depends in part on whether team members trust each other. The more trust, the more efficient the team; the more efficient the team, the more successful individual team members are likely to be within the corporation. Race can be a barrier to establishing team trust. Blacks may question whether their white colleagues really want to work with them; whites may wonder whether blacks can be trusted to suppress their racial identity commit-ments for the greater good of the team.

Blacks in leadership positions can reduce racial distrust and facilitate racial cooperation. Black managers and executives can provide input into the forma-tion of teams to maximize opportunities for racial cooperation and minimize the likelihood of racial tensions and anxieties. Also, the presence of senior black man-agers might suggest to whites that blacks can work effectively in teams and can be trusted. Blacks, for their part, might conclude from senior black presence that racial cooperation is possible. In short, the greater the presence of senior black employees, the greater the likelihood that blacks and whites will be more trusting of each other.

Related to trust is comfort. The more comfortable African Americans are within an institution and the more comfortable their co-workers are with them, the more likely African Americans are to succeed. Here, too, the presence of African Americans in leadership positions can be helpful. People are generally most comfortable working with others who are like them. The more different a black person is perceived to be, the more discomfort her identity produces. Think back to our discussion of Marlene and Fay in chapter 7. The successes of senior black managers reduce the likelihood that the junior executives will be perceived as different. Whites at the firm might conclude that if, for example, Lee, Phillip and Brenda, each of whom are black partners, fitted in, integrated themselves within the workplace, and worked their way up the corporate lad-der, the juniors can do the same. The more black success stories within the firm, the more comfortable whites are likely to be around the junior black employees. And the more comfortable white employees are with the black juniors, the less these juniors will have to work their identities, or supply what we called in chap-ter 1 "racial comfort" to fit in.

Role modeling and combating tokenism are two additional benefits that potentially flow from the presence of senior African American executives. The role modeling argument is typically linked to a more general argument for diversity.[10] Driving this argument is the view that one possible barrier to black people moving up the hierarchy is the difficulty of imagining themselves there.[11] The greater the black under-representation at the top of the hierarchy, the more

difficult the racial imagining. This claim is less about what people of color do at
the top of the corporation and more about the fact that they are there. Whille the
Supreme Court has disapproved of the idea that the benefits of role modeling
can justify affirmative action,[12] many still believe that. The basic insight is that
the presence of African Americans at the top of the corporate hierarchy sends
a positive message to African Americans at the bottom that they, too, can reach
the top.

Sometimes scholars and policy makers frame this diversity argument in terms
of combating tokenism. Tokenism refers to instances in which a firm hires few
people of color and does little to integrate them into the firm's culture.[13] Whether
or not a firm's reasons for practicing tokenism are illegitimate, firms that engage
in tokenism have a ready-made anti-discrimination defense: "It is true that most
of our associates are white. However, it is not true that we discriminate against
blacks. We hired Byron, an African American male, last year, and we hope that
we will hire more people like Byron in the future."

Tokenism burdens African Americans (and all people of color) in three ways.
First, it burdens the token with the weight of representing his race. The cost of
the token's failure is imposed not simply on him but on his race (here, black
people) as a whole.[14] Second, tokenism limits autonomy. To the extent that
the token believes he is representing his race, he does not feel free to interact
with whomever he pleases in the workplace. For example, Byron, the African
American executive, might avoid interacting with administrative support staff
out of fear that he will racially represent black managers as being more comfortable with the "low level" (black) workers than with "high level" (white) executives. With greater numbers of blacks at the workplace, Byron might feel both
less pressure to assimilate with the majority group and greater comfort expressing himself. A third problem is that tokenism might cause the token to question
whether he belongs within the institution, particularly given assumptions within
his workplace that blacks do not fit in as corporate executives. Why else would
he be alone at the top?

The success of the first generation (many of whom were likely tokens) and
their presence at the top of corporate hierarchies reduces the racial representation
burdens of later-generation employees. The conduct of the later group of employees will be less racially representative, giving these employees greater autonomy
to navigate the workplace and a greater sense of entitlement and belonging.

A final benefit that that theoretically derives from black executives at the top
of the corporation is information-sharing and networking. To succeed within
most large bureaucratic organizations, new employees must gain access to tacit
information about both the organization (for example, who are the power brokers within the institution) and the job (e.g., how to communicate with clients).[15]

Such information is often conveyed through personal interactions. This means that senior executives and managers have to take junior employees under their wing. Ideally, senior employees "group mentor" junior employees, providing a network of information for juniors.[16] This network then gives juniors knowledge about the institution, its governance structure, and power brokers.

The reason African Americans typically do not have access to this institutional knowledge is complicated; the problem is not simply conscious racial bias or dislike.[17] Part of it may be that mentorship resources are allocated to those with whom the mentors are most comfortable, and these will tend to be juniors of their same race and gender.[18] Moreover, tacit information is often conveyed in informal settings—settings in which people are relatively comfortable engaging in office gossip about the ins and outs of workplace politics. African Americans may have limited access to these settings, again because after-work socialization might tend to be same-race.[19]

First-generation blacks who succeeded, for example, probably did so despite minimal access to networks. In some cases their successes were a result of skill, in other cases it was luck, and in still other cases there was some non-black senior employee who was willing to reach out.[20] The presence and success of the first generation means that succeeding generations will have access to at least a minimal amount of mentorship and networks, reducing the need to rely on exceptional skill, luck, benevolence, and outside connections.

Those Most Likely to Succeed

Taken together, the foregoing "trickle down" benefits from the successes of first-generation African Americans at the top of the corporation should provide greater opportunities for black employees at the bottom. But whether junior African Americans actually experience these benefits depends on whether successful black executives and managers deploy their positions to both change corporate culture and to extend opportunities. There is reason to doubt that they will do so. The African Americans who succeed in climbing the corporate ladder tend to be (a) risk-takers, (b) lucky, and (c) overconfident. Remember, the odds are against them; these characteristics help them beat the odds. But these same characteristics may also increase the likelihood that the African Americans who ascend the corporate hierarchy will pull their ladder up behind them when they arrive at the top. In other words, the "trickle down" benefits might be more illusory than real.

Consider risk-taking first. We have seen that black employees have an incentive to work their identities to counteract the negative stereotype about competence. One way they can do this is to take on high-risk tasks, tasks that are beyond their skill level and that have the potential to make them stand out among their peers. When performed successfully, high-risk tasks can yield high returns. Successfully completing a difficult project that people with low levels of experience do not usually attempt might catch the attention of the corporate leaders and cause them to rethink their racial assumptions. African Americans seeking advancement have a big incentive to perform just such high-risk strategies. But they need luck to succeed because the odds are against them.

This is not necessarily the case for whites. Because whites are not subject to negative stereotypes, they will experience less pressure to take on high-risk assignments. If we assume that whites and African Americans are in a competitive race, one way for African Americans to gain a competitive edge, or at least mitigate a racial disadvantage, is to perform high-risk tasks.

Successful risk-taking helps explain a subset of African American corporate success, but another factor also plays a role: overconfidence. If the firm attributes an employee's successful risk-taking to luck, it probably will not promote that employee. Nor is it likely to look favorably upon excessive risk-taking behavior, if it leads to failures for the firm. Consequently, the employee who is seeking to outperform her colleagues cannot stop at taking higher-risk gambles. She must also be able to persuade the firm's decision-makers that the successes that result from these gambles were earned and not the product of luck. Excessively self-confident African Americans will be more persuasive on this score. The firm will perceive these employees to be "authentic" in their claim that their success was a function of talent, not luck. In sum, risk-taking, luck, and overconfidence together affect whether African Americans will ascend the corporate hierarchy.

Realizing the Trickle-Down Benefits

Given the characteristics we have attributed to African Americans at the top of the corporation, there is reason to believe that they will not provide the trickle-down benefits to junior minority workers. Plus, there are barriers that prevent them from doing so, including, but not limited to, stereotype negation.

Stereotype Negation

Senior African American managers and executives can negate stereotypes at the group level (through strategies that signal that blacks as a group are not lazy) or at the individual level (through strategies that signal that the particular senior black manager is not lazy). As we will explain, seniors have a greater incentive to perform individualized stereotype negation strategies than group negation strategies. The former, unfortunately, do little to improve the advancement opportunities of junior minorities. Imagine that Terrance, an African American, is interested in convincing the decision-makers at his firm that African Americans are not lazy, that they are just as hardworking as whites. Assume that he is present at one of the firm's hiring meetings, where all the attorneys weigh in on who the firm should hire. One way for Terrance to demonstrate that African Americans are not lazy is to remind his colleagues of the subtle ways in which stereotypes work and to urge them to be vigilant about not incorporating stereotypes into their decision-making. This need not be done in a confrontational manner. Terrance might even use humor to raise the racial consciousness of his colleagues.

This kind of direct intervention—speaking out about racial stereotypes in the context of a hiring meeting—is not likely to occur, however. As explained in chapter 2, hiring meetings are high-visibility events in which one's institutional identity is salient. Recall now the composite of the people of color who are most likely to ascend the corporate hierarchy; these people will probably be overconfident about their abilities, be willing to take high levels of risk, and be able to credibly demonstrate an affinity for the dominant group. Recall also the description of the modern corporation in earlier chapters—complex hierarchies with decentralization. These features of contemporary corporate cultures render high-visibility moments few and far between. They are occasions, therefore, in which an incentive exists for employees, especially non-white employees, to behave in ways that positively construct their *individual* workplace identity. This incentive makes the hiring meeting an inopportune time for Terrance to confront authority—even via humor.[21] Terrance will want to use the hiring meeting instead to bolster his reputation as an affable but tough African American who is loyal to the firm and committed to its institutional projects.

One might ask why Terrance's risk-taking tendencies would not make him likely to intervene. Being silent during a hiring meeting in which stereotyping could limit opportunities for African Americans hardly seems like something a risk-taker would do. But note that Terrance takes risks with respect to his own job assignments, not on overall institutional politics. He engages in risk-taking to the extent that he perceives a stereotype negation payoff. And none seems to flow from admonishing his colleagues to avoid using stereotypes. This suggests that Terrance has two choices: (1) silence, passive conduct that leaves his racially affable identity intact, or (2) speaking out against the racial stereotyping, active conduct with the potential to disrupt his "positive" racial image. However,

Terrance has a third option: to subtly sanction his colleagues' utilization of stereotypes. In the context of the meeting, he might say something like:

> Some of you have expressed concerns about the small number of peo-
> ple of color—especially African Americans—in the pool. One of you
> made the point that we cannot have another year in which we fail to hire
> at least one African American. As a black person myself and a member
> of this firm for over twelve years, I would certainly like to see others of
> us at this firm. But I don't think we should lower our standards, and I
> don't think we should be paternalistic. Let's not forget that, up until
> two years ago, there were three other African Americans in this firm.
> Two left to pursue other opportunities, and one was denied partnership
> for good reason. He simply was not a team-player, and he did not have
> the best work ethic. That's not a bad racial record. Could it be better?
> Perhaps. I would need to do some more thinking about it. To be clear:
> none of this is to say that we should ignore the possibility that our hir-
> ing process results in fewer minorities at the firm. What I am suggesting
> is that there is no indication here that this is the case. From where I sit,
> then, I think we should stop beating ourselves up about this. I say all of
> this as an African American who is deeply concerned about the well-
> being of African Americans inside and outside of this firm.

Terrance's speaking out in this way solidifies his image as a team player who is
loyal to the institution, invested in merit, and willing to subordinate racial group
identity politics for the good of the firm. His colleagues could read his comments
to say, with respect to hiring, the firm is doing nothing wrong; to the extent that
there are few African Americans at the firm, that is because of a pool problem,
the limited number of qualified African Americans, not a racial discrimination
problem. If so, Terrance will have demonstrated to his white colleagues in power
that (a) even in the context of African American under-representation at the firm,
he will not play the race card, and (b) he subscribes to the meritocratic nature
of the firm's decision-making.[22] Importantly, none of this challenges Terrance's
authenticity as an African American. At no time does he disidentify with the
identity category "black" or with the idea of race or racial organization. Terrance
is not speaking in the voice of colorblindness or post racialism. He says expressly
that race matters to him.

Terrance's subtle intervention could signal an even stronger commitment
to the firm and a weaker commitment to racial group identification. Terrance
could make the point that, given affirmative action, it is particularly important
to pay attention to the institution's standards when hiring minorities. This might
translate into Terrance applying a higher level of scrutiny to minority applicants;

he may insist that marginal minority candidates not be hired, even when marginal candidates from other groups are hired. This strategy could potentially allay concerns about Terrance's institutional commitment, on the one hand, and racial group loyalty, on the other. But it also provides those colleagues with an external justification for their negative actions regarding minority issues. For example, it is a lot easier for a law firm to defend some egregiously discriminatory position being advanced by a client if it is able to assert that its minority lawyers insisted, on the grounds of principle, that they not deny that client representation. Along similar lines, it would help the firm defend a discrimination case filed by a former employee of color if the people who led the charge for the denial of promotion were themselves members of a minority group.

Whether Terrance would go so far as to lead the charge against hiring another African American is not clear. What is clear is that there is little incentive for him to employ an interventionist strategy to negate racial stereotypes at the group level. That strategy carries the cost of disrupting the impression of him as the "good" black; the one with standards who also happens to be a good institutional citizen.

A different way for Terrance to negate racial stereotypes might be through his own work performance. Specifically, the quantity and quality of Terrance's work may suggest to the firm's decision-makers not only that Terrance is a smart, hardworking, and conscientious worker but also that these characteristics apply to African Americans as a group. Terrance's work performance might well be outstanding enough to send that signal. But, if Terrance is perceived to be exceptional—a superstar—or even just good, the firm might engage in exceptionalism. The firm could tell itself: "Terrance may be a black, but he is not like other African Americans. The stereotypes we hold about African Americans should not be applied to Terrance." Under this narrative, the firm may engage in "racial exceptionalism," a phenomenon we discussed in chapter 1.

Assuming that Terrance is not a superstar, he can still attempt to negate group-based stereotypes through the choices he makes about work. Terrance can be even more high-risk with respect to work assignments than he otherwise would be. The problem with this strategy is that the greater Terrance's risk-taking, the greater the possibility of failure that would confirm, rather than disrupt, racial stereotypes. The problem is compounded if other African Americans (or other minorities) in the firm also adopt this strategy. The failure rate of the group will rise, creating the overall impression that African Americans or minorities are irrational and rash. The end result is an exacerbation rather than an elimination of negative racial presumptions.

Another problem with group-based negation strategies that rely on work performance is that most jobs do not involve tasks where each employee's production can be separated and ranked against that of others. Many high-level jobs tend to involve production in teams and have fuzzy individual outputs. This limits the extent to which one individual can, through the quality of his work, challenge racial stereotypes at the group level. Often, the best individuals can do is to preempt the application of the negative stereotype to themselves. Returning to Terrance, although his work performance may rebut assumptions about *his* competence and work ethic, his effect on negative assumptions about his group, at best, will be minuscule. Terrance's incentives, even assuming that he cares about remedying perceptions of his group, will be to focus on altering perceptions of him, not the group.

Given both the cost and difficulty of negating stereotypes at the group level, African Americans will rationally focus on remedying stereotypes at the individual level. We discussed one barrier to fixing group perceptions: racial exceptionalism. There is also another, more problematic barrier. If Terrance's individual stereotype-negation strategy takes the form of distancing himself from his racial group, it can exacerbate rather than ameliorate negative stereotypes about African Americans as a group. Assume, for example, that Terrance informs his majority colleagues that he is frustrated with the low standards of work among other minorities in the firm and their failure to act as team players.[23] This hardly seems to be the kind of stereotype-negation strategy that will "trickle down" to benefit other people of color and blacks in particular.

But what about other "trickle down" benefits? Recall the assumption that the presence of successful minorities will have the effect of racially monitoring the institution. The assumption is that when making decisions white colleagues will be more conscious of racial issues in the presence of their successful minority colleagues than they would in their absence. This monitoring effect could impact both the firm's labor-market decisions, including those relating to promotion and hiring, and its other interactions with the outside world, including choices about what products to manufacture and how to market them. The question is how plausible are these racial monitoring assumptions?

Imagine that Terrance has been promoted to partner. Assume that hiring decisions are made by partners, that Terrance is about to participate in his first hiring meeting, and that he is only one of two minorities present. Will Terrance's presence have a monitoring effect? There are reasons to expect otherwise. First, Terrance has likely participated in numerous firm socialization rituals (including firm-wide meetings) in which he provided racial comfort. Terrance's very success within the firm could have derived from his ability to supply racial comfort, negate racial stereotypes, and present himself as a racially palatable African American. Members of the partnership, then, would not feel racially policed by Terrance's presence. His past Working Identity would have signaled to those partners that Terrance is not a troublemaker, does not play the race card, and is "one of the boys."

Second, if this is Terrance's first partnership meeting about hiring, he has an incentive to use the moment to assure his partners that his status as a partner will not change his institutional or racial identity. Terrance might view this meeting as a moment in which he, as a partner, needs to solidify positive perceptions about his institutional fit, loyalty, and team orientation.[24] Further, he will want to find ways to convey the idea that he is not interested in disrupting the selection and socialization processes that (racially) produced him. Rather than signaling to the white partners at the firm that he is monitoring them, Terrance will want to send a message to those partners that he is monitoring other African Americans to ensure that they, too, become appropriately socialized into the firm.

In a similar vein, one can question whether senior African American executives will produce the racial accountability benefits we described earlier. The idea, again, is that the presence of these African Americans would require the firm to account for—explain or justify—apparent racial inequalities in the firm. The reasons African American managers may not produce racial monitoring also explains why racial accountability may not occur. In short, the firm would expect that the African Americans it promotes (a) are committed to the norms of the firm, even norms that adversely affect minorities in hiring and promotion, and (b) would continually demonstrate that commitment.[25] As a result, the presence of senior African American executives would not necessarily exert any pressure on the firm's decision-makers to account for racial disparities or inequalities within the firm.

Let us now turn to racial cooperation—and more specifically, the suggestion that the presence of black executives and managers would facilitate racial cooperation. The notion was twofold. First, these individuals would help form teams that would maximize opportunities for racial trust; and second, their very success would eliminate or mitigate racial anxieties and suggest to nonwhites and whites alike that racial cooperation is possible. Here, too, the question is whether firms can realize these theoretical benefits. The answer is, only marginally so.

Senior black executives are not likely to structure teams in a race-conscious manner. Their firm socialization would tell them that this is a bad thing to do. It would confirm the idea that they are racially conscious (and not institutionally conscious) actors. Further, if African American executives have worked hard to demonstrate their capacity for racial cooperation on their own, they may expect other minorities to do the same.

Nevertheless, the presence of successful black managers might still provide some racial cooperation payoff. Their presence will suggest that racially palatable African Americans (not all African Americans) can work cooperatively with whites. This has the potential to diminish the perception that no African American can work cooperatively with whites. This is the sense in which the racial cooperation payoff from the mere presence of African American managers is likely to be marginal.

A related assumption we made is that African American managers will reduce the supply of and demand for racial comfort work in predominantly white corporations. Our thinking was that the presence of these senior executives would diminish anxieties about racial difference, thus reducing the need for juniors to make whites feel comfortable. Just the opposite may be true. As we explained earlier, African Americans and minorities who succeed in climbing the corporate hierarchy will probably have adopted strategies that negate racial stereotypes only as they apply to them. Some of these African Americans, who strategically positioned themselves as the "good" black, or the "but for" black, may not want to alter the view of their colleagues that they are special, racial exceptions, and that most other blacks are going to be difficult to work with. This would cause the institution to continue to screen its black employees for their willingness and capacity to supply racial comfort.

Moreover, even if black senior executives do not position themselves in that way, there is still an incentive for junior black employees to perform racial comfort. This is because, and as we have discussed earlier, a large amount of corporate work is performed in teams and African American employees might believe that corporate leaders will presume that African Americans do not work well in team-oriented environments.[26] This creates pressure for African Americans to demonstrate that in fact they do.[27] Some will want to demonstrate that they can do so more effectively than their white male counterparts.[28] These are the African Americans whom the firm is likely to promote. Their presence at the top of the corporation would not diminish the expectation that junior African Americans supply racial comfort but rather create racial precedent for the supply of racial comfort.

There is another reason to believe that, even with the presence of African Americans at the top of the corporation, the firm's decision-makers will continue to scrutinize junior African Americans—the employer's concerns about the friction costs of racial salience in the workplace. This concern will motivate the firm's leaders to guard against the promotion of black employees whose racial difference will bring the wheels of an institution to a grinding halt and to promote the black employees whose racial comfort greases those same wheels. The African Americans at the top of the corporation are racial windows on the types of African Americans who are likely to supply this grease. Rather than reducing the intra-racial screening of African Americans for racial comfort, then, the presence of successful African Americans might increase it, exerting pressures on junior African Americans to work their identity to supply that comfort.

Perhaps our story about the presence of African Americans at the top of the corporation gets better if we shift the focus to a cluster of benefits that relate to the idea that the presence of these African Americans at the top of the corporation sends a message to those on the bottom that they can also succeed. African Americans can serve as role models, and they can also diminish the extent to which junior African Americans feel like tokens. But whether an institution can realize these benefits turns on the type of African Americans in leadership positions. The African Americans at the bottom of the corporation may view those at the top as sell-outs who sold their racial identities for career opportunities. Even where this is not the case, the racial palatability of African American managers may make it difficult for the junior people of color to identify with them. For example, many black men and women might not perceive either Justice Clarence Thomas or former Secretary of State Condoleezza Rice as role models because of the compromises some think they have made to succeed.[29]

There is another problem. The role modeling argument assumes that the African Americans at the bottom of the corporation will want to forge a racial connection with those at the top. But this may not be the case, particularly if the corporation is successful in screening for racial palatability. The more successful the corporation is at performing this screening, the less likely African Americans at the top will have any racial relationship with those on the bottom. If Terrance, a junior black executive, was the product of the corporation's successful screening for racial palatability, he will probably not be concerned that senior executive Raheem (who goes by Ray) does not seem to be motivated by an affinity for his racial group. Still, Terrance might see Ray as a role model precisely because Ray lacks this kind of racial investment. In this respect, one could argue that the role modeling payoff is greater than zero. How much so is up for grabs.

With respect to tokenism, here, too, there is reason to question whether the presence of African Americans in leadership positions would yield a benefit. Our assumption was that the presence of these black executives would reduce the costs of tokenism—the weight of representing one's race and a diminishment in one's sense of workplace autonomy and belonging. But this may not be so. Consider the burden of racial representation. Assume that Terrance has just been promoted to partner. If one of the reasons the partners promoted Terrance is that they perceived him to be different from other African Americans, his presence will do little to reduce the racial representation burden of junior African Americans. They, too, will have to prove that they are not like other African Americans, and they assume the risk that their job performance and overall institutional identity will suggest that they are. Because Terrance's promotion was based, at least in part, on racial exceptionalism, other African Americans will have to prove either that they, like Terrance, are exceptional or that racial

stereotypes about African Americans are inaccurate. Terrance's success, therefore, will not necessarily ameliorate the racial representation burdens of junior
African Americans.

Terrance's success, depending on how it was achieved, might also serve to
decrease, rather than increase, the workplace autonomy or sense of belonging of
junior African Americans. Paradoxically, the more entrenched the firm's perception of Terrance as a racial exception, the heavier the burden on junior African
Americans might be to repudiate negative stereotypes. If the firm's decision-
makers tend to use simplified categorizations of their minorities into "good" and
"bad," the fact that Terrance is already in the "good" category might add to the
presumption that the newer junior minorities must be more normal, or "bad."

A final benefit we attributed to the presence of senior African American
managers is that they would facilitate networking and share information. Two
of the characteristics we attribute to African Americans at the top of the corporation suggest that they might not deliver these benefits: overconfidence and
the need to demonstrate affinity for the dominant group. Consider overconfidence. Recall our suggestion that African American managers will believe,
or convey the idea that they believe, that they deserve their success; that it
was not a product of happenstance.[30] This overconfidence enables an African
American who employs high-risk strategies to succeed and to persuade others that her success was not the product of luck but of merit. But an African
American who succeeds without mentoring may believe that other minorities
do not or should not need any mentorship; after all, she made it on her own
merit. She may even construe mentoring as special help, help that could function to confirm the very stereotypes she spent much of her time attempting to
disrupt.

The second characteristic that cuts against mentorship is that the successful
African American needs to continually demonstrate that she is a team player.
Sharing her human capital with other African Americans might suggest that she
is a special-interest player. If the senior minority perceives that her colleagues
are scrutinizing her mentorship choices for signs of racially specific mentorship, she may avoid mentoring too many or, indeed, any minorities. Plus, to the
extent one's status as a senior within the firm derives in part from one's success at
competing for the best mentees, this creates an additional incentive for African
American managers to seek out white mentees. Finally, if an African American
manager perceives that African American juniors have a poor success rate,
and if having a stable of successful mentees is important to long-term success,
there is a disincentive for the senior to mentor junior African Americans.[31] The
African American manager could believe that whether or not he mentors junior

minorities, they are less likely to succeed. His thinking in this respect need not be based solely on assumptions about the abilities of minority juniors but also on the fact that these juniors are less likely than their white counterparts to be mentored by senior white managers of the firm.

***

The story in this final chapter is not exactly uplifting. We have suggested that there is reason to question the assumption that African Americans at the top of the corporation will "lift as they climb." A key to understanding this story is recognizing that an employee's ability to race to the top of the corporation is not solely dependent upon traditional qualifications and capability. Producing more widgets than one's competitors is not enough. To succeed, employees have to effectively negotiate the political landscape of the institution. They have to appease individual corporate officers, co-opt and make allies with powerful interest groups, and undermine competitors. The more bureaucratic the organization and the more opaque the promotion process, the more important this institutional game is to climbing the corporate ladder.

Focusing on African Americans, our aim has been to identify the racial minority types who are likely to play this game well and, consequently, get to the top of the corporation. Because the racial minorities at the top of the corporation are in a position to ameliorate discrimination for those on the bottom, identifying these racial types is crucial to making corporations more welcoming to racial minorities. This intuition helps explain why many corporate governance and employment-discrimination scholars rest hope for the establishment of racially inclusive and nondiscriminatory corporate cultures on the assumption that successful racial types will actively seek out and perform antidiscriminatory institutional work.

However, there is reason to be skeptical. Incentives exist for minorities to get to the top of the corporation and pull the ladder up behind them when they get there. We are not making an empirical claim. People act against incentives all the time. The two of us would probably not have our jobs had others not lifted while they climbed (actually, lifting our weight probably impeded any hope they might have had of *really* climbing). And, certainly, we like to think that we have carried this forward and engaged in quite of bit of "lifting" activities ourselves. That said, our goal has been to question what we perceive to be a widespread assumption that the presence of racial minorities at the top of the hierarchy will produce significant benefits for those further down. This assumption is not harmless. It can result in society investing scarce resources in getting more minorities to the top. If, for example, the better strategy in terms of achieving greater racial equality and opportunity is to facilitate the entrance of larger numbers of junior minorities at the bottom of the hierarchy, that is important to know. Our broader point is that we remain cynical that having more minorities at the top of the hierarchy will necessarily improve the conditions of those on the bottom.

But we refuse to end on that pessimistic note. Thus, in the context of responding to some criticisms we heard as we circulated drafts of this book, the Epilogue explains why, notwithstanding what we have argued in this chapter, there may be reason for some optimism.

Acting Beyond
Black and White

There are a handful of questions and criticisms about this book that we heard on multiple occasions while it was in the draft stage. This epilogue engages them. As will become clear, some of the objections, we think, are more compelling than others and almost all of them we have discussed in some form in the preceding chapters. Nevertheless, compiling the criticisms in one place enables us to step back—with the reader—and think about *Acting White?* holistically.

The first concern we heard, typically from our academic colleagues, was that some (other) readers might misinterpret some of our claims along the lines of the following questions: Were we saying that race is mere behavior—that people could act in and out of racial categories? Were we articulating a "blame the victim" story—that people of color invite discrimination by failing to properly work and perform their identity? Was it our claim that identity performances were always conscious, that people were always being strategic about working their identity? Were we arguing for some basic right to be different? Were we suggesting that there were true ways to be black or white? The prior chapters were supposed to have answered these questions. But in case they did not, the answer is, no.

The second set of concerns we heard had to do with our focus on the black versus white experience. While we have attempted not to conflate "black" with "people of color," one might still fault us for not being more racially inclusive in our analysis. For us, this is not solely a matter of coverage in the sense of turning to other groups to provide other examples of a phenomenon framed largely with reference to African Americans. Taking up Working Identity vis-à-vis other racial groups could shape how we think about the phenomenon in the first place. Consider our focus on the concept of the racial double bind. Recall our discussion of how Obama is constrained by its existence. Lost in that discussion is the fact that Obama has had to respond to other racial constituencies as well—for purposes of our discussion, let us take the group of Latinas/os. In this respect, he is not negotiating a double racial bind. He is negotiating multiple racial binds. Being black enough is not necessarily going to satisfy the concern of Latinas/os. This is because Obama's racial commitments to African Americans would not answer (but invite) the question about his commitment to Latinas/os. Nor would Obama's refraining from being "too black" necessarily have traction with Latinas/os; that could signal that Obama is not interested in civil rights or immigration reform, areas of concern to many Latinas/os. At bottom, we concede that our focus on black and white experiences presents a decidedly incomplete picture of the Working Identity phenomenon.

Part of the reason we focus on African Americans is our perception that discussions of black people acting out their racial identity are more salient in today's society. From controversies about whether the underperformance of black youth is a function of black adolescents associating studying and academic success with "acting white" to questions about whether Obama is not black enough, public and academic discussions of racial performance are framed largely along some dimension of the "acting black"/"acting white" line discussed in this book.

To repeat, this does not mean that Working Identity dynamics are exhausted by the black experience. Take the example of Muslim Americans in the aftermath of the 9/11 terrorist attacks. They have experienced increased pressure to perform a mainstream American identity. And performing that identity might (for a man) mean shaving before taking a plane trip. Or for a woman it might mean refraining from wearing a head scarf. For the family, it might mean placing an American flag outside the home. It also might mean refraining from doing the traditional Muslim prayers at work. Each of the foregoing would diminish the extent to which a Muslim is perceived to be a Muslim and thus reduce the likelihood that one is imagined as a terrorist or a terrorist sympathizer. But they all involve costs; depending on the individual, high costs.

The analysis extends easily to other groups as well. The less "Mexican appearing" a Latina is, the more hassle-free her travels across the border likely will be. The more assimilationist an Asian American, the less likely she is to be considered a foreigner (although she might still be told that she speaks English well). The more phenotypically white a Native American appears to be, the more that person might need to be performatively Indian. Consider this last point with respect to Harvard Law professor and senatorial candidate, Elizabeth Warren. As of this writing, Warren is under attack for having claimed to be Native American in her early years as an academic. Warren seems to have demonstrated that she legitimately believed that she was part-Cherokee by descent (1/32nd, according to most news reports).[1] But her belief in her own Native American ancestry has not been enough for many critics.[2] She does not get to claim to be Native American, they say, unless she also acted (worked her identity) as a Native American.[3] This performance demand, some of these critics argue, is especially important because Warren looks "so white." The assumption here is that if Warren looked more Cherokee, people would demand less from her in terms of Working Identity.[4] These questions about Warren's racial authenticity are one more example that the Working Identity phenomenon transcends the borders of the black experience.

And the phenomenon transcends race. As we discussed in chapter 4, scholars, policy makers, and judges have been expressing a gender version of this Working Identity story for some time. A version of it also exists with respect to sexual orientation. Don't Ask, Don't Tell, the policy the military employed for many years to regulate gay and lesbian participation in the Armed Forces, was, at least in part, based on Working Identity. Under the policy, lesbians and gay men could serve in the military so long as they neither announced nor otherwise engaged in conduct that expressed their sexual orientation. Significantly, the conduct concern under Don't Ask, Don't Tell was not just about sex. Indeed, many of the servicewomen and men who the military dismissed under this policy were "outed" not based on sexual activity per se but on gender non-conformity, In this sense, what prompted the military to investigate whether particular military personnel were gay or lesbian was whether service men acted like men and whether servicewomen acted like women. All of this is to say, the Working Identity phenomenon is broader than the contours of *Acting White?*.

A third concern some critics raised about the book is that our Working Identity thesis blurs the line between race and culture.[5] But that line has always been grey. Take the historical arguments about primitive Native American and African civilizations. Are they racial arguments or cultural claims? Take the culture of poverty arguments about African American laziness, criminality, and sexual immorality. Are they racial arguments or cultural claims? Take the model minority arguments about Asian Americans? Cultural or racial? Concepts like race and culture are not easily separable; they are interconnected.[6] It is impossible, then, to know where to draw the line between the two. What we can say is that calling everything that is racially associative, other than phenotype, "culture" is too narrow a conception of race. An alternate approach might be to formulate a typology of race-discrimination claims, with claims in certain categories receiving more or less anti-discrimination protection. Under the existing system, claims based on phenotype appear to receive the maximal protection. Claims based on accent, by contrast, receive a much lower level of protection. We need to do better than simply assert that the former is about race and the latter is about culture.

A final concern we heard was that we were airing dirty laundry—not about African Americans but about predominantly white institutions. As many of you know, the airing dirty laundry concern is typically raised to query whether it is appropriate for African Americans to discuss some aspect of black community life or politics in the presence of people who are not African American. That iteration of the airing dirty laundry problem is not what we were hearing. The concern was that we were highlighting racial dynamics about predominantly white institutions to a general audience—and that the story we were telling implicates our own institutions. To switch metaphors, the worry was that we were telling stories out of school. This was not our first time hearing this concern. Colleagues raised it after we circulated drafts of our very first article on the topic over a decade ago. Naively, we initially gave the issue short shrift. After all, we were academics discussing a social phenomenon that academics were interested in understanding. It was not until a senior colleague literally sat us down and explicitly told us that we would be at risk of being denied tenure if we kept writing about Working Identity that we processed the objection. How could we not have anticipated that pursuing this project would make some of our colleagues uncomfortable?

It would be too easy for us to say that we refused to make our colleagues racially comfortable, that we refused to produce the racial double blind performance, that we refused to compromise our identity. It would be too easy for us to say that we simply "kept it real," to borrow from Dave Chappelle, that we decided to let the chips fall where they may. Perhaps we supplied racial comfort in other ways. Perhaps notwithstanding the racial discomfort our scholarship produced, our racial ledger remained in the black, so to speak.

Truth be told, we'd just as soon not think about the matter. But that, of course, is exactly what we have to do. The topic of Working Identity continues to engender anxieties. People don't like talking about "acting black" or "acting white." Laughing about Working Identity with reference to a *Saturday Night Live* skit is one thing. Talking seriously about the phenomenon is quite another. And yet our hope is that *Acting White?* will encourage people to do just that; that the book will put Working Identity squarely on the table; and that when we think about race and racial discrimination going forward we will understand that all of us judge people based not only on the color of their skin but on the content of their Working Identity.

NOTES

Prologue

1. Nancy Leong, *Racial Capitalism*, 126 Harvard L. Rev., (forthcoming 2012).
2. *Saturday Night Live* (NBC television broadcast Feb. 10, 2007), transcript available at http://snltranscripts.jt.org/06/06mupdate.phtml.
3. Barack Obama, Candidate for U.S. Senator for Illinois, Keynote Address at the Democratic National Convention in Boston (July 27, 2004) (transcript available at http://www.washingtonpost.com/wp-dyn/articles/A19751–2004Jul27.html).
4. *See* Angela Onwuachi-Willig & Mario Barnes, *The Obama Effect: Understanding Emerging Meanings of "Obama" in Anti-Discrimination Law*, 87 Ind. L.J. 325, 332 (2012) (discussing the relevant cases)
5. *See* Xuan Thai &Ted Barrett, *Biden's Description of Obama Draws Scrutiny* (CNN television broadcast Jan. 31, 2007), available at http://articles.cnn.com/2007–01–31/politics/biden. obama_1_braun-and-al-sharpton-african-american-presidential-candidates-delaware-democrat?_s=PM:POLITICS.
6. Eugene Robinson, *An Inarticulate Kickoff*, The Washington Post, Feb. 2, 2007, available at http://www.washingtonpost.com/wp-dyn/content/article/2007/02/01/AR2007020101495.html.
7. *See* Adam Nagourney, *Biden Unwraps His Bid for '08 with an Oops!*, N.Y. Times, Feb. 1, 2007, available at http://www.nytimes.com/ 2007/02/01/us/politics/ 01biden.html.
8. *Id.*
9. David Gregory, *Sen. Biden Apologizes for Remarks on Obama*, NBC News, Jan. 31, 2007, available at http://www.msnbc.msn.com/ id/16911044/.
10. *See* Richard Ford, *Barack Is the New Black*, 6 Du Bois Rev. 37 (2009).
11. *See, e.g.,* Kimberly D. Krawiec, *Is Obama a UNC Fan: Or a Savvy Politician?*, The Faculty Lounge Blog, March 17, 2012, available at http://www.thefacultylounge.org/2012/03/is-obama-a-unc-fan.html.
12. Rick Chandler, *Jalen Rose: "I Hated Duke: They Only Recruited Uncle Toms,"* NBC Sports: Off the Bench, March 8, 2011, available at http://offthebench.nbcsports.com/2011/03/08/jalen-rose-i-hated-duke-they-only-recruited-black-players-who-were-uncle-toms/.
13. *Real Time with Bill Maher* (HBO television broadcast May 28, 2010).
14. Debra J. Dickerson, *Colorblind*, The Salon (January 22, 2007), available at http://www.salon.com/news/opinion/feature/2007/01/22/obama.
15. Interview by Stephen Colbert with Debra J. Dickerson, *The Colbert Report* (Comedy Central television broadcast Feb. 8, 2007). *See also* Dickerson, *supra* note 14.
16. *See* Marc Sheppard, *Obama, Lincoln and the Reformation of Black History*, Am. Thinker Blog (Feb. 15, 2007), available at http://www.americanthinker.com/2007/02/obama_lincoln_and_the_reformat.html.

17. *See* Leslie Fulbright, *Obama's Candidacy Sparks Debate on Race/Is He African American if His Roots Don't Include Slavery?*, SF Gate (Feb. 19, 2007), *available at* http://articles.sfgate.com/2007–02–19/news/17232968_1_african-americans-black-mayors-black-candidate.

18. *Id.*

19. *Id.*

20. For a discussion of racial authenticity, black community politics, and Justice Thomas's jurisprudence, *see* Angela Onwuachi-Willig, *Just Another Brother on the SCT? What Justice Clarence Thomas Teaches Us About the Influence of Racial Identity*, 90 Iowa L. Rev. 931 (2005).

21. *See* Russell Robinson, *Racing the Closet*, 61 Stan. L. Rev. 1463 (2009).

22. *See* 6 Du Bois Rev., Issue 1, a special issue focusing on Obama. *See also*, Symposium, *Perspectives on Obama, Race and the Law*, Rutgers Race and the L. Rev. (2008); Symposium, *Defining Race*, 72 Albany L. Rev. 855 (2009).

23. *See generally* Angela Onwuachi-Willig & Mario Barnes, *The Obama Effect: Understanding Emerging Meanings of "Obama" in Anti-Discrimination Law*, 87 Ind. L.J. 325, 332 (2012). *See also* Angela Onwuachi-Willig & Osamudia James, *The Declining Significance of Presidential Race?*, 72 Law. & Contemp. Probs. 89 (2009).

24. Onwuachi-Willig & Barnes, *supra* note 23.

25. Eduardo Bonilla-Silva & Victor Ray, *When Whites Love a Black Leader: Race Matters in Obamerica*, 13 J. Afr.-Am. Stud. 176, 178 (2009).

26. Fredrick Harris, *Still Waiting for Our First Black President*, The Washington Post, June 1, 2012, *available at* http://www.washingtonpost.com/opinions/still-waiting-for-our-first-black-president/2012/06/01/gJQARsT16U_story.html.

27. Senator Barack Obama, *A More Perfect Union* (March 18, 2008), (transcript available at http://www.barackobama4us.com/56/obama-race-speech-a-more-perfect-union).

28. *See* Brian Ross & Rehab El-Buri, *Obama's Pastor: God Damn America, U.S. to Blame for 9/11*, ABC News, March 13, 2008, *available at* http://a.abcnews.com/Blotter/DemocraticDebate/story?id=4443788&page=1; Reverend Wright's sermon took place in 2003, but was aired and "exposed" in 2008 by ABC News.

29. Senator Barack Obama, *supra* note 27.

30. *Id.*

31. *Id.*

32. *Id.*

33. *Id.*

34. *Id.*

35. Adam Nagourney, Jim Rutenberg & Jeff Zeleny, *Near-Flawless Run From the Start to Finish is Credited in Victory*, N.Y. Times, Nov. 5, 2008, at P1.

36. Katherine Fung, *Geraldo Rivera: Trayvon Martin's Hoodie Is as Much Responsible for His Death as Is George Zimmerman*, The Huffington Post, March 23, 2012, available at http://www.huffingtonpost.com/2012/03/23/geraldo-rivera-trayvon-martin-hoodie_n_1375080.html.

37. Ann Oldenburg, *Geraldo Rivera Blames Hoodie for Trayvon Martin's Death*. USA Today, May 19, 2012, available at http://content.usatoday.com/communities/entertainment/post/2012/03/geraldo-rivera-blames-hoodie-for-trayvon-martins-death/1#.T7hg7mB2dNx.

38. *Id.*

39. *Id.*

40. *Id.*

41. Joseph Williams, *Trayvon Martin Shooting: Black Leaders Press White House*, Politico, March 22, 2012, available at http://www.politico.com/news/stories/0312/74385.html.

42. Sam Stein, *Obama on Trayvon Martin Case*, The Huffington Post, March 23, 2012, available at http://www.huffingtonpost.com/2012/03/23/obama-trayvon-martin_n_1375083.html.

43. Thomas B. Edsall, *Anti-Establishment Strategy*, N.Y. Times, Dec. 26, 2011, available at http://campaignstops.blogs.nytimes.com/2011/12/25/the-anti-entitlement-strategy/.

44. Alan Bjerga & Jennifer Oldham. *Gringrich Calling Obama "Food-Stamp President" Draws Critics*, Bloomberg Businessweek, 2012, May 19, 2012, available at http://www.businessweek.com/news/2012–01–25/gingrich-calling-obama-food-stamp-president-draws-critics.html.

45. Michael Luo, *In Job Hunt, College Degree Can't Close Racial Gap*, N.Y. TIMES, November 9, 2009, available at http://www.nytimes.com/2009/12/01/us/01race.html

46. *Id.*

47. Michael Luo, *Whitening the Resume*, N.Y. TIMES, December 5, 2009, available at http://www.nytimes.com/2009/12/06/weekinreview/06Luo.html

48. *Id.*

49. *See* Luo, *supra* note 45.

50. *See* Luo, *supra* note 47.

51. *Id.*

52. *Id.*

53. *Id.*

54. *E.g.,* Taunya Lovell Banks, *The Black Side of the Mirror/The Black Body in the Workplace*, in SISTER CIRCLE: BLACK WOMEN AT WORK (SUSAN HARLEY ET AL., ED. 2002).

Chapter 1

1. The focus on employees is not intended to suggest that the workplace is the only location for identity performances.

2. Actions sufficient to demonstrate collegiality in one institutional setting, like attending faculty meetings, may be insufficient to demonstrate collegiality in another.

3. ERVING GOFFMAN, THE PRESENTATION OF SELF IN EVERYDAY LIFE 77 (1959).

4. *See, e.g.,* BRUCE WILSHIRE, ROLE PLAYING AND IDENTITY: THE LIMITS OF THEATRE AS METAPHOR (1982).

5. It is possible for the employee to either be wrong about the institution's existing values or to miscalculate the relative importance of the criteria involved in the institution's values.

6. People always are already engaged in a series of performances. *See* JUDITH BUTLER, BODIES THAT MATTER, 136–39 (1993); *See also* Judith Butler, *Imitation and Gender Insubordination, in* INSIDE/OUT: LESBIAN THEORIES, GAY THEORIES 13, 19 (DIANA FUSS ED., 1991).

7. A tension or a conflict may not always exist, and employees' sense of identity may on occasion comport with workplace norms. *See* Herminia Ibarra, *Making Partner: A Mentor's Guide to the Psychological Journey*, 78 HARV. BUS. REV. 147, 152–53 (2000).

8. Our argument is about self-perception and self-definition, although expressions like, "That's so unlike Susan!" suggest that people form idealized impressions of others as well.

9. SAMMY DAVIS JR., *I'VE GOTTA BE ME, ON* I'VE GOTTA BE ME: THE BEST OF SAMMY DAVIS JR. (1996).

10. WILLIAM SHAKESPEARE, THE TRAGEDY OF HAMLET, PRINCE OF DENMARK ACT 1, SC. 3, L.78 (SUSANNE L. WOFFORD ED., 1994).

11. The performance of racial-comfort strategies can be understood as an unstated racial term of employment, "shadow work." *See* ELIZABETH V. SPELMAN, INESSENTIAL WOMAN 209–10 (1990).

12. An example is the controversy of suspected Chinese nuclear espionage against the United States. *See* Neil Gotanda, *Racialization of Asian Americans and African Americans: Racial Profiling and the Wen Ho Lee Case*, 47 UCLA L. REV. 6 (2000).

13. *See* Marina Angel, *Women in Legal Education: What It's Like to Be Part of a Perpetual First Wave or the Case of the Disappearing Women*, 61 TEMP. L. REV. 799, 831 (1988).

14. Certain mimicking actions—such as Outsider men dating white women—may cause discomfort to Insiders. *See, e.g.,* Devon W. Carbado, *The Construction of O.J. Simpson as a Racial Victim*, 32 HARV. C. R.-C. L. L. REV. 49, 72–73 (1997).

15. CRASH (LIONS GATE ENTERTAINMENT 2005).

16. This leads to the question of when a person begins to internalize the role he is playing to such an extent that the role takes over his identity.

17. Russell K. Robinson, *Racing the Closet*, 61 STAN. L. REV. 1463 (2009).

18. For a discussion of the complex relationship between cosmetic surgery, race and identity performance, see Stephen R. Munzer, *Cosmetic Surgery, Racial Identity and Aesthetics*, 19 CONFIGURATIONS 243 (2011).

19. People can pass into other identities as well. So, people can partially pass as black or Asian American. We are focusing largely in partial passing in the direction of whiteness.

20. *See*, e.g., Charles R. Lawrence III, *The Id, the Ego, and Equal Protection: Reckoning with Unconscious Racism*, 39 STAN. L. REV. 317, 318 (1987)

21. *See George Zimmerman's Father Claims Trayvon Martin Beat His Son, Threatened His Life*, FOXNEWS.COM, March 29, 2012, available at http://www.foxnews.com/us/2012/03/29/g eorge-zimmermans-father-claims-trayvon-martin-beat-his-son-threatened-his-life/.

22. This suggests that the often-made claim, "I am not prejudiced because I am friends with X, Y, & Z, who are all from that group," means something different when X, Y, and Z have engaged in partial passing strategies, than when they have not.

23. See Devon W. Carbado, *Black Rights, Gay Rights, Civil Rights*, 47 UCLA L. REV. 1467 (2000).

24. An example here is the case of an Outsider who plays basketball with the awareness that it makes him "one of the boys." Our point is not to suggest that this employee should not play basketball. The employee might enjoy playing ball. Basketball might be part of his social identity.

25. Kenji Yoshino, *Assimilationist Bias in Equal Protection: The Visibility Presumption and the Case of "Don't Ask, Don't Tell,"* 108 YALE L.J. 485, at 500 (1998). Yoshino offers a typology similar to the passing/partial-passing typologies employed in this paper.

26. UNDERCOVER BROTHER (UNIVERSAL PICTURES 2002).

27. For discussions of some of the Korean American stereotypes, see ELAINE H. KIM & EU-YOUNG YU, EAST TO AMERICA: AMERICAN LIFE STORIES (THE NEW PRESS 1996).

28. Compare this with the situation in which the Outsider is arguing that there is discrimination. Here, the Outsider story is suspect and needs white racial authentication.

29. *See* Manning Marable, *Clarence Thomas and the Crisis of Black Political Culture, in* RACE-ING JUSTICE, EN-GENDERING POWER: ESSAYS ON ANITA HILL, CLARENCE THOMAS, AND THE CONSTRUCTION OF SOCIAL REALITY 61, 62 (TONI MORRISON ED., 1992).

30. For a canvassing of the implicit bias literature, see Jerry Kang et al., *Implicit Bias in the Courtroom*, 50 UCLA L. REV. 1125 (2012).

31. The story that we tell about the incentives that Outsiders have to work their identities to negate stereotypes and persuade employers that they will fit into the workplace culture implicates an argument that Richard Epstein has made for abolishing Title VII. Epstein's argument is premised on the idea that workplace norms matter and that the effective operation of these norms is more likely when the workforce shares a common culture. *See* RICHARD A. EPSTEIN, FORBIDDEN GROUNDS: THE CASE AGAINST EMPLOYMENT DISCRIMINATION LAWS 61–67 (1992). Having a racially homogeneous workforce is an easy and cheap way to produce a workforce with a common culture. *Id.* at 61–67. Epstein argues that Title VII's restriction on race-based hiring, therefore, causes inefficiencies by making it much more expensive for an employer to create a workforce with a common culture. *Id.* at 76–78. The argument is flawed, however, in that it is not the employer, but rather the Outsider employees who incur the cost of acquiring the requisite amounts of cultural capital so as to fit in. *Cf.* Drucilla Cornell & William W. Bratton, *Deadweight Costs and Intrinsic Wrongs of Nativism: Economics, Freedom, and Legal Suppression of Spanish*, 84 CORNELL L. REV. 595, 602, 620, 628, 645 (1999). Assuming a scarcity of jobs, the employer will then be able to choose those Outsider employees who demonstrate that they will fit into the workplace culture. Title VII, for the most part, does not restrict an employer's ability to define its workplace culture. At the least, the phenomenon of Outsiders working their identity ameliorates Epstein's concerns about Title VII.

32. Performing identity can even involve direct expenditures of cash. For example, imagine a black man who walks into a fancy clothing store in a hurry because he has a meeting to attend soon. None of the salespeople pay him any attention. To get the salespeople's attention, he might be forced to purchase one of the expensive wallets in the display case.

33. For a general discussion of how stereotypes affect the employment prospects and experiences of black men, *See* Floyd D. Weatherspoon, *Remedying Employment Discrimination Against African-American Males: Stereotypical Biases Engender a Case of Race Plus Sex Discrimination*, 36 WASHBURN L.J. 23 (1996).

34. *See* Kimberlé Williams Crenshaw in *Race, Reform, and Retrenchment: Transformation and Legitimation in Antidiscrimination Law,* 101 HARV. L. REV. 1331, 1373 (1988),
    Historical Oppositional Dualities:

White Images	Black Images
Industrious	Lazy
Intelligent	Unintelligent
Moral	Immoral
Knowledgeable	Ignorant
Enabling Culture	Disabling Culture
Law-Abiding	Criminal
Responsible	Shiftless
Virtuous/Pious	Lascivious

35. 392 U.S. 1 (1968).
36. *Id.* at 30
37. *Id.*
38. *See* Lani Guinier, *Transcript: Keynote Address by Lani Guinier,* 25 U. TOL. L. REV. 875, 885 (1995) (encouraging law professors to move away from Socratic engagement to a more conversational and less hierarchical approach); John M. Rogers, *Class Participation: Random Calling and Anonymous Grading,* 47 J. LEGAL EDUC. 73 (1997) (suggesting that class participation should play an important part in the delivery of legal education).
39. In the context of the classroom, perhaps the most pervasive stereotypes students will have about the professor is that he is not competent. But, even to the extent that students do not hold this negative view, they will likely not assume that the professor is competent. *See* Derrick A. Bell, *Diversity and Academic Freedom,* 43 J. LEGAL EDUC. 371, 377 (1993); Joyce Anne Hughes, *Neither a Whisper or a Shout, in* REBELS IN LAW: VOICES IN HISTORY OF BLACK WOMEN LAWYERS 90, 98 (J. CLAY SMITH JR. ED., 1998).
40. For a discussion of how the employment of nontraditional classroom pedagogy can create (or solidify) the impression of a black professor's incompetence, *see* Bell, *supra* note 54, at 377; *see also* Reginald Leamon Robinson, *Split Personalities: Teaching and Scholarship in Non-stereotypical Areas of Law,* 19 W. NEW ENG. L. REV. 73, 74–77 (1997).
41. *See, e.g.,* Phillip E. Areeda, *The Socratic Method,* 109 HARV. L. REV. 911, 922 (1996).
42. Note that the professor might also be worried that the use of the lecture format would result in the impression that he is unreceptive to student ideas. Such an approach might also encourage his colleagues to take the position that he "spoon feeds" or "condescends to" students.
43. For a discussion of the link between the pedagogical choices law professors make and the experiences of students of color in the classroom, *see generally,* Kimberlé Williams Crenshaw, *Foreword: Toward a Race-Conscious Pedagogy in Legal Education,* 11 NAT'L BLACK L.J. 1 (1989).
44. For example, to the extent that there are few black students in a particular class, students and sometimes faculty members look to these students for the "black perspective." And even when students and faculty members do not expect black students to provide the black perspective, black students will still carry the burden of "representing" race.
45. *See* SARA LAWRENCE-LIGHTFOOT, RESPECT 155–69 (1999).
46. Significantly, the employment of the Socratic method does not mean that the professor escapes any of these criticisms. Clarity can be interpreted as condescension or spoon feeding; a great amount of student engagement can be interpreted as disorganization or unpreparedness; asking lots of questions can be interpreted as providing little guidance.
47. 392 U.S. at 52.
48. The Court's recitation of the facts does not mention the defendant's race. *Id.* at 52. However, the trial court record reveals that John Terry was black.
49. For a discussion of the extent to which this historical context of the 1960s shaped the Court's doctrinal approach in Terry, *see* Tracey Maclin, *Terry v. Ohio's Fourth Amendment Legacy: Black Men and Police Discretion* 72 ST. JOHN'S L. REV. 1271 (1998).
50. *See* Anthony C. Thompson, *Stopping the Usual Suspects: Race and the Fourth Amendment,* 74 N.Y.U. L. REV. 956, 962–73 (1999).
51. *Id.* at 962–73.

52. The importance of teaching evaluations varies from institution to institution. And even within a specific institution, teaching evaluations may not be as important in all cases.

53. For example, he may fear that the students will think that as a black professor he is obsessed with race. *See* Hughes, *supra* note 39, at 101 n.61 ("A survival strategy employed by some [people of color] is 'racelessness.'").

54. Linda Crane, *Can We Talk?: Reflections of Seven Female African American Law Professors, in* 6 National Bar Assoc. Magazine 16, 19 (July 1992); Elaine Martin, *Power and Authority in the Classroom: Sexist Stereotypes in Teaching Evaluations,* 9 SIGNS: J. WOMEN IN CULTURE & SOCIETY 482, 486–87, 491–92 (1984).

55. Chief Justice Warren characterized the question before the Court as "whether it is always unreasonable for a policeman to seize a person and subject him to a limited search for weapons unless there is probable cause for an arrest." Terry v. Ohio, 392 U.S. 1, 15 (1968).

56. The extra work that Outsiders often do in negotiating identity in the classroom extends beyond the obvious classes like Constitutional Criminal Procedure and Criminal Law, where it is almost impossible to ignore race and gender issues (although we have seen it done).

57. This is not to deny that there are likely to be identity performance pressures on, for example, a white male conservative professor who is trying to negotiate his identity within a liberal educational institution. A white male professor teaching rape, for example, might be worried about the extent to which his status as a (white) man might shape the way students respond to him and the material. *See* James J. Tomkovicz, *On Teaching Rape: Reasons, Risks, and Rewards,* 102 YALE L.J. 481, 501 (1992). Our point is that a white male professor is not likely to have to think about identity negotiations to the same extent as a professor who is not white and male.

58. For criticisms of extant notions of colorblindness, *see* e.g., Neil Gotanda, *A Critique of "Our Constitution Is Color-Blind,"* 44 STAN. L. REV. 1 (1991); Gary Peller, *Race Consciousness,* 1990 DUKE L.J. 758; Patricia Williams, *The Obliging Shell: An Informal Essay on Formal Equal Opportunity,* 87 MICH. L. REV. 2128 (1989).

59. *See generally* BEVERLY DANIEL TATUM, WHY ARE ALL THE BLACK KIDS SITTING TOGETHER IN THE CAFETERIA? (1997).

60. *See* Angela P. Harris, *On Doing the Right Thing: Education Work in the Academy,* 15 VT. L. REV. 125, 128 (1990).

61. One can articulate this point more broadly by arguing that colorblindness is a racial preference for whites. See Devon W. Carbado & Cheryl I. Harris, *The New Racial Preferences,* 96 CAL. L. REV 1139 (2008).

62. *See* Kimberlé Crenshaw, *Playing Race Cards: Constructing a Pro-Active Defense of Affirmative Action,* 16 NAT'L BLACK L.J. 196, 199–202 (1999); *See also* Harris, *supra* note 5, at 1738.

63. A relatively recent article by Amy Wax, *The Discriminating Mind: Define it, Prove it,* 40 CONN. L. REV. 979, 1199 (2008), suggests that it may be efficient for people of color to bear this type of burden.

64. At some point, compromise becomes the denial of a person's self. *See* generally Susan E. Babbitt, *Moral Risk and Dark Waters, in* RACISM AND PHILOSOPHY AT 235 (SUSAN E. BABBITT & SUE CAMPBELL EDS., 1999).

65. The skill necessary to negotiate a cultural context is a productive asset for the individual and therefore is described as a form of "cultural capital." Pierre Bourdieu used the term to refer to forms of cultural knowledge, competencies, or dispositions. RANDAL JOHNSON, EDITOR'S INTRODUCTION TO PIERRE BOURDIEU, THE FIELD OF CULTURAL PRODUCTION 7 (RANDAL JOHNSON ED., 1993).

66. For discussions of Asian American stereotypes, see, e.g., Yuko Kawai, *Stereotyping Asian Americans: The Dialectic of the Model Minority and the Yellow Peril,* 16 HOWARD J. COMM.16 (2005).

67. Though not framed in this way, incentives along the lines we discussed are explored in Nancy Leong, *Racial Capitalism,* 126 HARV. L. REV. (forthcoming 2013).

68. *See* e.g., Jerry Kang & Mahzarin R. Banaji, *Fair Measures: A Behavioral Realist Revision of "Affirmative Action,"* 94 CAL. L. REV. 1063 (2006) (exploring the implications of the implicit bias literature for the affirmative action debate).

69. Jerry Kang's *Trojan Horses of Race* 118 HARV. L. REV. 1489, 1503 (2005).

70. MALCOLM GLADWELL, BLINK: THE POWER OF THINKING WITHOUT THINKING (2007).
71. Cheryl Harris, *Whiteness as Property*, 106 HARV. L. REV. 1707, 1711 (1993).
72. On the use of the accident analogy to analyze discrimination, see, e.g., Amy Wax, *Discrimination as Accident*, 74 IND. L.J. 1129 (1999); Michael Selmi, *Response to Amy Wax: Old Whine, New Bottle*, 74 IND. L.J. 1233 (1999).
73. In essence, this cheapest-cost-avoider analysis is what drives the doctrine of immutability in discrimination cases. Under this doctrine, plaintiffs were allowed to sue for discrimination only if the characteristics in question were immutable (or a fundamental right, like the right to marry or practice one's religion). This is an issue we tackle in chapter 3. There, we discuss the *Renee Rogers* case, in which a black female employee asserted an employment discrimination claim based on an American Airlines grooming policy that prohibited its employees from wearing braided hair. .

Chapter 2

1. *E.g.*, Chris Cillizza, *Reid Apologizes for "Light Skinned" Remark About Obama*, WASHINGTON POST, January 9, 2010, available at http://voices.washingtonpost.com/thefix/senate/harry-reid-apologizes-for-ligh.html.
2. *Dr. Boyce Watkins Takes Issue with Senator Harry Reid over Racist Comments*, HIPHOP WIRED, January 10, 2010, available at http://hiphopwired.com/2010/01/10/dr-boyce-watkins-takes-issue-with-senator-harry-reid-over-obama-comments/.
3. JOSEPH C. PHILLIPS, HE TALK LIKE A WHITE BOY 15–16 (2006).
4. *See* Mari J. Matsuda, *Voices of America: Accent, Antidiscrimination Law and Jurisprudence for the Last Reconstruction*, 100 YALE L.J. 1329 (1991).
5. Some scholars refer to this as linguistic profiling. *See* Dawn L. Smalls, *Linguistic Profiling and the Law*, 15 STAN. L. & POL'Y REV. 579, 582–83 (2004).
6. *See id.* describing United States v. Ferrill, 168 F.3d 468 (11th Cir. 1999).
7. *See* Jon Hanson & Douglas A. Kysar, *Taking Behavioralism Seriously: The Problem of Market Manipulation*, 74 N.Y.U. L. REV. 630 (1999) (in the context of behavioral anomalies, rational actors will seek to exploit the vulnerabilities of others).
8. For a classic critique of the extent to which antidiscrimination law is structured by notions of causation and intentionality, see Alan David Freeman, *Legitimizing Racial Discrimination Through Antidiscrimination Law: A Critical Review of Supreme Court Doctrine*, in CRITICAL RACE THEORY: THE KEY WRITINGS THAT FORMED THE MOVEMENT 29 (KIMBERLÉ W. CRENSHAW ET AL. EDS., 1995).
9. For a discussion of the ways in which implicit biases work, see Jerry Kang's *Trojan Horses of Race* 118 HARV. L. REV. 1489 (2005). *See also*, Charles R. Lawrence III, *The Id, the Ego, and Equal Protection: Reckoning with Unconscious Racism*, 39 STAN. L. REV. 317, 322–24 (1987); Linda Hamilton Krieger, *The Content of Our Categories: A Cognitive Bias Approach to Discrimination and Equal Employment Opportunity*, 47 STAN. L. REV. 1161 (1995).
10. 517 U.S. 806 (1996).
11. *Id.* at 812–13.
12. For a racial critique of the Fourth Amendment, see generally Devon W. Carbado, *E-racing the Fourth Amendment*, 100 MICH. L. REV. 946 (2002).
13. For relevant discussions, see Neil Gotanda, *A Critique of "Our Constitution is Color-Blind,"* 44 STAN. L. REV. 1 (1991); Cheryl I. Harris, *Whiteness as Property*, 106 HARV. L. REV. 1707 (1993); Kimberlé W. Crenshaw, *Race, Reform, and Retrenchment: Transformation and Legitimation in Antidiscrimination Law*, 101 HARV. L. REV. 1331 (1988); Kenneth L. Karst, *Myths of Identity: Individual and Group Portraits of Race and Sexual Orientation*, 43 UCLA L. REV. 263 (1995).
14. For a discussion of "Driving While Black" and pretextual traffic stops, see Katheryn K Russell, *"Driving While Black": Corollary Phenomena and Collateral Consequences*. 40 B.C. L. REV. at 717–22 (1999); David A. Harris, *"Driving While Black" and All Other Traffic Offenses: The Supreme Court and Pretextual Traffic Stops*, 87 CRIM. L. & CRIMINOLOGY 544 (1997). For news stories about the "Driving While Black" and other racial profiling problems around the United States, see Jeffrey Goldberg, *The Color of Suspicion*, N.Y. TIMES, June 20, 1999, at 51;

Debra Dickerson, *Racial Profiling: Are We Really Equal in the Eyes of the Law?*, L.A. Times, July 16, 2000, at M1; ACLU & The Rights Working Group, The Persistence of Racial and Ethnic Profiling in the United States (2009), *available at* http://www.aclu.org/pdfs/humanrights/cerd_finalreport.pdf.

15. For an examination of the difficulties of litigating racial profiling charges under both the Fourth and Fourteenth Amendments, see Phyllis W. Beck & Patricia A. Daly, *State Constitutional Analysis of Pretext Stops: Racial Profiling and Public Policy Concerns*, 72 Temple L. Rev. 597 (1999); *see also* David Crump, *Evidence, Race, Intent and Evil: The Paradox of Purposelessness in the Constitutional Racial Discrimination Cases*, 27 Hofstra L. Rev. 285 (1998); Abraham Abramovsky & Jonathan I. Edelstein, *Pretext Stops and Racial Profiling After Whren v. United States: The New York and New Jersey Responses Compared*, 63 Alb. L. Rev. 725 (2000).

16. Behavioral theorists suggest that employers are likely to go beyond interpreting ambiguous information through the lens of their prior assumptions to interpreting ambiguous evidence as confirmation of their prior conceptions. *See* Michael Selmi, *Family Leave and the Gender Wage Gap*, 78 N.C. L. Rev. 707, 752 n.162 (2000) (citing studies).

17. This perception has been examined in the sexual harassment context. Studies show that "many men tend to have the attitude that mild forms of sexual harassment such as suggestive looks, repeated requests for dates, and sexist jokes, [are] harmless social interactions to which only overly-sensitive women would object." J. Tod Hyche, Comment, *The Reasonable Woman Standard in Sexual Harassment Cases. Is it Reasonable?*, 24 Cumb. L. Rev. 559, 568 (1993/1994) (quoting Nancy S. Ehrenreich, *Pluralist Myths and Powerless Men: The Ideology of Reasonableness in Sexual Harassment Law*, 99 Yale L.J. 1177, 1207 n.110 (1990)); Richard Cohen, *What's Harassment? Ask the Woman*, Wash. Post, July 5, 1988, at A19.

18. *See* Devon W. Carbado & Mitu Gulati, *Working Identity*, 85 Cornell L. Rev. 1259, 1291–93 (2000).

19. *See* George P. Baker et al., *Compensation and Incentives: Practice vs. Theory*, 63 J. Fin. 593, 598–99 (1988) (where evaluation of performance allows for significant amounts of bias, those performances (and evaluations) tend not to be directly tied to compensation and promotion).

20. In addition to taking additional time and effort, lumpy tasks will also often put the employee in unavoidable, high conflict situations. For example, take the task of sitting on a hiring committee at a firm. Discussions about credentials, what they mean, and how they should be weighed, are often scenes of conflict. The junior employee stuck on such a committee is almost inevitably going to have disagreements with the others and those disagreements can destroy relationships that could perhaps have otherwise been finessed.

21. *See* Catherine R. Albiston & Laura Beth Nielsen, *Welfare Queens and Other Fairy Tales: Welfare Reform and Unconstitutional Reproductive Controls*, 38 How. L.J. 473 (1995); *see also* Pamela J. Smith, *Teaching the Retrenchment Generation: When Sapphire Meets Socrates at the Intersection of Race, Gender, and Authority*, 6 Wm. & Mary J. Women & L. 53 (1999).

22. *See* Charles R. Lawrence III, *The Id, the Ego, and Equal Protection: Reckoning with Unconscious Racism*, 39 Stan. L. Rev. 317, 322–24 (1987).

23. For discussion of assumptions and attitudes towards women in the workforce and conflict with traditional notions of the family, see Marion G. Crain, *Feminizing Unions: Challenging the Gendered Structure of Wage Labor*, 89 Mich. L. Rev. 1155, 1179 (1991); *see also* Joan Williams, *Implementing Antiessentialism: How Gender Wars Turn Into Race and Class Conflict*, 15 Harv. BlackLetter L.J. 41 (1999); Kathryn Branch, *Note, Are Women Worth as Much as Men?: Employment Inequities, Gender Roles, and Public Policy*, 1 Duke J. Gender L. & Pol'y 119 (1994); Jerry A. Jacobs & Kathleen Gerson, *Rethinking Law in the Twenty-First Century Workplace: Toward a Family-Friendly, Gender-Equitable Work Week*, 1 U. Pa. J. Lab. & Emp. L. 457 (1998).

24. For treatments of screening in the literature on discrimination, *see* Drucilla Cornell & William W. Bratton, *Deadweight Costs and Intrinsic Wrongs of Nativism: Economics, Freedom, and Legal Suppression of Spanish*, 84 Cornell L. Rev. 595, 646–53. (1999); Bradford Cornell & Ivo Welch, *Culture, Information, and Screening Discrimination*, 104 J. Pol. Econ. 542, 556–58 (1996). Although the authors of these articles use the concept of screening somewhat differently than we do, the underlying premise—that Insiders are likely to have a nuanced view of

the categories of Insiders, but a simplistic and crude view of the categories of Outsiders—is the same in both our work and theirs.

25. The gender gap in the taking on of family responsibilities is described at length in Selmi, *supra* note 16 and Williams *supra* note 23.

26. Nancy Leong, *Racial Capitalism*, 126 HARV. L. REV. (forthcoming 2013)

27. Lila A. Coleburn & Julia C. Spring, *Socrates Unbound: Developmental Perspectives on the Law School Experience*, 24 LAW & PSYCHOL. REV. 5, 18 (2000).

28. On the dynamics of reciprocity, see Ernst Fehr & Simon Gächter, *Fairness and Retaliation: The Economics of Reciprocity*, 14 J. ECON PERSP. 159 (2000).

29. For a discussion of informal networks within the workplace, often crucial to career advancement, see generally Cynthia Fuchs Epstein et al., *Glass Ceilings and Open Doors: Women's Advancement in the Legal Profession; A Report to the Committee on Women in the Profession, the Association of the Bar of the City of New York*, 64 FORDHAM L. REV. 291 (1995); Herminia Ibarra, *Race, Opportunity, and Diversity of Social Circles in Managerial Networks*, 38 ACAD. MGMT. J. 673 (1995); Patricia Digh, *The Next Challenge: Holding People Accountable-Organizational Commitment Towards Diversity*, HR MAG., Oct. 1998, at 63.

30. For self-reported statistics on the percentage of women and minorities among major law firm associates, *see* http://www.infirmation.com/shared/insider/payscale.tcl; *see also* http://www.nalp.org/lawfirmdiversity.

31. *Kobe Bryant Rape Case Collapses*, BBC NEWS, Sept. 2, 2004, http://news.bbc.co.uk/2/hi/americas/3620018.stm.

32. Mark Star, *Duds Go Out of Bounds*, NEWSWEEK, Oct. 31, 2005, *available at* http://www.newsweek.com/id/50857.

33. Mike Wise, *Opinions on the NBA's Dress Code are Far from Uniform*, WASH. POST, Oct. 23, 2005, *available at* http://www.washingtonpost.com/wp-dyn/content/article/2005/10/22/AR2005102201386.html.

34. *See, e.g.,* Associated Press, *Pacers' Jackson: Dress Code Is "Racist,"* NBC SPORTS, Oct. 20, 2005, http://nbcsports.msnbc.com/id/9730334/.

35. Jamie Wilson, *NBA's "No Bling" Dress Code Prompts Racism Accusations*, THE GUARDIAN, Oct. 31, 2005, *available at* http://www.guardian.co.uk/world/2005/oct/31/usa.americansports.

36. *See* Noah D. Zatz, *Managing the Macaw: Third-Party Harassers, Accommodation, and the Disaggregation of Discriminatory Intent* 109 COLUM. L. REV. 1357 (2009).

37. Scholars in other contexts have posited that the workplace choices of Outsider employees are often a response to organizational constraints not of the employees' own making. *See, e.g.,* Vicki Schultz, *Telling Stories About Women and Work: Judicial Interpretations of Sex Segregation in the Workplace in Title VII Cases Raising the Lack of Interest Argument*, 103 HARV. L. REV. 1749, 1815–16 (1990); Selmi, *supra* note 16, at 739.

Chapter 3

1. Rogers v. Am. Airlines, Inc., 527 F. Supp. 229 (S.D.N.Y. 1981).

2. *Id.* at 232.

3. *Id.* at 231–32.

4. *Id.* at 231.

5. Angela Onwuachi-Willig, *Another Hair Piece: Exploring New Strands of Analysis Under Title VI*, 98 GEO. L. J. 1079, 1093 (2010).

6. Paulette M. Caldwell, *Intersectional Bias and the Courts: The Story of Rogers v. American Airlines*, in RACE LAW STORIES 571, 573 (RACHEL F. MORAN & DEVON W. CARBADO EDS., 2008); *see also* Taunya Lowell Banks, *The Black Side of the Mirror/The Black Body in the Workplace*, in SISTER CIRCLE: BLACK WOMEN AND WORK (SHARON HARLEY AND BLACK WOMEN'S COLLECTIVE EDS., 2002).

7. *See e.g.,* Kimberlé Crenshaw, *Demarginalizing the Intersection of Race and Sex: A Black Feminist Critique of Antidiscrimination Doctrine, Feminist Theory and Antiracist Politics*, 1989 U. CHI. LEGAL F. 139 (1989).

8. This comparison to white men has become more complex since discrimination law was expanded to recognize claims by white men themselves.

9. Crenshaw, *supra* note 7.

10. Crenshaw's article is one of the most cited law review pieces of all time. *See* Fred R. Shapiro & Michelle Pierce, *The Most-Cited Law Review Articles of All Time*, 110 MICH. L. REV. 1483, 1489 at Table 1 (2012). At or around the time Crenshaw was developing her theory, other scholars were also thinking about the relationship between race and gender in the context of antidiscrimination law. Among the other classic pieces, are, Angela P. Harris, *Race and Essentialism in Feminist Legal Theory*, 42 STAN. L. REV. 581 (1990); Regina Austin, *Sapphire Bound!*, 1989 WIS. L. REV. 539 (1989); Paulette M. Caldwell, *A Hair Piece: Perspectives on the Intersection of Race and Gender*, 1991 DUKE L.J. 365 (1991); Judy Scales-Trent, *Black Women and the Constitution: Finding Our Place; Asserting Our Rights*, 24 HARV. C.R.-C. L. L. REV. 9 (1989).

11. Crenshaw, *supra* note 7, at 139.

12. *See* Peter Kwan, *Jeffrey Dahmer and the Cosynthesis of Categories*, 48 HASTINGS L. J. 1257, 1280 (1997).

13. *See* Darren Lenard Hutchinson, *Out Yet Unseen: A Racial Critique of Gay and Lesbian Legal Theory and Political Discourse*, 29 CONN. L. REV. 561 (1997).

14. *See* Mari J. Matsuda, *When the First Quail Calls: Multiple Consciousness as Jurisprudential Method*, 14 WOMEN'S RTS. L. REP.297 (1992).

15. *See* Devon W. Carbado, *Black Rights, Gay Rights, Civil Rights*, 47 UCLA L. REV. 1467 (2000).

16. *See* Francisco Valdes, *Sex and Race in Queer Legal Culture: Ruminations on Identities & Inter-connectivities*, 5 S. CAL. REV. L. & WOMEN'S STUD. 25 (1995).

17. *See* Adrien Katherine Wing, *Brief Reflections Toward a Multiplicative Theory and Praxis of Being*, 6 BERKELEY WOMEN'S L.J. 181 (1990–91).

18. Civil Rights Act of 1964, 42 U.S.C. § 2000(e-2).

19. Degraffenreid v. Gen. Motors Assembly Div., St. Louis, 413 F. Supp. 142, 145 (E.D. Mo. 1976).

20. *Id.*

21. The actual case analyzed in Crenshaw's article, *supra* note 7, was *DeGraffenreid*, *supra* note 19, where five black women had brought a discrimination claim against their employer, General Motors. In Crenshaw's words, "[b]ecause General Motors did hire women—albeit white women—during the period that no Black women were hired, there was, in the court's view, no sex discrimination that the seniority system could conceivably have perpetrated." Crenshaw, *supra* note 7, at 142.

22. *See* Harris, *supra* note 10

23. *See* Caldwell, *supra* note 6.

24. *Lam v. University of Hawaii*, 40 F.3d 1551, 1562 (9th Cir. 1994)

25. *See* Civil Rights Act of 1964, 42 U.S.C. § 2000e-2(a)(2). (2000) (prohibiting an employer from "limit[ing]...or classify[ing]...applicants for employment in any way which would deprive or tend to deprive any individual of employment opportunities..."); Connecticut v. Teal, 457 U.S. 440, 455 (1982) ("It is clear that Congress never intended to give an employer license to discriminate against some employees on the basis of race or sex merely because he favorably treats other members of the employees' group.... [T]he statute's focus on the individual is unambiguous.")

26. *See* Furnco Constr. Corp. v. Waters, 438 U.S. 567, 579 (1978); see also *Teal*, *supra* note 25.

27. Furnco Constr. Corp. *supra* note 26, at 580. Consider also *Espinoza v. Farah Mfg. Co.*, 414 U.S. 86 (1973). In *Espinoza*, a Mexican woman was not hired for a position in a workplace in which there was a very high percentage of employees of Mexican descent (96%). *Id.* at 87. While the Court explained that such statistics "do not automatically shield an employer" from a discrimination claim, the Court essentially implied that statistics were sufficient to negate a discrimination claim because the Court did not rely on any other evidence. "[T]he plain fact of the matter is that [the employer] does not discriminate against persons of Mexican national origin...In fact, the record shows that the worker hired in place of [the plaintiff] was a citizen with a Spanish surname." *Id.* at 93. Espinoza and Furnco suggest that courts some-times do deny plaintiff's discrimination claims if members of the plaintiff's protected class are

represented in the workplace or if someone of plaintiff's protected class was hired instead of the plaintiff.

28. *See e.g.*, Elizabeth M. Adamitis, *Appearance Matters: A Proposal to Prohibit Appearance Discrimination in Employment*, 75 WASH. L. REV. 195 (2000); *Cf.* Mary Nell Trautner & Samantha Kwan, *Gendered Appearance Norms: An Analysis of Employment Discrimination Lawsuits 1970–2008*, 20 RESEARCH IN THE SOCIOLOGY OF WORK 127 (2010).

29. DALE CARNEGIE, HOW TO WIN FRIENDS AND INFLUENCE PEOPLE (1936).

30. *Rogers, supra* note 1, at 231.

31. *Id.* at 232.

32. *Id.*

33. *Id.*

Chapter 4

1. The litigation is described in a number of articles, including Devon Carbado et al., *Makeup and Women*, in EMPLOYMENT DISCRIMINATION STORIES (JOEL W. FRIEDMAN, ED., 2006); Tracey George et al., *The New Old Legal Realism*, 105 NORTHWESTERN L. REV. 689 (2011).

2. We are not the only ones to observe the disjunction between gender and race cases in this area. *E.g.,* Kimberly A. Yuracko, *The Antidiscrimination Paradox: Why Sex Before Race?* 104 NORTHWESTERN L. REV. 1 (2010); *see also* Barbara J. Flagg, *Fashioning a Title VII Remedy for Transparently White Subjective Decisionmaking*, 104 YALE L. J. 2009, 2029–30 (1995).

3. A search on Google Images for "Darlene Jespersen" should pull up photographs of Darlene in her black and white bartender uniform, bow tie and all. Available at http://www.google.com/search?q=darlene+jespersen&hl=en&client=safari&rls=en&prmd=imvnso&tbm=isch&tbo=u&source=univ&sa=X&ei=1d24T4icEtHk6QGiuZjcCg&ved=0CHYQsAQ&biw=1023&bih=650.

4. *Jespersen v. Harrah's Operating Co., Inc.*, 444 F.3d 1104 (9th Cir. 2006).

5. *Id.* at 1111.

6. *Id.* at 1113.

7. *See* Carbado et al. *supra* note 1 at 114.

8. *General Elec. Co. v. Gilbert*, 429 U.S. 125 (1976). For a discussion and additional cites, see Carbado et al. *supra* note 1 at 114.

9. *See* Carbado et al., *supra* note 1 at 114–15; Ann C. McGinley *Babes and Beefcake: Exclusive Hiring Arrangements and Sexy Dress Codes*, 14 DUKE J. GENDER L. & POL'Y 257; Daniela M. de la Piedra, *Flirting with the PDA: Congress Must Give Birth to Accommodation Rights That Protect Pregnant Working Women*, 17 COLUMBIA J. GENDER & L. 275 (2008).

10. *See* Carbado et al., *supra* note 1 at 115.

11. Phillips v. Martin Marietta Corp. 400 U.S. 542 at 544; *See also* Carbado et al., *supra* note 1 at 115.

12. *Price Waterhouse v. Hopkins*, 490 U.S. 228 (1989). For discussions of this case, *see, e.g.,* Cynthia Estlund, *The Story of Price Waterhouse v. Hopkins*, in EMPLOYMENT DISCRIMINATION STORIES (JOEL FRIEDMAN, ED., 2006); Joel Wm. Friedman, *Gender Nonconformity and the Unfulfilled Promise of* Price Waterhouse v. Hopkins, 14 DUKE J. GENDER L. & POL'Y 205 (2007).

13. *Jespersen v. Harrah's Operating Co. Inc.* 444 F.3d 1104 at 1107 (9th Cir. 2004).

14. *Jespersen*, 444 F.3d 1104 at 1111.

15. *Id.* at 1112.

16. *Id.* at 1112.

17. *Id.* at 1116.

18. PAULA BLACK, THE BEAUTY INDUSTRY: GENDER, CULTURE, PLEASURE 34 (2004).

19. *Id.*

20. MARY-ALICE WATERS, INTRODUCTION TO COSMETICS, FASHIONS, AND THE EXPLOITATION OF WOMEN 3, 15 (JOSEPH HANSEN & EVELYN REED EDS., 1986).

21. Black, *supra* note 18, at 34.

22. KATHY PEISS, HOPE IN A JAR: THE MAKINGS OF AMERICA'S BEAUTY CULTURE, 241–242 (1999).

23. *Id.* The fear of the perception that women's sports are a haven for lesbians or other men haters has, in many contexts, led sports associations to impose grooming and appearance rules on the players as part of the attempt to feminize these players. *See, e.g.,* A. Burroughs et al., *Add Sex and Stir: Homophobic Coverage of Women's Cricket in Australia,* 19 J. Sport & Social Issues 266 (1995).

24. Black, *supra* note 18, at 34; *see also* Peiss, *supra* note 22, at 241–42.

25. Transcript of Video Presentation by Sheridan Harvey, *Rosie the Riveter: Real Women Workers in World War II,* Library of Congress Virtual Programs and Services, available at http://www.loc.gov/rr/program/journey/rosie-transcript.html.

26. *Id.* For a fuller account of this history, see Devon Carbado et al., *supra* note 1 at 108.

27. The doctrine was first announced in *Frank v. United Airlines,* 216 F.3d 845 (9th Cir. 2000).

28. *Jespersen,* 444 F.3d 1104 at 1117 (Kozinski, J., dissenting).

29. *Id.* at 1109.

30. *Id.* at 1110.

31. For an exploration of this tension, see Katherine T. Bartlett, *Tradition as Past and Present in Substantive Due Process Analysis,* Duke L. J. (forthcoming 2013).

Chapter 5

1. Charles Ogletree, *Lawyer's Statement on the Arrest of Henry Louis Gates Jr.,* The Root, July 20, 2009.

2. *TRANSCRIPT: 911 Call and Police Radio Dispatches in the Arrest of Henry Louis Gates Jr.,* ABC News, July 27, 2009, http://abcnews.go.com/Politics/story?id=8185376&page=1; *RAW DATA: Transcript of Cambridge 911 Call,* Fox News, July 27, 2009, available at http://www.foxnews.com/politics/2009/07/27/raw-data-transcript-cambridge/.

3. Laurel J. Sweet, et. al., *Officer in Henry Gates Flap Tried to Save Reggie Lewis,* Boston Herald, July 23, 2009, http://www.bostonherald.com/news/regional/view/20090722cop_who_arrested_henry_gates_im_not_apologizing/srvc=home&position=0.

4. *Cop Who Arrested Harvard Professor Teaches Racial Profiling Class,* New York Post, July 23, 2009, available at http://www.nypost.com/seven/07232009/news/nationalnews/cop_who_arrested_harvard_professor_gave___180902.htm.

5. Lynn Sweet, *The Story Behind My Obama Question,* Chicago Sun Times, July 24, 2009 at 4.

6. *Id.*

7. Huma Khan, et. al., *Obama Called Police Officer Who Arrested Gates, Still Sees "Overreaction" in Arrest,* ABC News, July 24, 2009, http://abcnews.go.com/Politics/story?id=8163051&page=1.

8. Cassie M. Chew, *Harvard Professor and Filmmaker Henry Louis Gates May Make Documentary about Racial Profiling,* The Examiner, July 22, 2009, http://www.examiner.com/x-13622-DC-Indie-Movie-Examiner~y2009m7d22-Filmmaker-Henry-Louis-Gates-may-pursue-legal-action-after-arrest.

9. Presumably, whites feel pressured to comport themselves respectably in the context of police encounters as well. The point is that stereotypes operate differently for blacks.

10. *Charge Against Harvard Professor Dropped,* CNN, July 21, 2009, http://www.cnn.com/2009/CRIME/07/21/massachusetts.harvard.professor.arrested/.

11. Krissah Thompson & Cheryl W. Thompson, *Officer Tells His Side of The Story in Gates Arrest,* Washington Post, July 24, 2009, http://www.washingtonpost.com/wp-dyn/content/article/2009/07/23/AR2009072301073.html?sid=ST2009072301777.

12. *Id.*

13. *Charge Against Harvard Professor Dropped, supra* note 10 ("According to his lawyer, Gates told the officer he lived there and showed him his Massachusetts driver's license and Harvard University identification card. The officer followed him into his house and said he had received a report of a possible break-in, the lawyer said. Gates grew frustrated that the officer was continuing to question him in his home and asked for the officer's name and badge number, Ogletree said.")

14. Schneckloth v. Bustamonte, 412 U.S. 218 (1973).

15. *Id.* at 220.
16. *Id.*
17. *Id.*
18. *Id.*
19. *Id.*
20. *Id.*
21. *Id.* at 222.
22. *Id.* at 220.
23. *Id.* at 227–28.
24. Robert L. Johnson & Dr. Steven Simring, The Race Trap: Smart Strategies For Effective Racial Communication in Business and in Life (2000); *see also* Kenneth Meeks, Driving While Black: Highways, Shopping Malls, Taxicabs, Sidewalks: What to Do If You Are a Victim of Racial Profiling 138, 142, 148 (2000).
25. *See* David Dante Trout, *The Race Industry, Brutality, and the Law of Mothers*, in Not Guilty: Twelve Black Men Speak Out on Law, Justice and Life 60 (Jabari Asim ed., 2001).
26. Johnson & Simring, *supra* note 24, at 121–22.
27. *Id.* at 121.
28. *Id.*
29. *Id.* at 125.
30. *Id.* at 121; *see also* Katheryn K. Russell, The Color of Crime 34 (1998).
31. Drayton v. United States, 536 US 194 (2002)
32. *Id.* at 199.
33. 412 U.S. 218, 220 (1973).
34. *Id.*
35. *See id.* According to 1990 Census figures, 71.7% of Sunnyvale's 117,229 residents were white, 19.4% were Asian or Pacific Islander, 12.8% were Hispanic, and 3.4% were black.
36. Three of the occupants have surnames that do not explicitly signify Latino/a identity.
37. In 1970, the Chicano Moratorium movement held a series of rallies in California. The most famous of these rallies took place in East Los Angeles in August 1970, when a crowd of 20,000 gathered to protest U.S. involvement in the Vietnam War. The rally ended in violence as participants clashed with LAPD officers and Los Angeles County Sheriff's deputies. Three people died in the conflict, including Mexican-American journalist Ruben Salazar, who was killed by a tear gas canister fired by law enforcement. *See Mexican-Americans March in California to Mark '70 Protest*, N.Y. Times, Aug. 28, 1995, at A12.
38. *See* Russell, *supra* note 30, at 34.
39. *See* Rohan Preston, *Police State of Mind*, in Not Guilty: Twelve Black Men Speak Out on Law, Justice and Life 158 (Jabari Asim ed., 2001).
40. For example, one study found that "[b]etween January 1995 and September 1996, of the 823 citizens detained for drug searches on one stretch of Interstate 95, over 70% were African American." Anthony C. Thompson, *Stopping the Usual Suspects: Race and the Fourth Amendment*, 74 N.Y.U. L. Rev. 957–58 (1999); *see also* James Warren, *Driving While Black*, The Atlantic (2009), available at http://www.theatlantic.com/magazine/archive/2009/07/driving-while-black/7625/; Kate Antonovics & Brian Knight, *A New Look at Racial Profiling: Evidence from the Boston Police Department*, NBER Working Paper (2004), available at http://www.nber.org/papers/w10634.pdf; Jennifer A. Larrabee, *"DWB (Driving While Black)" and Equal Protection: The Realities of an Unconstitutional Police Practice*, 6 J.L. & Pol'y 291, 297 (1997); Iver Peterson, *Turnpike Data Show Decline in Searches*, N.Y. Times, Apr. 24, 2001, at B1; David A. Harris, *The Stories, the Statistics, and the Law: Why "Driving While Black" Matters*, 84 Minn. L. Rev. 265 (1999).
41. As Katheryn Russell notes: "Many Black men have developed protective mechanisms to either avoid vehicle stops by the police or to minimize the potential for harm during these stops. The primary shield they use is an altered public persona. This includes a range of adaptive behaviors, e.g., sitting erect while driving, driving at the precise posted speed limit, avoiding certain neighborhoods, not wearing certain head gear (e.g., a baseball cap), and avoiding flashy cars. Another preemptive strategy that is available to a select few is vanity license plates

that indicate professional status (e.g., M.D. or ESQ). Of course, vanity tags can work as both a magnet and a deterrent for a police stop." Russell, *supra* note 30, at 34; *see also* Michael A. Fletcher, *Driven to Extremes: Black Men Take Steps To Avoid Police Stops*, WASH. POST, Mar. 29, 1996, at A1.

42. *See* Harris, *supra* note 40, at 265–66 (suggesting the actors Wesley Snipes, Will Smith, Blair Underwood, and LeVar Buron, and the attorney Johnnie Cochran have been racially profiled).

43. *Id.* at 269.

44. ACLU, DRIVING WHILE BLACK 5 (1999).

45. *See* MARK V. TUSHNET, MAKING CIVIL RIGHTS LAW: THURGOOD MARSHALL AND THE SUPREME COURT, 1936–1961, 28–29 (1994).

46. For an overview of the relationship between civil rights and the politics of respectability, see Regina Austin, *"The Black Community," Its Lawbreakers, and the Politics of Identification*, 65 S. CAL. L. REV. 1791 (1992).

47. In his account of the infamous Scottsboro trials of the early 1930s, in which nine black youths were accused of raping two white women in Alabama, James Goodman notes that Walter White, the NAACP's secretary at the time, was reluctant to involve his organization in the youths' defense partly because he feared that the NAACP's image was at risk.

48. RANDALL KENNEDY, RACE, CRIME, AND THE LAW 17 (1997).

49. *Id.* at 20. For critiques of Kennedy's employment of the politics of respectability, see Paul Butler, *(Color)Blind Faith: The Tragedy of Race, Crime, and the Law*, 111 HARV. L. REV. 1270 (1998) and Sheri Lynn Johnson, *Respectability, Race Neutrality, and Truth*, 107 YALE. L. J. 2619 (1998).

50. 517 U.S. 806 (1996).

51. *Id.* at 808.

52. *Id.*

53. *Id.*

54. *Id.*

55. *Id.* at 809.

56. *Id.*

57. The Supreme Court often has questioned the efficacy of an inquiry into hidden, improper motives in the Fourteenth Amendment context. See, e.g., *Palmer v. Thompson*, 403 U.S. 217, 224 (1971) (stating, in upholding a Jackson, Mississippi ordinance that closed city-owned swimming pools to stave off their desegregation, that "it is extremely difficult for a court to ascertain the motivation, or collection of different motivations, that lie behind a legislative enactment"); *see also Rogers v. Lodge*, 458 U.S. 613, 647 (1982) (Stevens, J., dissenting) ("Assuming that it is the intentions of the 'state actors' that is critical, how will their mental processes be discovered?").

58. Kevin R. Johnson, *The Song Remains the Same: The Story of* Wren v. United States, *in* RACE LAW STORIES 419, 426 (RACHEL F. MORAN & DEVON C. CARBADO EDS., 2008).

59. 532 U.S. 318 (2001).

60. *Id.* at 324.

61. *Id.*

62. *Id.* at 345–46.

63. *Id.* at 346.

64. *Id.* at 360 (O'Connor, J., dissenting).

65. For a discussion of the devaluation of black motherhood in comparison to white motherhood, see Cheryl I. Harris, *Myths of Race and Gender in the Trials of O.J. Simpson and Susan Smith—Spectacles of Our Times*, 35 WASHBURN L. J. 225 (1996).

66. 532 U.S. at 324, 370.

67. The analysis raises the question of whether and to what extent Justice O'Connor's discourse about the case would have been different if Atwater had been black. One response might be that the facts of Atwater could neatly fit into political narratives about black women as irresponsible mothers. Under this view, Justice O'Connor would not have objected so vociferously, if at all, to Officer Turek's conduct. Nor would she have discussed racial profiling. Another, perhaps more plausible response is that while Justice O'Connor's critique of Turek's

conduct likely would have been more restrained, she would nevertheless have discussed racial profiling. Under this view, ideologies about black motherhood would limit but not completely undermine Atwater's ability to function as an icon of victimization.

68. *Atwater*, 532 U.S. at 372 (O'Connor, J., dissenting).
69. According to the booklet, "[T]he constitutionality of pretextual traffic stops—using minor traffic infractions, real or alleged, as an excuse to stop and search a vehicle and its passengers—reached the Supreme Court in 1996 in a case called Whren v. United States." ACLU Booklet on file with authors. The literal language in the booklet appears to be taken from a June 1999 report by David A. Harris on the Driving While phenomenon. David A. Harris, Driving While Black: Racial Profiling on Our Nation's Highways, American Civil Liberties Union (June 7, 1999).
70. David A. Sklansky, *Some Cautious Optimism About the Problem of Racial Profiling*, 3 Rutgers Race & L. Rev. 293 (2001).
71. Muneer I. Ahmad, *A Rage Shared by Law: Post-September 11 Racial Violence as Crimes of Passion*, 92 Cal L. Rev. 1259–79 (2004) (explaining that post-September 11, "Muslim-looking" emerged as a new racial construct, based largely on phenotype as compared to faith, which functions to conflate "Muslim" with "terrorist" and renders many communities who fall under the category "Muslim-looking"—including "Arab Muslims, Arab Christians, Muslim non-Arabs … and even Latinos and African Americans, depending on how closely they approach the phenotypic stereotype of the terrorist"—highly suspect and dangerous).
72. John Tehranian, *Compulsory Whiteness: Towards a Middle Eastern Legal Scholarship*, 82 Ind. L.J. 20 (2007).
73. *See* Marc Mauer & Tracy Huling, Young Black Americans and the Criminal Justice System: Five Years Later 1, 3 (1995).
74. This is not to say that whiteness is never conceptualized under good/bad binaries. Certainly in the context of Jim Crow, there were discourses—that both whites and blacks deployed—to the effect that not all whites are bad, the presumption being that most whites in the South were.
75. Kennedy, *supra* note 48, at 21.
76. *Id.*
77. *See generally* Devon W. Carbado & Mitu Gulati, *Working Identity*, 85 Cornell L. Rev. 1259 (2000).

Chapter 6

1. *See* Julianne Hing, *Sonia Sotomayor on the Cover of Latina Magazine*, Colorlines, November 11, 2009, available at http://colorlines.com/archives/2009/11/sonia_sotomayor_on_the_cover_of_latina_magazine.html.
2. *See* Jesse Washington, *Sotomayor poses in court for Latina magazine cover*, Associated Press, November 11, 2009.
3. *See id.*
4. *See Lecture: "A Latina Judge's Voice,"* N.Y. Times, May 14, 2009 (republication of the Mario G. Olmos Lecture from 2001, given at U.C. Berkeley).
5. *See* Lani Guinier, *Our Preference for the Privileged*, Boston Globe, July 9, 2004; Sarah Rimerand & Karen W. Arenson, *Top Colleges Take More Blacks, but Which Ones?*, N.Y. Times, Jun. 24, 2004; *see also* Angela Onuachi-Willig, *The Admission of Legacy Blacks*, 60 Vand. L. Rev. 1141 (2007). For data on the topic, see Douglas Massey, Camille Charles, Margarita Mooney & Kim Torres, *Black Immigrants and Black Natives Attending Selective Colleges and Universities in the United States*, 113 Am. J. Ed. 243 (2007).
6. Angela Onwuachi-Willig, *The Admission of Legacy Blacks*, 60 Vand. L. Rev. 1141 (2007); Kevin Brown & Jeannine Bell, *Demise of the Talented Tenth: Affirmative Action and the Increasing Underrepresentation of Ascendant Blacks at Selective Higher Educational Institutions*, 69 Ohio St. L. J.1229 (2008).
7. University of California v. Bakke, 438 US 265 (1978).
8. *Id.* at 311–14.
9. Thomas H. Lee, *University Dons and Warrior Chieftains: Two Concepts of Diversity*, 72 Fordham L. Rev. 2301, 2305–06 (2004).

10. Peter H. Schuck, Diversity In America 164–65 (2003).
11. Grutter v. Bollinger, 539 U.S. 306, 330 (2003).
12. *Grutter,* 539 U.S. at 306. Clear rules take away that discretion.
13. *Id.*at 316.
14. *See* Donald C. Langevoort, *Overcoming Resistance to Diversity in the Executive Suite: Grease, Grit and the Corporate Tournament,* 61 Wash. & Lee L. Rev. 1615, 1630 (2004).
15. *Grutter,* 539 U.S. at 328.
16. Fisher v. University of Texas, No. 11–345.
17. *See* Order Denying Rehearing, Fisher v. University of Texas, No. 09–50822 (Fifth Circuit Court of Appeals, 2012); *see also* Adam Liptak, *Justices Take Up Race as Factor in College Entry,* N.Y. Times, Feb. 21, at A1.

Chapter 7

1. "The Politics of Fear," cover of The New Yorker, July 21, 2008. http://www.newyorker.com/online/covers/slideshow_blittcovers.
2. As an earlier version of this chapter was in the works, we came across a report of a racial discrimination case filed by Patricia Russell Brown, a Harvard-educated lawyer, against the law firm Dorsey & Whitney. The report in the *Washington Post* quoted Brown's lawyer as saying: "My client is a double-Ivy League graduate, a JAG [Judge Advocate General] lawyer…[and] a real-life 'Cosby Show' lawyer, married to a medical doctor. If they treat her this way, imagine how they treat other people." James V. Grimaldi, *Well-Credentialed Lawyer Accuses Minneapolis Firm of Racial Discrimination,* Wash. Post, Jan. 13, 2003, at E10 (first alteration in original).
3. For an analysis of one such story, see David B. Wilkins, *On Being Good and Black,* 112 Harv. L. Rev. 1924 (1999). *See also* Kenji Yoshino, *Covering,* 111 Yale L.J. 769, 879–87 (2002).
4. This is a caricature of the narrative of Larry Mungin's discrimination case. *See* Mungin v. Katten Muchin & Zavis, 116 F.3d 1549 (D.C. Cir. 1997); Wilkins, *supra* note 3, at 1935 (exploring the implications of the "just fell through the cracks" excuse in the Mungin case).
5. A critic might validly ask whether, to the extent the black employee takes pains to conform his behavior to that of the white employees, it will be easier for the black employee to argue that his failure to receive the promotion was based on race alone. After all, the black employee did everything as if he were white and still did not receive the promotion. An example illustrates why the answer is no. If the black associate brings a discrimination lawsuit against the firm, the firm will counter by saying that although they liked the associate, things just did not work out. Their promotion process involves sponsorship and a vote by all the current partners, and at the end of the day Johnny simply did not have enough support. Nothing racial occurred because white male associates slip through the cracks all of the time, too. This explanation, as illustrated by the appellate court opinion in the Mungin case, works to negate any starting presumption of racism. Instead, the claim is that it was just the system. Thus, the black plaintiff is likely to lose.
6. *See* Alan B. Krueger, *Sticks and Stones Can Break Bones, but the Wrong Name Can Make a Job Hard to Find,* N.Y. Times, Dec. 12, 2002, at C2.
7. "Terms" and "Conditions" are key words in Title VII. The statute makes it an unlawful employment practice for an employer to "discriminate against any individual with respect to his compensation, terms, conditions, or privileges of employment because of such individual's race, color, religion, sex, or national origin. Civil Rights Act of 1964 Sec. 2000(e)-2(a)(1). Performance claims are often found to fail the requirements of the statute on the ground that they constitute "de minimis" discrimination. *See* Rebecca Hanner White, *De Minimis Discrimination,* 47 Emory L.J. 1121, 1122–23 (1998).
8. *See* Willingham v. Macon Tel. Publ'g Co. 507 F.2d 1084, 1091–92 (5th Cir. 1975) (holding that employers cannot discriminate against employees based on immutable characteristics or fundamental rights); Gerdom v. Continental Airlines, Inc., 692 F.2d 602, 605–06 (9th Cir. 1982) (concluding that employers can promulgate rules that are different for men and women as long as they "do not significantly deprive either sex of employment opportunities, and are even-handedly applied to employees of both sexes"). Fundamental rights include the right to have children or to marry. Immutable characteristics include the protected

categories themselves. *See* Willingham, 507 F. 2d at 109. The scope of the third category—
policies that have a significant burden on only one sex that deprive that sex of employment
opportunities—is less clear. *See,* e.g., Carroll v. Talman Fed. Sav. & Loan Ass'n of Chicago,
604 F. 2d 1028, 1033 (7th Cir. 1979) (finding employer's policy requiring women, but not
men, to wear uniforms violated Title VII because "when some employees are uniformed
and others are not there is a natural tendency to assume that the uniformed women have
a lesser professional status than their male colleagues attired in normal business clothes");
Priest v. Rotary, 634 F. Supp. 571, 581. Fed. Dist. Ct., N.D. Cal. 1986 (holding that the
employer's policy requiring female employees to wear sexually suggestive clothing violated
Title VII); EEOC v. Sage Realty Corp., 507 F.Supp. 599, 608–09. Fed. Dist. Ct., S.D.N.Y.
1981 (same); *See also* Allen v. Lovejoy, 553 F. 2d 522, 524 (6th Cir. 1977) (holding that the
employer's rule requiring women to change their last names to their husband's names when
they got married violated Title VII because "[a] rule which applies only to women, with no
counterpart applicable to men, may not be the basis for depriving a female employee who
is otherwise qualified of her right to continued employment"). *But cf.* Stroud v. Delta Air
Lines, Inc., 544 F. 2d 892 (5th Cir. 1977) (holding that a rule prohibiting flight attendants
from being married did not violate Title VII because there were only female flight attendants, even though the no-marriage rule did not apply to other job classifications in which
men were employed).

9. The case most often cited for the immutability requirement is Willingham v. Macon Tel.
   Publ'g Co., 507 F.2d 1084, 1091–92 (5th Cir. 1975). For examples of other performance
   claims that were rejected by the courts as minimal, see, e.g., Tavora v. New York Mercantile
   Exch., 101 F.3d 907 (2d Cir. 1997); Barker v. Taft Broad Co., 549 F.2d 400 (6th Cir. 1977);
   Dodge v. Giant Food, 488 F.2d 1333. D.C. Cir. 1973.

10. *See,* e.g., City of Los Angeles v. Manhart et al., 435 U.S. 702, 705 n.13. (1978) (citing Sprogis
    v. United Air Lines Inc., 444 F.2d 1194, 1198 (7th Cir. 1971)).

11. Exceptions in the legal literature include, Margaret E. Montoya, *Mascaras, Trenzas, y Grednas:
    Un/Masking the Self While Un/braiding Latina Stories and Legal Discourse,* 15 CHICANO-LATINO
    L. REV. 1 (1994) and Kevin R. Johnson, *"Melting Pot" or "Ring of Fire"?: Assimilation and the
    Mexican-American Experience,* 85 CAL. L. REV. 1259, 1261 (1997).

12. *See generally* Philomena Essed & David Theo Goldberg, *Cloning Cultures: The Social Injustices
    of Sameness,* 25 ETHNIC & RACIAL STUD. 1066 (2002).

13. *Cf.* SHELBY STEELE, THE CONTENT OF OUR CHARACTER (1990).

14. One can argue that it is the homogeneity incentive that reduces efficiency because it cuts out
    real talent, skill, and experience.

15. Judges are already in the business of determining race. Our point is that these determina-
    tions are more complicated to the extent that they involve performative evidence. *See* Ariela J.
    Gross, *Litigating Whiteness: Trials of Racial Determination in the Nineteenth-Century South,* 108
    YALE L.J. 109 (1998); John Tehranian, *Compulsory Whiteness: Towards a Middle Eastern Legal
    Scholarship,* 82 INDIANA L. J. 1 (2007).

16. Richard T. Ford, *Race as Culture? Why Not?,* 47 UCLA L. REV. 1803, 1807 (2000). For a cri-
    tique of Ford's essay, see Leti Volpp, *Righting Wrongs,* 47 UCLA L. REV. 1815 (2000).

17. Ford, *supra* note 16, at 1805.

Chapter 8

1. *See* Kathleen M. Tangenberg, *Linking Feminist Social Work and Feminist Theology in Light of
   Faith-Based Service Initiatives,* 18 AFFILIA: J. WOMEN & SOC. WORK 379, 381 (2003).

2. *See* Mary Church Terrell, 15 *The Progress of Colored Women (1898),* in DANIEL MURRAY
   PAMPHLET COLLECTION (Library of Congress), *at* http://memory.loc.gov/cgi-bin/query/
   r?ammem/murray:@field(DOCID+@lit(lcrbmrpt0a13div2)).

3. So much so, in fact, that black public figures are vulnerable to criticism for failing to practice the commitment. Consider, for example, one commentator chastising University of
   California regent Ward Connerly for his anti-affirmative action advocacy and organizing:
   "It astounds me that this man, a black man, has forgotten where he has come from. He has
   completely neglected the idea that we have in our community to 'lift as we climb.' Instead,

he is kicking as he climbs, kicking those hot on his heels. He is a disgrace to the beneficiaries of affirmative action, and as a member of the black community." Bari al-Hakim, *Letters to the Editor: UC Regent: A Disgrace to His Race*, THE DAILY CALIFORNIANONLINE, Jan. 18, 2001.

4. This has been one of the most consistent criticisms of the Supreme Court's conceptualization of racism as a problem of conscious intentionality. *See* Washington v. Davis, 426 U.S. 229, 239–40 (1976) (holding that to establish an equal protection claim, the plaintiff must prove intentional racial decision-making on the part of the state).

5. Because racial stereotypes often have gender specificity, Johnny's success would not necessarily send a strong signal about the capacity for black women to succeed in that corporate environment.

6. On the subject, *see generally* Claude M. Steele & Joshua Aronson, *Stereotype Threat and the Intellectual Test Performance of African Americans*, 69 J. PERSONALITY & SOC. PSYCHOL. 797 (1995), and Joshua Aronson et al., *Stereotype Threat and the Academic Underperformance of Minorities and Women*, in PREJUDICE: THE TARGET'S PERSPECTIVE 83 (JANET K. SWIM & CHARLES STANGOR EDS., 1998).

7. *See, e.g.*, Gary Blasi, *Default Discrimination: Law, Science, and Unintended Discrimination in the New Workplace*, in BEHAVIORAL ANALYSES OF WORKPLACE DISCRIMINATION (MICHAEL J. YELNOSKY & MITU GULATI EDS., 2007); Nilanjana Dasgupta & Anthony G. Greenwald, *On the Malleability of Automatic Attitudes: Combating Automatic Prejudice with Images of Admired and Disliked Individuals*, 81 J. PERSONALITY & SOC. PSYCHOL. 800, 803–04 (2001).

8. The obligation to act affirmatively is discussed in a series of articles by David Wilkins about the "obligation thesis." *See* David B. Wilkins, *Essay: Identities and Roles: Race, Recognition, and Professional Responsibility*, 57 MD. L. REV. 1502, 1556 (1998); David B. Wilkins, *Two Paths to the Mountaintop? The Role of Legal Education in Shaping the Values of Black Corporate Lawyers*, 45 STAN. L. REV. 1981 (1993).

9. Some research suggests that the effect of making salient the danger that decision makers might be acting in a prejudiced manner can reduce the amount of prejudice. *See generally* Steven J. Spencer et al., *The Role of Motivation in the Unconscious: How Our Motives Control the Activation of Our Thoughts and Shape Our Actions*, in SOCIAL MOTIVATION: CONSCIOUS AND UNCONSCIOUS PROCESSES (JOSEPH P. FORGAS ET AL. EDS., 2005).

10. *See* Richard Delgado, *Essay: Affirmative Action as a Majoritarian Device: Or, Do You Really Want to Be a Role Model?*, 89 MICH. L. REV. 1222, 1223 n.5 (1991).

11. *See, e.g.*, Sherrilyn A. Ifill, *Racial Diversity on the Bench: Beyond Role Models and Public Confidence*, 57 WASH. & LEE L. REV. 405, 481 (2000); Adeno Addis, *Role Models and the Politics of Recognition*, 144 U. PA. L. REV. 1377, 1384 n.20 (1996).

12. *See* Wygant v. Jackson Bd. of Educ., 476 U.S. 267, 275–76 (1986) (refusing to utilize the role model theory); Regents of the Univ. of Cal. v. Bakke, 438 U.S. 265, 305–10 (1978) (refusing to consider remedying the amorphous effects of past "societal discrimination" absent a compelling state interest).

13. The classic work on tokenism and the burdens that come associated with it is ROSABETH MOSS KANTER, MEN AND WOMEN OF THE CORPORATION (2d ed. 1993). Kanter's focus was on women, and the dynamics with respect to other groups such as racial minorities are likely to be different. For more recent discussions, *see* Louise Marie Roth, *The Social Psychology of Tokenism: Status and Homophily Processes on Wall Street*, 47 SOC. PERSP. 189, 208–10 (2004); Michael J. Yelnosky, *The Prevention Justification for Affirmative Action*, 64 OHIO ST. L.J. 1385, 1389–99 (2003).

14. *See* Yelnosky, *supra* note 13, at 1390–99 (describing the dynamics of tokenism).

15. In the law firm context, this information is described in David B. Wilkins & G. Mitu Gulati, *Why Are There So Few Black Lawyers in Corporate Law Firms? An Institutional Analysis*, 84 CAL. L. REV. 496 (1996). *See generally* Pamela J. Smith, *Failing to Mentor Sapphire: The Actionability of Blocking Black Women from Initiating Mentoring Relationships*, 10 UCLA Women's L.J. 373, 389–90 (2000); Margo Murray & Marna A. Owen, *Beyond the Myths and Magic of Mentoring* (1991); Scott E. Seibert et al., *A Social Capital Theory of Career Success*, 44 ACAD. MGMT. J. 219 (2001).

16. Individuals rely on not just a single mentor for developmental support, but on a "relationship constellation." Monica C. Higgins & Kathy E. Kram, *Reconceptualizing Mentoring at Work: A Developmental Network Perspective*, 26 ACAD. MGMT. REV. 264, 264 (2001).

17. Wilkins describes the importance of having access to networks that can provide such information in the context of the story of Lawrence Mungin, a black lawyer who makes a number of strategic errors in his attempt to move up the corporate hierarchy. *See* David B. Wilkins, *On Being Good and Black*, 112 HARV. L. REV. 1924, 1966 (1999) (book review); *see also*, Glenn C. Loury, *Discrimination in the Post-Civil Rights Era: Beyond Market Interactions*, J. ECON. PERSP., Spring 1998, at 119–21 (arguing that social networks, which largely determine one's access to resources, allow past discrimination to persist over time and can have deleterious impacts on skills among minorities and significantly contribute to racial inequalities).

18. *See* DAVID A. THOMAS & JOHN J. GABARRO, BREAKING THROUGH: THE MAKING OF MINORITY EXECUTIVES IN CORPORATE AMERICA 26 (1999). *See generally* Raymond A. Friedman & Brooks Holtom, *The Effects of Network Groups on Minority Employee Turnover Intentions*, 41 HUM. RESOURCES MGMT. 405 (2002) (describing the background literature on the barriers to mentorship for minority employers and finding that the presence of "network groups" can help alleviate that problem); David A. Thomas, *Racial Dynamics in Cross-Race Developmental Relationships*, 38 ADMIN. SCI. Q. 169 (1993) (describing the barriers that racial differences can erect to the creation of effective mentorship relationships). On the importance of mentorship relationships for lawyers in general and minority lawyers in particular, *see generally* Monica C. Higgins & David A. Thomas, *Constellations and Careers: Toward Understanding the Effects of Multiple Developmental Relationships*, 22 J. ORG. BEHAV. 223 (2001); David Thomas & Monica Higgins, *Mentoring and the Boundaryless Career: Lessons from the Minority Experience*, in THE BOUNDARYLESS CAREER: A NEW EMPLOYMENT PRINCIPLE FOR A NEW ORGANIZATIONAL ERA 268 (MICHAEL B. ARTHUR & DENISE M. ROUSSEAU EDS., 1996).

19. *See* Wilkins & Gulati, *supra* note 15, at 569–70; *see also* Nijole V. Benokraitis & Joe R. Feagin, *Sex Discrimination: Subtle and Covert*, in DOWN TO EARTH SOCIOLOGY 334, 334–35 (JAMES M. HENSLIN ED., 7th ed. 1993) (describing the informational inadequacy problem that arises as a result of being excluded from informal social groups at the workplace).

20. *See, e.g.*, Jonathan Kaufman, *Inside Outsiders: As Blacks Rise High in the Executive Suite, CEO is Often Jewish*, WALL ST. J., Apr. 22, 1998, at A1. What Wilkins interestingly finds in the law firm context is that the first generation of minority successes often came in laterally, after what was usually a distinguished career in public service. David B. Wilkins, *Partners Without Power?: A Preliminary Look at Black Partners in Corporate Law Firms*, 2 J. INST. FOR STUDY LEGAL ETHICS 15, 30–31 (1999). Wilkins argues that minority associates and partners, because of their reduced access to intrafirm networks, often have to tap into networks outside their firm—networks that often involve public service to the larger minority community. David B. Wilkins, *Doing Well by Doing Good? The Role of Public Service in the Careers of Black Corporate Lawyers*, 41 HOUS. L. REV. 1, 29–30 (2004).

21. *Cf.* DERRICK A. BELL, CONFRONTING AUTHORITY: REFLECTIONS OF AN ARDENT PROTESTOR 9–25 (1994) (providing "models for confrontation").

22. *See* Elijah Anderson, *The Social Situation of the Black Executive: Black and White Identities in the Corporate World*, in THE CULTURAL TERRITORIES OF RACE: BLACK AND WHITE BOUNDARIES 3, 9 (MICHÈLE LAMONT ED., 1999); *cf.* David A. Thomas, *Diversity as Strategy*, HARV. BUS. REV., Sept. 2004, at 98, 102 (noting, in a description of IBM's recent strategic initiative to improve diversity at the firm, how members of the black task force advocated for a conservative approach to diversity because of the fear that they would be perceived as asking for "unearned preferences, and, even worse, might encourage the stereotype that blacks are less capable").

23. On the distancing strategies adopted by Outsiders in a variety of contexts, including race, gender, and sexual orientation, see Angela Onwuachi-Willig, *Volunteer Discrimination*, 40 U.C. DAVIS L. REV. 1895, 1898, 1921–25 (2007); Frank Rudy Cooper, *Intersectional Assimilation, Identity Performance and Hierarchy*, 39 U.C. DAVIS L. REV. 853, 859–60 (2006); Angela Onwuachi-Willig & Mario L. Barnes, *By Any Other Name?: On Being "Regarded as" Black, and Why Title VII Should Apply Even if Lakisha and Jamal Are White*, 2005 WIS. L. REV. 1283, 1306–07. More generally, *see* Donna Chrobot-Mason et al., *Sexual*

Identity Management Strategies: An Exploration of Antecedents and Consequences, 45 SEX ROLES 321 (2001); John F. Dovido et al., *Reducing Contemporary Prejudice: Combating Explicit and Implicit Bias at the Individual and Intergroup Level*, in REDUCING PREJUDICE AND DISCRIMINATION 137 (STUART OSKAMP ED., 2000); Naomi Ellemers et al., *Self and Social Identity*, 53 ANN. REV. PSYCHOL. 161 (2002); Teresa LaFromboise et al., *Psychological Impact of Biculturalism: Evidence and Theory*, in THE CULTURE AND PSYCHOLOGY READER 489 (NANCY RULE GOLDBERGER & JODY BENNET VEROFF EDS., 1995); Robin J. Ely, *The Effects of Organizational Demographics and Social Identity on Relationships Among Professional Women*, 39 ADMIN. SCI. Q. 203 (1994) [hereinafter Ely, *The Effects of Organizational Demographics*]; Robin J. Ely, *The Power in Demography: Women's Social Constructions of Gender Identity at Work*, 38 ACAD. MGMT. J. 589 (1995); Laurie A. Rudman, *Self-Promotion as a Risk Factor for Women: The Costs and Benefits of Counter-stereotypical Impression Management*, 74 J. PERSONALITY & SOC. PSYCHOL. 629 (1998); Laurie A. Rudman & Peter Glick, *Feminized Management and Backlash Toward Argentic Women: The Hidden Costs to Women of a Kinder, Gentler Image of Middle Managers*, 77 J. PERSONALITY & SOC. PSYCHOL. 1004 (1999).

24. In her classic work, Kanter describes this (in the gender context) as women being subject to "loyalty tests" where, as a requirement of fitting in, women are expected to put down other women on occasion. Kanter describes three ways in which women can pass loyalty tests: they can let slide biased statements about other women, they can allow for jokes about women to be made without resistances, and they can accept their situation. *See* Kanter, *supra* note 13, at 227–29 (explaining loyalty tests); *see also* Ramit Mizrahi, Note, *"Hostility to the Presence of Women": Why Women Undermine Each Other in the Workplace and the Consequences for Title VII*, 113 YALE L.J. 1579, 1602 (2004).

25. Hewlin and Rosette argue that even white male employees will often feel pressured to avoid pointing out instances of discrimination (even while thinking that it is wrong) so as to avoid being stigmatized as non-team players. *See generally* Patricia Faison Hewlin & Ashleigh Shelby Rosette, *Stigma Avoidance: A Precursor to Workplace Discrimination* (Aug. 2004) (unpublished draft). Hewlin and Rosette draw on a larger literature on organizational silence. For examples of articles in this area, *see* Frances J. Milliken et al., *An Exploratory Study of Employee Silence: Issues That Employers Don't Communicate Upward and Why*, 40 J. MGMT. STUD. 1453 (2003); C.C. Pinder & Karen P. Harlos, *Employee Silence: Quiescence and Acquiescence as Responses to Perceived Injustice*, 20 RES. HUM. RESOURCES & PERSONNEL MGMT. 331 (2001); Janet P. Near & Marcia P. Miceli, *Whistle-Blowers in Organizations: Dissidents or Reformers?*, 9 RES. ORG. BEHAV. 321 (L.L. CUMMINGS & BARRY M. STRAW EDS., 1987).

26. The development of open, trusting, and genuine relationships is crucial for the setting up of effective teams. *See* Amy Edmonson, *Psychological Safety and Learning Behavior in Work Teams*, 44 ADMIN. SCI. Q. 350, 354–55 (1999). There are two bodies of research that bear on this point that racial minorities are likely to have difficulty in matching up to their white male counterparts on these criteria. First, research shows that perceived similarity and in-group-ness positively influences the likelihood of trust and liking, crucial precursors for setting up effective teams. *See generally* Roderic M. Kramer et al., *Collective Trust and Collective Action: The Decision to Trust as a Social Decision*, in TRUST IN ORGANIZATIONS: FRONTIERS OF THEORY AND RESEARCH 357 (RODERIC M. KRAMER & TOM R. TYLER EDS., 1996); Charlan Jeanne Nemeth, *Differential Contributions of Majority and Minority Influence*, 93 PSYCHOL. REV. 23 (1986); Jeffrey T. Polzer et al., *Capitalizing on Diversity: Interpersonal Congruence in Small Work Groups*, 47 ADMIN. SCI. Q. 296 (2002). And then there is a large body of research on the types of negative stereotypes racial minorities face that, depending on the minority identity in question, can include laziness, untrustworthiness, lack of intelligence, lack of creativity, and foreignness. *See generally* Patricia G. Devine, *Stereotypes and Prejudice: Their Automatic and Controlled Components*, 56 J. PERSONALITY & SOC. PSYCHOL. 5 (1989); Sandy Jeanquart-Barone, *Implications of Racial Diversity in the Superior-Subordinate Relationship*, 26 J. APPLIED SOC. PSYCHOL. 935 (1996); Lisa Sinclair & ZivaKunda, *Reactions to a Black Professional: Motivated Inhibition and Activation of Conflicting Stereotypes*, 77 J. PERSONALITY & SOC. PSYCHOL. BULL. 885 (1999).

27. *See* Francis J. Flynn et al., *Getting to Know You: The Influence of Personality on Impressions and Performance of Demographically Different People in Organizations*, 46 ADMIN. SCI. Q. 414, 419 (2001) (finding that demographically different persons who are better able to self monitor are more likely to be able to succeed in workplace settings).

28. Along these lines, a number of commentators recommend that Outsiders—those with different social identities—de-emphasize those social identity differences and instead emphasize work-related commonalities so as to achieve cohesion and unity at the workplace. *See generally* Scott Allison & Caryn E. Herlocker, *Constructing Impressions in Demographically Diverse Organizational Settings*, 37 AM. BEHAV. SCIENTIST 637 (1994); Jennifer A. Chatman et al., *Being Different Yet Feeling Similar: The Influence of Demographic Composition and Organizational Culture on Work Processes and Outcomes*, 43 ADMIN. SCI. Q. 749 (1998); John F. Dovidio et al., *Reducing Contemporary Prejudice: Combating Explicit and Implicit Bias at the Individual and Intergroup Level*, inREDUCING PREJUDICE AND DISCRIMINATION (STUART OSKAMP ED., 2000). There is a body of research that finds that the above prescriptions do not always need to hold for diverse teams to function effectively. If the organizations themselves set up structures that value social identity differences, then employees will feel less of a need to adopt the kinds of strategies mentioned above. Instead, their differences can, in some cases, be harnessed to achieve productivity gains. *See* Robin J. Ely & David A. Thomas, *Cultural Diversity at Work: The Effects of Diversity Perspectives on Work Group Processes and Outcomes*, 46 ADMIN. SCI. Q. 229, 240–43 (2001) [hereinafter Ely & Thomas, *Cultural Diversity at Work*] (examining the potential value of diverse individual cultural experiences to the group process); Robin J. Ely & David A. Thomas, *Team Learning and the Racial Diversity-Performance* Link 26–31 (Aug. 2004) (unpublished manuscript, on file with *Washington and Lee Law Review*) (analyzing the impact of racial learning environments on performance measures).

29. On the labeling of prominent African Americans such as Clarence Thomas as "sell outs," see RANDALL KENNEDY, THE POLITICS OF RACIAL BETRAYAL (2008).

30. *See* Anderson, *supra* note 22, at 12 ("For…blacks [at the higher status levels of an organization] there is a strongly felt need to believe they are present in the organization not solely because of the color of their skin but because of their own excellence in the general business world.").

31. The phenomenon of inadequate mentorship by out-group members has been observed at length in the literature on gender. *See* Mizrahi, *supra* note 24, at 1590–92 (examining the phenomenon of "female-on-female workplace hostility"). More broadly, *see generally* Pat Heim & Susan Murphy, IN THE COMPANY OF WOMEN: TURNING WORKPLACE CONFLICT INTO POWERFUL ALLIANCES (2001). Research by scholars such as Ely and Thomas, however, suggests that there is nothing necessary about this dynamic. *See generally* Ely and Thomas, *Cultural Diversity at Work, supra* note 28. Organizations can be structured in ways that women (and other Outsiders) are comfortable enough in their difference that they are able to help others of their group. *See* Ely, *The Effects of Organizational Demographics, supra* note 23, at 206.

32. For discussions of these diversity initiatives and perceived benefits, *see, e.g.,* Lissa Broome et al., *Dangerous Categories: Narratives of Corporate Board Diversity*, 89 N.C. L. REV. 759 (2010); *Narratives of Diversity in the Corporate Boardroom: What Insiders Say About Why Diversity Matters*, in DISCOURSE PERSPECTIVES ON ORGANIZATIONAL COMMUNICATION (forthcoming, 2012).

Epilogue

1. *See, e.g.,* Noreen Malone, *Do Elizabeth Warren's Cherokee Roots Really Matter?*, NEW YORK MAGAZINE, May 3, 2012, available at http://nymag.com/daily/intel/2012/05/elizabeth-warrens-cherokee-roots-matter.html.

2. *E.g.,* David Bernstein, *Elizabeth Warren Herself Claimed Minority Status*, April 28, 2012, available at http://volokh.com/2012/04/28/elizabeth-warren-herself-claimed-minority-status/. In his piece, Bernstein cites to an interesting case involving two fair-complexioned, fair-haired Boston firefighters claimed they were black based on ancestry. They were determined not

to be black, in part, as a function of their identity performances. *See* Susan Diesenhouse, *Boston Case Raises Questions on Misuse of Affirmative Action*, N.Y. Times, Oct. 9, 1988, available at http://www.nytimes.com/1988/10/09/us/boston-case-raises-questions-on-m isuse-of-affirmative-action.html?pagewanted=all&src=pm.

3. *E.g.,* Gayle Fee & Laura Raposa, *Liz Skips Harvard Powwow*, Boston Herald, May 8, 2012, available at http://bostonherald.com/track/inside_track/view/20220508inside_ track_headline_3/.

4. *E.g.,* Jamarhl Crawford, *Elizabeth Warren: Native to Privilege*, Blackstonian, May 1, 2012, available at http://blackstonian.com/news/2012/05/elizabeth-warren-native-to-privilege/.

5. Richard T. Ford, Racial Culture: A Critique (2005).

6. *See* Leti Volpp, *Righting Wrongs*, 47 UCLA L. Rev. 1815, 1833–34 (2000).

INDEX

ACLU. *See* American Civil Liberties Union (ACLU)

Admissions policy, diversification, 122–25
applicant's perspective, 130–31
differentiation, 128–30
interaction with others, comfort of applicant, 127–28
interviewing diversity, 125–26
negating stereotypes, 122–24
process, admissions, 126–30
quotas, 132
racially cooperative citizenry, promoting, 124–25
reasons for concerns, 131–33
"risky" candidates, determining, 128–30
and similarity, 126–27
University of Michigan Law School, 119

Advancement tasks (work), "talking white" and, 54–56

Affirmative action, 18–19
diversity through, 118–21. *See also* Diversity
Gratz v. Bollinger, 119–21
Grutter v. Bollinger, 119, 132
University of California v. Bakke, 118–21

African Americans. *See specific topic*

Alcala, Joe, 101–2, 105

The All-American Girls Professional Baseball League, 87

Als, Hilton, 28

American Airlines, policy on braids, 67–69, 77–78, 92, 143

American Airlines, Rogers v., 67–69, 77–78, 92, 143

American Civil Liberties Union (ACLU), 18
"Driving While Black," 111–112
racial profiling, campaign against, *107,* 107–8, 113

Anti-discrimination solutions, 19, 134–48
assimilation costs, 146–47

assimilationist model, 140–41, 148
choice of model, 146
difference model, 141–48
hypothetical cases, 136–40
race plus discrimination, 143–44
sex plus regime, 143

Armed Forces, gays and lesbians in, 169

Ascriptive identity, 23

Asian Americans
stereotypes, 41
women, discrimination against, 70

Assimilation costs, 146–47

Assimilationist model, anti-discrimination solutions, 140–41, 148

Atwater, Gail, 110, 111, 184–85n66

Atwater v. City of Lago Vista, 110, 111, 184–85n66

Backfire costs, 40–41

Bakke, University of California v., 118–21

Barnes, Mario, 10

Basketball
and Obama, 8–9, 63
outsider playing, 174n24

Bell, Jeannine, 118

Biden, Joseph, 6–7

"Black enough," 8–10

Black Panther Party, 16

Blacks. *See specific topic*

Black women, Working Identity, 17–18, 68–79
families, commitment to, 57
gender gap, 73
negative stereotypes of, countering, 145
race-gender intersection, 71
Rogers v. American Airlines, 77–78, 92, 143
Title VII, 74–75

Blink (Gladwell), 42

Bollinger, Gratz v., 119–21

Bollinger, Grutter v., 119, 132

Bonilla-Silva, Eduardo, 10
BP. *See* British Petroleum (BP)
Braids, policy on (American Airlines),
    67–69, 77–78, 92, 143
Braun, Carol Moseley, 7
British Petroleum (BP), 9
Brown, Kevin, 118
Brown, Patricia Russell, 186n2
Brown v. Board of Education, 12
Bryant, Kobe, 63
Bush, George W., 34
Bustamonte, Schneckloth v., 101–2, 105
Buying back, 34–35

Caldwell, Paulette, 69
Cambridge Police Department, 97, 106, 114,
    182n13
Campbell, Timothy, 108–9, 112
Carnegie, Dale, 77
Carolina Tar Heels, 8–9
Chappelle, Dave, *21,* 21–23, 25–26
    "When Keeping It Real Goes Wrong," 114
The Chappelle Show (tv show), 21–23,
    25–26
Chicago Bulls, 8
Chicago Sun-Times, 98
Chinese accents, stereotyping, 27
Chinese nuclear espionage, suspected,
    173n12
Citizenship tasks, talking white, 58–62
City of Lago Vista, Atwater v., 110, 111,
    184–85n66
Clinton, Bill, 7
Clinton, Hillary, 5
Clooney, George, 5
Coleburn, Lila, 59
Collegiality, 24, 77
Colorblindness, 38–39, 43
Comforting, racial, 27–28
Complete passing, 29, 32
Compromising, costs of, 40
Concerns regarding "acting white," 167–70
Connerly, Ward, 188n3
Corporate leaders, black, 152–55,
    161–65
The Cosby Show (tv show), 47–48
Crash (film), 28
Crenshaw, Kimberlé, 70–71
Criminal, not acting, 96–115. *See also* Racial
    profiling
Crowley, James, 96, 97–98, 101, 106, 114, 182n13

Darlene Jespersen v. Harrah's Casino, 80–82,
    85–92, 95
    Price Waterhouse, application of doctrine to,
        84, 145
Davis, Sammy, Jr., 25

*Demarginalizing the Interaction of Race and Sex: A
    Black Feminist Critique of Antidiscrimination
    Doctrine, Feminist Theory, and Antiracist
    Politics* (Crenshaw), 70–71
Democratic National Convention (2004), 5–6
Derek, Bo, *68,* 68–69
Dickerson, Debra, 9
Difference model, anti-discrimination solutions,
    141–48
Discomfort, providing, 33–34
Discrimination. *See also* Gender discrimination;
    Race discrimination
    doctrine of immutability, 177n73, 187n8
    generally, 2
    intra-group discrimination, 2
Distancing strategies, Outsiders, 190n23
Diversity, 116–33
    admissions policy, universities. *See* Admissions
        policy, diversification
    affirmative action, 118–21
    and paper records, 121–22
    reasons for concerns, 131–33
    and Working Identity, 1–2, 116–33
Doctrine of immutability, 177n73, 187n8
Dorsey & Whitney, 186n2
Double bind, 167–68. *See also* Racial double
    bind
    effeminacy cases, 91, 95
    women employees, 54
Drayton, United States v., 104–5
"Driving While Black" (ACLU), 112
Driving while black/brown (DWB), 100, 106–15
    Atwater v. City of Lago Vista, 110, 111,
        184–85n66
    differences between blacks and whites, 103–4
    "Driving While Black" (ACLU), 112
    Whren v. United States, 50, 109–12
Duke Blue Devils, 8–9
DWB. *See* Driving while black/brown (DWB)

Ebony, "Power 150" article, 149–50
Edwards, John, 7
Effeminacy cases, 91, 95. *See also Darlene
    Jespersen v. Harrah's Casino; Price
    Waterhouse v. Hopkins*
Epstein, Richard, 174n31
Exploitation, "talking white," 50

First-generation blacks, 155
Fourteenth Amendment, 184n57
Fourth Amendment, 50, 102

Gates, Henry Louis, 63, 97, *97,* 106, 114, 182n13
Gaye, Marvin, 80
Gay plaintiffs, 89–91, 95
Gays and lesbians, Armed Forces, 169
Gender discrimination, 82–84. *See also* Title VII

Gingrich, Newt, 14
Gladwell, Malcolm, 42
"God Damn America" speech (Wright),
    11–12
Gonzalez, Carlos, 108–9, 112–14
"Good" and "bad" blacks. *See* Racial profiling
"Good" and "bad" women, Working Identity,
    93–95
Gratz v. Bollinger, 119–21
Grooming requirements. *See* Black women,
    Working Identity; White women, Working
    Identity
Grutter v. Bollinger, 119, 132
Guinier, Lani, 118

Hampton University, 16
Harrah's Casino
    Beverage Department Image Transformation
        Program, 81
    grooming requirements policy, 85–88
Harrah's Casino, Darlene Jespersen v., 79, 80–82,
    85–92, 95
Harris, Cheryl, 43
Harris, Frederick, 10
Harvard Law Review, 5
Helping other blacks, "acting white" for purposes
    of, 149–66
    corporate leaders, black, 152–55
    intervention, direct, 157
    role modeling, 153–54
    success, 155–56
    tokenism, combating, 153–54
    "trickle-down" benefits, 150–52, 156–65
He Talk Like a White Boy (Phillips), 47–48
High visibility settings, conversations in, 50–52
Hiring, interviews, 62–65
Hopkins, Ann, 84–92, 95, 144–45
Hopkins, Price Waterhouse v., 84–92, 95, 144–45
Howard, Terrance, 28

Identity, defined, 23–24
Identity performances ("acting white"),
    35–42
    Asian Americans, stereotypes of, 41
    backfire costs, 40–41
    colorblindness, 38–39, 43
    compromising, costs of, 40
    Indians, stereotypes of, 41
    poor performances, costs of, 40
    racial cliquishness, 39
    racial stereotypes, 36, 37–38
    Socratic method, 36–37, 175n46
    women, stereotypes of, 40
    Working Identity as work, 35–38
"I Have a Dream" (King), 10
Immutability, 177n73, 187n8
Incarceration of blacks, statistics, 185n73

Institutional fit, 77
Institutional "goodies," "talking white" in
    workplace, 60–61
Institutional speech and criticism," talking white,"
    52–54
Intersectionality , 69, 74
intervention, direct, 157
Interviews, hiring
    Outsiders, 62
    "talking white," 62–65
Intra-group discrimination, 2

Jackson, Jesse, 4, 6–7
Jarrett, Valerie, *149,* 149–50
Jespersen, Darlene, 80–82, 85–91, 95
    photos of, 181n3
Jespersen v. Harrah's Casino, 79
Johnson, Robert, 102
Jones, Edith, 133
Jordan, Michael, 8, 147

Kang, Jerry, 42
"Keeping it real," 114
Kennedy, Randall, 108–9, 113
King, Martin Luther, Jr., 10, 123
Korean Americans, stereotypes, 33
Kozinski, Alex, 80, *80,* 93

LAMBDA Legal, 92
LAPD, 108
Latina magazine, 117
Latinas
    and appearance, 168
    Supreme Court. *See* Sotomayor, Sonia
Legal intervention, Outsiders, 65
Leong, Nancy, 58
Limbaugh, Rush, 11
Lincoln, Abraham, 9–10
"Loyalty tests," 190n24
Luo, Michael, 15, 19

Maher, Bill, 9
Makeup, gender discrimination claim
    regarding wearing to work, 80–82,
    85–91, 94–95
Malcolm X, 123
Marshall, Thurgood, 118
Martin, Trayvon, 13–14, 31
Mentorship, inadequate, 191n31
Mexican Americans
    appearance of, and traveling, 168
    hiring, 180–81n27
Michigan, University of
    Law School, 118
Miranda warnings, 35–36
Mungin, Lawrence, 189n17
Muslim Americans, 168

National Association for the Advancement of
    Colored People (NAACP), 108, 184n47
National Association of Black Accountants, 150
National Association of Colored Women's Clubs,
    150
National Review, 136
Native Americans, appearance, 168–69
NBA, 63–65
NCAA tournament, 9
Negotiation, racial, 25–26
Negro dialect, 46–47, 67
New Yorker, 28, *134*
New York Times, 13, 15–16, 19
"Not too black," 5–7
"N-word," 47

Obama, Barack, *46*
    acting white versus acting black, 91–92
    background of, 4–5
    basketball, relation to, 8–9, 63
    as "black enough," 8–10
    Democratic National Convention (2004)
        speech, 5–6
    and double bind, 167–68
    Gates, Henry Louis case, 98–99
    on Martin, Trayvon, 14
    Negro dialect and, 46–47, 67
    New Yorker, 134
    as "not too black," 5–7
    race, speech on, 11–12
    Sotomayor, Sonia, appointment of,
        115–18
    Wright, Reverend and, 11–12
Obama, Michelle, *134–36*
O'Brien, Soledad, 99
O'Connor, Sandra Day, 11, 110, 119–21, 132,
    184–85n66
Ohio, Terry v., 35–37
Onwuachi-Willig, Angela, 10, 69, 118
Orr, Yvonne, 16
Outsiders
    basketball players, 174n24
    distancing strategies, 190n23
    identities of, 174n3124
    interviews, hiring, 62
    legal intervention, 65
    social identities, 191n28
    workplace, 58–61

Indian, stereotypes, 41
Parker, Sarah Jessica, 5
Partial passing, 29, 32
Passing, strategic, 29–32, 43
    complete passing, 29, 32
    partial passing, 29, 32
    racial exceptionalism, 31
    stuffwhitepeoplelike.com, 29–31

Performance
    poor performances, costs of, 40
    and Working Identity differences, 76–77
Performing identity, 174n31
Phillips, Joseph, 47–48
Powell, Lewis F., 118–20
"Power 150" article *(Ebony),* 149–50
Pregerson, Harry, 87
Pregnancy Discrimination Act, 83
Price Waterhouse v. Hopkins, 84–92, 95, 144–45
Privacy, racial profiling and, 102–3
Promotions (work)
    black employees, 186n4
    and "talking white," 54–55

Quotas, admissions policies, 132

Race discrimination, idealized model of, 43
Raceplus discrimination, 143–44
*The Race Trap: Smart Strategies for Effective Racial
    Communication* (Johnson and Simring),
    102
"Racial capitalism," 58
Racial cliquishness, 39
Racial comforting, 27–28
Racial cooperation, 161
Racial double bind, 1–20. *See also* Working
    Identity
    racial performance, 10–15
Racial exceptionalism, 31
Racial negotiation, stages of, 25–26
Racial performance, 10–15
Racial profiling, 18, 96–115
    ACLU campaign against, *107,* 107–8, 113
    driving while black/brown (DWB), 100,
        106–15
    Gates, Henry Louis case, 63, 97, 106, 114
    "good" and "bad" blacks, 96, 99–100, 106–7,
        112–14, 130, 144
    and privacy, 102–3
    public campaign against, 106–7
    Schneckloth v. Bustamonte, 101–2, 105
    and stop-and-ask, 100–106
    and terrorism, 112, 168
    United States v. Drayton, 104–5
Racial stereotypes, *36,* 37–38
Rand, Officer, 101–2, 105
Ray, Victor, 10
Rehnquist, William, 83
Reid, Harry, 46–47, 67
"Reverse discrimination," 114
Rivera, Geraldo, 13
Robinson, Eugene, 6–7
Rogers, Renee, 68–69, 77–78, 92, 143
Rogers v. American Airlines, 67–69, 77–78, 92,
    143
Role modeling, 153–54

Romney, Mitt, 14
Rose, Jalen, 8

Saturday Night Live (tv program), 4, 8, 170
Scalia, Antonin, 50
Schneckloth v. Bustamonte, 101–2, 105
Schroeder, Mary, 80, *80*
Seattle Navy Yard, 87
Segregation, 12
Self-identity, 23
Self-image, 23
Selling out, 34
September 11, 2001, 112, 168
Sex as biology, 82–84
Sex discrimination. *See* Gender discrimination
Sex plus regime, anti-discrimination solutions,
    143
Sexual harassment, 178n17
Sharpton, Al, 6–7, 9–10
Signaling, 2–3, 23–24
Simring, Steven, 102
"Single axis frameworks," 70–71
Sisters Reading Group, 122
Socratic method, 36–37, 175n46
Solutions (anti-discrimination), 19,
    134–48
Sotomayor, Sonia, 115–18, *116*
Souter, David, 116
Sperry, Boeing, 87
Spring, Julia, 59
Steele, Claude, 151
Stereotypes and stereotyping
    admissions policy, diversification, 122–24
    anti-stereotyping theory, 91, 95
    of Asian Americans, 41
    black women, 145
    Chinese accents, 27
    exploiting stereotypes, 33
    families, black women committed to, 57
    Korean Americans, 33
    negation, 44, 151, 156–65
    of Indians,, 41
    professors, incompetency of, 175n39
    racial, *36,* 37–38
    sex-object stereotyping, 88
    success, trickle-down benefits, 151
    and talking white, 48–50
    white women, Working Identity, 91
    of women, 40
    workplace conversations, 49–50
"Stereotype threat," 151
Stop-and-ask, racial profiling and,
    100–106
Stuffwhitepeoplelike.com, 29–31
Success, "acting white" for purposes of helping
    other blacks, 155–56
Sweet, Lynn, 98

"Talking white," 17, 46–67
    advancement tasks (work), 54–56
    citizenship tasks, 58–62
    exploitation, 50
    high visibility settings, conversations in, 50–52
    identification of problem, 66–67
    institutional speech and criticism, 52–54
    interviews, hiring, 62–65
    legal intervention, 65
    and stereotypes, 48
    workplace and. *See* Workplace, "talking white"
        and
Terrell, Mary Church, 150
Terrorism, 112, 168
Terry v. Ohio, 35–37
Texas, University of, 133
Thomas, Clarence, 10, 34
Title VII, 72, 74–75
    black women, Working Identity, 74–75
    white women, Working Identity, 82–84, 89,
        91, 93, 95
Tokenism
    combating, 153–54
    defined, 154
    first-generation blacks, 155
Traffic analogy, "acting white," 44
"Trickle-down" benefits, 150–52, 156–65
    racial cooperation, 161
    stereotype negation, 156–65
Trust, 153, 190n26
Turek, Officer, 110, 111, 184–85n66

"Unequal burdens" doctrine, 92–93
United States v. Drayton, 104–5
United States, Whren v., 50, 109–12
University of California v. Bakke, 118–21

Vogue, 135

"War on terror," 112, 168
Warren, Earl, 37, 176n55
Warren, Elizabeth, 168
Washington Post, 6–7
Watkins, Boyce, 47
West, Cornel, 9–10
"When Keeping It Real Goes Wrong"
    (Chappelle), 114
White, Walter, 184n47
White women, Working Identity, 18,
    80–95
    Darlene Jespersen v. Harrah's Casino, 80–82,
        84–92, 95
    gay plaintiffs, 89–91, 95
    "good" and "bad" women, 93–95
    makeup, gender discrimination claim regarding
        wearing to work, 80–82, 85–91, 95
    sex as biology, 82–84

White women, Working Identity (*cont.*)
  stereotyping, 91
  Title VII, 82–84, 89, 91, 93, 95
  "unequal burdens" doctrine, 92–93
Whren v. United States, 50, 109–12
Williams, Johnny, 15–16
Women. *See also* Black women; White women,
    Working Identity
  Asian Americans, discrimination against, 70
  black women, Working Identity, 17–18,
    68–79. *See also* Black women, Working
    identity
  "double bind," employee situations, 54
  stereotypes, 40
  white women, Working Identity, 18, 80–95.
    See also White women, working identity
  Working Identity, 3
Working Identity
  acting white, 21–45
  anti-discrimination solutions, 134–48
  black women, effect on, 17–18, 68–79
  buying back, 34–35
  central question, 16–17
  costliness of, 3
  criminal, not acting. *See* Criminal, not acting;
    Racial profiling

  defined, 1
  and diversity, 1–2, 116–33
  helping other blacks, "acting white" for
    purposes of, 149–66
  Obama, Barack, 8, 10
  overview, 3–4
  performance issues, examples, 76–77
  questions raised for law, 3
  racial negotiation and, 26
  self-presentation, 82
  and "talking white," 66
  white women, 18, 80–95. *See also* White
    women, Working Identity
  women, 3
  as work, 35–38
Workplace, "talking white" and
  complaining, 60–62
  conversations, generally, 52–54
  institutional "goodies," 60–61
  Outsiders, 58–61
  stereotypes in workplace conversations,
    49–50
  types of work, 54–60
Wright, Reverend, 11–12

Zimmerman, George, 13, 31